CHAUCER

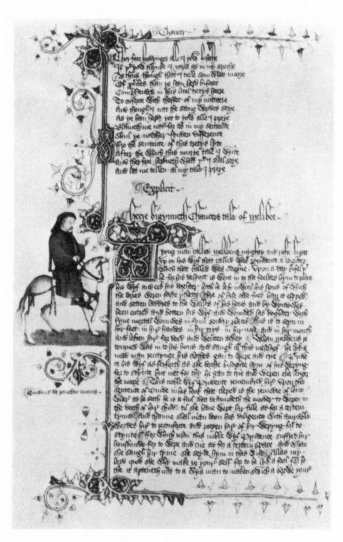

PORTRAIT OF CHAUCER
From the Ellesmere MS.

CHAUCER

BY
GEORGE H. COWLING

WITH SIX ILLUSTRATIONS

 BOOKS FOR LIBRARIES PRESS
FREEPORT, NEW YORK

First Published 1927
Reprinted 1971

INTERNATIONAL STANDARD BOOK NUMBER:
0-8369-5692-3

LIBRARY OF CONGRESS CATALOG CARD NUMBER:
74-150179

PRINTED IN THE UNITED STATES OF AMERICA

TO
MY WIFE

CONTENTS

vii

LIST OF ILLUSTRATIONS

CHAUCER

I

THE LIFE OF CHAUCER

§ 1

IN a poem entitled *The Governance of Princes*, which was written about 1412 by a poetic disciple of Chaucer named Thomas Hoccleve, the author in filial reverence caused to be inserted a miniature portrait of his " mayster dere." Two manuscripts of this poem containing tiny coloured pictures of Chaucer have survived the vandalism of those early friends of culture who collected such illuminations to stick like foreign postage-stamps in scrap-albums. The one which we reproduce (from MS. Harley 4866, British Museum) is the best-known portrait—the gentle face and scanty white beard of an old man clad in a dark stuff gown and hood. He is facing half-left, and he points with his right hand as if reciting something. This picture in all probability was the original of the not too flattering painting in the National Portrait Gallery. The other, also a British Museum manuscript, Royal 17 D VI, contains a full-length portrait of the same individual facing right ; but neither the drawing nor the colouring are so attractive as the Harleian portrait.

Another picture of Dan Chaucer, this time riding as a pilgrim to Canterbury, is found as an illumination to the Tale of Melibeus in the celebrated Ellesmere MS. of *The Canterbury Tales*. The manuscript is now " in utmost longitude " in the United States of America, but there is a published facsimile, thanks to the Manchester University Press, and there can be no doubt that either the Ellesmere

I

is a copy of the Harleian portrait, or both are copies of the same original. The Ellesmere picture portrays the same nose, the same eyes, and the same forked beard. The figure is made a little younger perhaps, but it represents the same individual, and, curiously enough, the pose is exactly the opposite of the Harleian portrait, except that the right hand holds reins instead of a rosary; which suggests that somehow the illuminator of this part of the Ellesmere MS. made a transfer from an earlier illumination like the Harley portrait, and then inserted the horse and the reins.

After we have made allowance for inevitable discrepancies, these portraits agree in representing a wise old man with a shy glance, a greybeard with a fresh but thinnish face, a long straight nose, and a forked beard—a rather corpulent old man dressed, according to the fashion of that age for well-to-do people, in a dark gown and hood. Perhaps it was his royal livery. The picture of the knight in the Ellesmere MS. shows a gentleman wearing a similar gown and hood. And in all these portraits the expression and figure of the person represented accord with "the murye wordes of the Host to Chaucer" which are prefixed to the Tale of Sir Thopas.

> *To Chaucer:*   " What man artow ? " quod he,
> " Thou lookest as thou woldest finde an hare,
> For ever upon the ground I see thee stare.
> Approche neer, and looke up murily."

> *To the Pilgrims:* " Now war yow, sires, and lat this man have
>   place.
> He in the waast is shape(n) as wel as I ;
> This were a popet in an arm t'embrace
> For any woman, smal and fair of face.
> He semeth elvish by his countenaunce
> For unto no wight dooth he daliaunce."

That was Chaucer in his old age.

Yet another portrait, showing Chaucer aged about

forty-five, is to be found, as Brusendorff recently pointed out [1] in one of the Parker MSS.—in the frontispiece to Troilus and Criseyde (MS. 61, Corpus Christi College, Cambridge). It occurs in a picture of the poet reciting his poems from an open-air pulpit to a very aristocratic audience, which appears to include King Richard II— defaced doubtless by some good Lancastrian—and plain Queen Anne herself wearing actually the petalled coronet around her golden hair which, more directly than French literary influences, may have suggested to Chaucer the personification of his sovereign lady as the daisy in the charming Prologue to *The Legend of Good Women*. In this picture Chaucer's face is younger. His hair and his short beard are brown ; but one has no difficulty in identifying the same grave but waggish individual of the other portraits.

We know almost exactly what Chaucer looked like— which is more than we can say about Shakespeare. Chaucer was not aristocratic in appearance. In our age he might have passed for a secretary, or a manager of some kind. Yet his appearance was unforbidding, and his features were well chiselled. He looked pensive, worldly wise, and rather tired ; but despite these indications of lack of enthusiasm and love of decency, one can easily see in fancy the grave eyes light up with a witty twinkle and the rather heavy and drooping mouth curl into a smile.

Chaucer was real enough to the men of the next generation : there is no doubt about that. But during the fifteenth century, though his fame as a poet endured, the record of his life became almost utterly lost. This strange fact seems to need an explanation ; for Chaucer ranked with Dante and Petrarch in the opinion of his countrymen as the chief exponent of the English equivalent of the *dolce stil nuovo*—the flower of eloquence rhetoriale, Ovid in fantasy, Virgil in diction—that was the popular sum of criticism. Perhaps the explanation of the loss of the

---

[1] *The Chaucer Tradition*, London, 1925, p. 19.

record of his life is that there was not much to remember. He began life as a valet, and married a poor woman of higher rank. Had she not been poor, probably she would never have married him. He became an official of the Crown ; not a law-officer, but a sort of steward or manager. She died. He died. He was taken prisoner once, and once he was robbed by a gang of sturdy knaves ; but these are hardly adventures which lend themselves to anecdote. Chaucer's eldest son, Thomas Chaucer, became a rich and important landowner in the fifteenth century. Perhaps like many others who have risen in the world, he was just a little ashamed of his middle-class origin, and from his manors of Ewelme and Woodstock made no attempt to enlighten ignorance or to correct error.

§ 2

And so the true story of Chaucer's life remained forlearned and forgotten, and conjecture built a wonderful tissue of guess-work and inference which became a tradition. The traditions about Chaucer were first collected and recorded by John Leland, the antiquary and topographer, in his *Commentarii de Scriptoribus Britannicis* (c. 1545). This early history of English literature remained in manuscript unpublished until 1709, when it was edited for the Clarendon Press by Anthony Hall ; but it was read by John Bale, who derived from it the first published life of Chaucer which appeared in Latin dress in Bale's compendium of English writers—*Illustrium Maioris Britanniae Scriptorum Summarium*—published at Basel in 1557.

According to Leland, Chaucer was born a scion of a noble house in either Berkshire or Oxfordshire. He attended " the Isiacan Schools "—for Leland's account is as rhetorical as it is untruthful. There pursuing his studies, he became " acutus dialecticus (logician), dulcis rhetor, lepidus poeta, gravis philosophus, ingeniosus mathematicus, et sanctus theologus "—from which it is clear that even in those days Oxford turned out some first-class men. But to continue : about the end of the reign of Richard II, to whom he was not unknown, Chaucer resided in France, where he won great renown by his frequent literary compositions, and absorbed also the grace, wit and elegance of the French language. When he returned to England, he found that his brilliant reputation came with him also. He delighted to attend the Inns of Court and the courts of law. John Gower the poet became his bosom friend ; and to him and to Strode, an alumnus of Merton College, Oxford, Chaucer subjected his *Troilus and Criseyde* for criticism. It must have been about this time that, according to Speght, he became a student of law of the Inner Temple, and was fined two shillings for trouncing a friar in Fleet Street.

Chaucer's ideal as a poet was (we are told) to make the English language the literary rival of the Italian of Petrarch and the French of Alain Chartier. Curiously enough, the very date of his death seems to have been forgotten, though his monument silently recording that he had died on October 25, 1400, was in the Abbey of Westminster for every passenger to read. Leland recorded that Chaucer was known and esteemed by three kings—Richard II, Henry IV and Henry V—which is no doubt true when we recollect that Prince Hal was born in 1388 and the Chaucers were clients of the House of Lancaster ; but false if it implies that the poet was alive in 1413 when Henry V came to the throne. Nevertheless Leland stated correctly that Chaucer was buried in Westminster, but he added, with probably much less correspondence to fact, that Chaucer left to his son Lewis his riches and his manor-house at Woodstock. To these traditions we might add one more, recorded this time by Edward Phillips, the author of *Theatrum Poetarum* (1675)—that Sir Geoffrey Chaucer was poet laureate.

These romantic traditions coloured all the early lives of the poet ; but some of Chaucer's early editors began to add facts based upon the scrutiny of official documents. In the edition of 1598, Thomas Speght, or his collaborator the antiquary John Stowe, conjectured that Chaucer's father was a city wine-merchant—a shrewd hit! He knew also that Geoffrey Chaucer wore the livery of Edward III as a valet, also as secretary to various embassies, and as a Customs official of the port of London. He recorded that Chaucer received pensions from Richard II and Henry IV ; and, most important fact of all, he stated on the authority of a pedigree compiled by Robert Glover, Somerset Herald, that Chaucer married a daughter of Sir Payne Roet, Guienne King-of-Arms. John Dart, or his collaborator William Thomas, in Urry's edition of 1721, was the first to state that John Chaucer the vintner was the father of the poet ; and he indicated first the importance of Chaucer's deposition in the Scrope-Grosvenor dispute. Nevertheless the early lives of Chaucer are in the main unreliable ; and, as far as Leland's contribution is concerned, it would appear that he confused the lives of Geoffrey Chaucer and of his son, Thomas Chaucer.

§ 3

After this preliminary let us begin to make the story fit the facts, which are quite plentiful, more numerous indeed than the facts of Shakespeare's life, but not always so significant. Any life of Chaucer must needs deal with probabilities and weigh possibilities, and to a certain extent it must inevitably be the product of historical imagination and intelligent guess-work, rather than of certain deductions.[1] But our ideal shall be truth.

[1] The first important life of Chaucer based upon facts ascertained from historical study was that written by Sir Harris Nicolas in 1844 for the " Aldine " Chaucer, and every life of Chaucer must now be based on the evidence of the public historical records published by Sir Harris Nicolas, and by his successors in this useful kind of research, especially Walford D. Selby, Frederick J. Furnivall, Edward A. Bond, and R. E. G. Kirk, the editors of the *Life-Records of Chaucer*, published by the Chaucer Society (1900). The " Forewords " to this work, written in 1901 by R. E. G. Kirk, are invaluable as a guide to the documents.

In October, 1386, when Geoffrey Chaucer was at the height of his worldly prosperity, being Controller of the Customs in the Port of London, Justice of the Peace and Knight of the Shire for the County of Kent, he was called as a witness before a court of chivalry holden in the refectory of the Benedictine Abbey of Westminster, and presided over by Sir John Derwentwater, to decide the important question whether Sir Robert Grosvenor or Sir Richard Scrope (lately Chancellor of Richard II) had a prior right to bear the arms described by the heralds as " d'azure ove (with) une bende d'or." In his deposition, which still remains amongst the Miscellaneous Rolls of Chancery, he described himself as " Esquier del age de xl ans et plus, armeez par xxvii ans." Questioned whether the arms were those of Sir Richard Scrope (whose witness he was), he replied: " Oil, qar il lez ad veu estre armeez en Fraunce, devant la ville de Retters, et M. Henry Le Scrop armez en mesmes lez armeez (arms) . . . et issint (so) il lez vist armez par (during) tout le dit viage, tanque (until) le dit Geffrey estoit pris." Whence emerge the interesting facts that Chaucer was more than forty in 1386, that he was an esquire and bore arms, that he had in 1359–1360 taken part in the Hundred Years' War in a skirmish near Réthel, and had been taken by the French.

If, as he bore witness, Chaucer was more than forty years old in 1386, he was probably born about 1340. His father, John Chaucer the vintner, whose house the poet sold during the Peasant Rising of June, 1381, occupied premises in Thames Street, London, adjoining the stream called the Walbrook. It was in all probability over this wine-warehouse, amidst the fume of the white wine and the red, that Geoffrey Chaucer was born. Here also probably his sister Katharine—who lived to marry Simon Manning of Cobham, Kent—first saw the light. Their father was a substantial vintner, not indeed one of the city magnates, but a man of some wealth and standing—an importer of wines from France and Spain, and perhaps from the Rhine ; also, during part of his career at least, a brewer.   He died in 1366, and Chaucer's mother, Agnes, made haste to marry another vintner named Bartholomew atte Chapel.

Where Chaucer was educated we do not know ; but as St. Paul's School was the nearest and the best, it would be there in all probability that he learned his Latin grammar, rhetoric, and logic.   There he would con the grammar of Donatus or of Priscian, and would begin to read Cato's *Moralia*, Æsop's *Fables*, his ever favourite *Metamorphoses* and *Heroides* of Ovid, and the earlier books of Virgil's *Æneid*.   There no doubt he read selections from Statius and Claudian, and possibly from Prudentius, Boëthius and Augustine.   He knew no Greek.   Greek was not introduced into the grammar schools until the beginning of the sixteenth century.   Chaucer's knowledge of the story of Troy came from Virgil, and from the medieval Latin prose *Historia Troiana* of Guido delle Colonne of Messina. Besides the elementary Trivium, he probably studied also the more advanced Quadrivium, namely, Arithmetic, which he used later in his official reckonings ; Geometry, for at least he knew the school name [1] of Euclid I, 47 ; some Astronomy he certainly knew, for his works teem with astronomical allusions, and did he not compile *The Treatise on the Astrolabe* ? and perhaps also he studied Music.   He spoke English and French from childhood. His family bore a French name [2] and was engaged in the wine-trade with French merchants.   At school his Latin was translated into the Anglo-French of the period.   It was not until after the Black Death of 1349 that the head-master of Merton College School instituted the novelty of construing Latin into English.

Thames Street was an important thoroughfare in those

---

[1] " Dulcarnon " : see *Troilus and Criseyde, III*, 930–936.
[2] The name means either shoemaker or hosemaker, and earlier in the fourteenth century there were Chaucers in Cordwainer Street, the district of the shoemakers, one of whom, William, was a taverner.

days—the chief highway of the wards of Dowgate and the Vintry. Cold Harbour, the town house of Sir John Holland, half brother of Richard II, was there ; and the mansions of the Earls of Worcester and Ormond. Therein also were the Vintry, the hall of the guild of Vintners, and the halls of the Cutlers, Plumbers and Glaziers. These Chaucer would pass by on his way to school. There was no aristocratic and fashionable quarter of London in the fourteenth century. Noble and guildsman dwelt side by side ; and if there were no slums, it was because the servants and craftsmen lodged near their masters in hall and shop as they best might. Perhaps, indeed, from our century we might regard comfortless, plague-ridden London of the Middle Ages—without heating, lighting or sanitation— as one vast slum, from the royal Wardrobe in the west to the royal Tower in the east ; but London Bridge with its chapels and its gate-guarded street, the century of parish churches with their varied steeples topped by old St. Paul's, and the great Tower, were buildings of magnificence and beauty beside the usual houses of wood and plaster, not even excelled by the great stone houses of the nobles. And the silently flowing broad expanse of the Thames with its picturesque shipping, seen from the Vintry wharf, must have increased the schoolboy's impression that London was " A per se " and " crown of cities all."

Whether young Chaucer attended Oxford, as Leland conjectured, is very doubtful. The cathedral school of London, the grammar school attached to St. Paul's, was one of the best schools in England, and adequate to furnish Chaucer with all the school learning which he displays. And indeed, unless he went to Oxford at a very early age, there seems no time in Chaucer's life for the study of philosophy ; for we find him, still in his teens, in the service of Elizabeth de Burgh, Countess of Ulster, first wife of Edward III's third son, Lionel Duke of Clarence. Together with an obscure young lady called Philippa Pan,

which, it is suggested, stands for " pantrymaid," Chaucer
figures in the household accounts for 1357 as the recipient
of divers odd florins by way of pocket-money, together
with a " paltok " or overcoat as part of his livery ; and, as
that Christmas was spent at Hatfield in the East Riding,
there is no doubt that at least once in his life Chaucer came
into immediate contact with the dialect of the North.
How a tradesman's son became a page in the service of
one of the highest in the land is an interesting speculation.
There can be no doubt that John Chaucer's wines brought
him, like those of John Ruskin's father, into a business
connexion with the grand ; and one must continue to
wonder whether young Geoffrey obtained his coveted post
as a royal favour, or at the premium of a free consignment
of tuns and butts. Henceforward Chaucer served the
great. His fellow-squires were often no richer than he, but
as a rule they had birth on their side. Commoners, like
William of Wykeham, might take their generation by
storm of genius, and compel it to recognize their talents :
the nobility, from youth up, owned and acquired place and
power by right of heraldry.

In the winter of 1359, after two years of truce following
upon the Battle of Poitiers, Edward III again invaded
France in order to force the Dauphin Charles to yield to the
terms which had been agreed to by the captive King John
of France. The King of England went in person, like the
stout old viking that he was, and his troop of sturdy sons
accompanied him. With that expedition went Chaucer,
probably as a squire in the retinue of Lionel, Duke of
Clarence. It was a military parade of a common type in
the annals of English-French warfare in the fourteenth
century. The French avoided a pitched battle against the
most destructive English archers and men-at-arms, but
the spirited mounted knights and squires engaged in petty
skirmishes ; and the army lived, or starved as might be, on
its line of march, and plundered and burnt farms at will.
The first objective of the expedition was Rheims. After a

seven weeks' unsuccessful siege, the English army, leaving Rheims intact, advanced southwards through Champagne, and then retired towards Paris. Edward's army was too small to besiege Paris. It had suffered severely from tempest, plague and famine ; and so the remnant retired downcast and damp to Chartres and Brétigny, where a treaty of peace was signed on May 8, 1360. Chaucer was captured by the French at Réthel, north of Rheims. He was ransomed on March 1st, the king contributing £16 towards his ransom. In October, King John of France came over from his captivity at Eltham to France to take steps towards raising his royal ransom ; and it will be remembered that, having failed to obtain it, he honourably returned to England in 1364 to die in exile. At Calais he was welcomed by Edward III, the Black Prince, and by Chaucer's liege, Lionel Duke of Clarence and Earl of Ulster ; and Chaucer appears to have been sent back to England with letters. In July, 1361, Lionel, Duke of Clarence, went into Ireland to act as the king's lieutenant. There is not a hint in Chaucer's writings which may suggest that he ever saw Ireland : Chaucer did not accompany him. Elizabeth, Countess of Ulster, died in 1363 ; and it is clear that Chaucer's connexion with the household of Clarence terminated soon after the campaign in France—" when, is not set "—but we might add that the heiress of the house, Philippa, married later Edmund Mortimer, Earl of March, whose son Roger afterwards became for a time Chaucer's patron.

§ 4

And now begins a period of five or six years of which there is no record. What Chaucer did between 1361 and 1367, when quite definitely he was employed in the household of Edward III, is unknown. Tradition speaks of travels in France and of legal studies in the Inner Temple. It may be : but more probably Chaucer was recognized as a useful clerk, skilled in French and Latin and in the primitive accountancy of the age, which appears to have been done miraculously in roman numerals with the aid of counters and a sort of draught-board : he had already obtained some reputation as a poet—he was translating *Le Roman de la Rose* and had composed the doleful tale of Ceyx and Halcione from the Latin of Ovid—and so was invited to join the household of the king. Perhaps in 1361 he took service with John of Gaunt, or, more probably, he became an inmate of the royal household after the death of the Countess of Ulster in 1363.

Three years later he married a wife. Edward III, it will be remembered, had married Philippa of Hainault ; and in her retinue came over a French knight named Sir Payne Roet. He remained attached to the English court as a herald, and became King-of-Arms for the Duchy of Guienne. To him were born two daughters : Philippa (*b.* 1348 ?) who married Geoffrey Chaucer, and Katharine (*b.* 1350) who married in 1368 Sir Hugh Swynford (*d.* 1372), a young knight in the service and retinue of the fourth son of Edward III, John of Gaunt, Duke of Lancaster. As a young girl, Philippa Roet obtained, no doubt through her father's influence, a post at court as waiting woman (*domicella camerae*) to old Queen Philippa. As coheiress, in the absence of an heir, of the estates in Hainault (and perhaps near Greenwich) of a blue-blooded knight with a genuine coat-of-arms—" gules, three Catherine wheels or " —she was a good match for a commoner with an improvised coat-of-arms—" parti per pale, a bend over all " ; and the vintner's son wedded himself to gentility when she married him. The marriage probably took place with the royal approval in September, 1366. On the twelfth of that month the king granted Philippa Chaucer a pension of 10 marks a year (£6 13s. 4d.) for her services to the queen. Nine months later the king granted to Galfridus Chaucer, *dilectus vallectus noster*, on June 20, 1367, an annuity of 20 marks a year (£13 6s. 8d.). Very possibly this was on the occasion of the birth of Chaucer's eldest son, Thomas, who afterwards became Chief Butler to Henry IV and Henry V, and held other important offices.[1]

Although it was a regulation of the royal household that no member should keep his wife at the court, Philippa remained—a clear indication that she was still employed as a demoiselle of the queen. And indeed the names of both Chaucer and his wife appear in a list of the members of the royal household made by the Keeper of the Wardrobe for official use, probably in 1368. Philippa Chaucer's name is fifth in the list of demoiselles of the queen : Geoffrey's stands seventeenth in the list of esquires of the king, in rank below the bachelors and the clergy, but above the sergeants-at-arms, the junior esquires, and the falconers, heralds, minstrels, waits, valets of the chamber, assistant butlers, bakers, kitcheners, grooms, etc., who composed a medieval court.

Two books of household ordinances for the duties of the royal servants are accessible,[2] yet Chaucer's services cannot be defined with accuracy. We do not even know whether he was always at court. We should probably be wrong to think of him merely as a footman or a bed-maker. We should be equally wrong to regard him as a gentleman-in-waiting. Probably his duties were partly clerical and secretarial. It is hardly likely that he was later chosen as

[1] As these relationships have been doubted, it is necessary to recount the evidence. 1. A pedigree compiled in the reign of Elizabeth by Robert Glover, Somerset Herald, asserted that Chaucer married a daughter of Sir Payne Roet. 2. Philippa is first said to be the wife of Chaucer in a grant by John of Gaunt, dated 12 June, 1374. He granted Chaucer £10 a year " pour la bone (service) que nostre bien aimé Geffray Chaucer nous ad fait, et auxint (also) pour la bon service que nostre bien aimée Philippe, sa femme, ad fait à nostre treshonorée Dame et Mère, la Royne." 3. Gaunt, who eventually married Philippa's sister Katharine, was a patron of Chaucer, Philippa Chaucer, Thomas Chaucer, and of an Elizabeth Chaucy (probably Chaucer's daughter or sister), whom Gaunt placed in a convent at Barking on May 12, 1381. 4. After Chaucer's death (e.g. on a deed of 1409) Thomas Chaucer used Geoffrey's seal. 5. The arms of Roet are found in Ewelme Church, on the tomb of Thomas Chaucer, whom Thomas Gascoigne (d. 1458) declared in his Liber Veritatum to be Chaucer's son. 6. In a letter to Henry IV, Henry Beaufort (son of Katharine Roet) alludes to Thomas Chaucer (son of Philippa Roet) as " my cousin " (Life Records, No. 287).

[2] " King Edward II's Household and Wardrobe Ordinances," etc., ed. Furnivall ; being Life Records of Chaucer, Part ii, Chaucer Society, 1876.

Secretary of Embassies and as Clerk of the Customs without previous evidence of his skill in languages and in keeping accounts. Possibly, owing to his father's connexion with the wine-trade, he was originally in the department of the King's Butler. It is worthy of note that Chaucer's son Thomas acted as Chief Butler to four successive kings. Chaucer would, besides doing his particular office, whatever it may have been, serve in the great hall at meals ; he would probably attend the king at Mass, and upon the royal outgoings and incomings. He was also liable to be sent on errands about household business by any of the great officials of the household—the Steward, the Treasurer of the Wardrobe, or the Chamberlain.

A medieval court was no place for an independent mind, and probably no place for an honest man. It offered promotion in rank and wealth, and all kinds of sinecures, from the wardship of a minor to an absentee stewardship, or a living ; but it offered them not only to men of proved ability, but also to the friends and favourites of the men of influence, who enjoyed their power for a shorter or a longer time partly by their rank or wealth, partly by their ability, and partly by the favour in which they were held by the king or queen, or by the influence of one of the royal dukes or of a minister of the Crown. There were no parties, but merely conflicting factions. Court life was a continual struggle for place and power ; the weapons being rarely arms, but rather flattery, bribes, or threats, and that ancient and modern form of underhand dealing which we call " wangling." Naturally there was much envy, and a good deal of backbiting and deceit. As Chaucer said— " Envie is lavendere of the court alway." The fact that he held his offices under the Crown, with one short break only, from about 1364 to 1391 indicates not only that he was a man of some ability : it indicates too that he was a man of the world who could be all things to all men.

In the summer of 1369 there was an outbreak of plague. Queen Philippa died on August 15th, and Blanche, Duchess of Lancaster, on September 12th. Possibly Chaucer carried the news to Calais, whence Gaunt was engaged in raiding Picardy. At least the keeper of the royal wardrobe, who acted as household treasurer, paid Chaucer £10 in 1371 for expenses incurred in 1370 during the war in Aquitaine. It was certainly during this period, the winter of 1369–1370, that he wrote *The Book of the Duchess* to condole with Gaunt for the death of Blanche the Duchess.[1] After the death of Blanche of Lancaster, Katharine Roet, the wife of Sir Hugh Swynford since 1368, became the governess of Gaunt's daughters, Philippa and Elizabeth of Lancaster. Gaunt married Costanza, the eldest daughter of King Pedro I of Castile in September 1371, and about the same time his royal brother Edmund Langley, Earl of Cambridge, afterwards Duke of York, married her younger sister Isabella. Henceforth until 1388, when he succeeded by force of arms in settling the Spanish succession by the marriage of his younger daughter Katharine to Enrique the eldest son of Juan I, King of Castile, John of Gaunt— or to give him his heraldic dues, Duke of Lancaster, Earl of Derby, Lincoln and Leicester, Lord of Beaufort and Nogent, Seneschal of England—assumed the title of King of Castile as consort of his wife Costanza ; and his London palace, The Savoy, was a scene of magnificence only surpassed by the court at Westminster.

To this second court, after the return of the King and Queen of Castile to England in November, 1371, Philippa Chaucer transferred her services ; and, together with Dame Senche Blount, and Dame Blanche de Trompington, became one of the *demoiselles* of Costanza. For these services past and to come she received on August 30, 1372,

---

[1] Scholars have been too prone to take Chaucer's words about his lovesickness " That I have suffred this eight yere " (l. 37) too literally. If Chaucer had really been seriously in love with a lady other than his own wife Philippa, he would not have told Gaunt about it. What Chaucer means in *The Book of the Duchess*, ll. 30–41, is that to see Blanche was to love her ; and that from the time when he first saw her, on his return from France in 1361, until her death, she was his sovereign lady—but " that is doon "—she was dead.

a pension of £10 a year from the Duchy of Lancaster. She still received her royal pension of 10 marks in half-yearly instalments at Easter and Michaelmas, which Chaucer frequently drew together with his own. Henceforth, except when Philippa obtained leave from Costanza's household, Chaucer lived apart from his wife. Probably he took it philosophically :

> Sin day by day thou mayst thyselven see
> That from his love, or elles from his wyf,
> A man mot twinnen of necessité,
> Ye, though he love her as his owne lyf.
> Yit nil he with himself thus maken stryf ;
> For wel thou wost, my leve brother dere,
> That alwey frendes may not ben yfere.
>
> (*T and C*, v. 337).

Did she not stand in the presence of a queen ? Every New Year's Day she received from Gaunt a splendid gift, like the Queen of Castile and the rest of her ladies—in 1373 a " buttoner " and six silver-gilt buttons, in 1380, 1381, and 1382 a splendid silver-gilt cup. If Gaunt succeeded in winning the Kingdom of Castile, there might be castles and honours in Spain ; and meanwhile (dated June 13, 1374) there was an earnest of future favours in the shape of a pension of £10 for Chaucer himself, in addition to Philippa's annuity. One of these favours (in all probability) was the placing of Elizabeth, the daughter of Chaucer (?), as a nun in Barking Abbey in 1381. This cost the Duchy of Lancaster £51 8s. 2d. It was perhaps as a compliment to his wife's mistress that Chaucer wrote the legend of Custance, which afterwards was included in *The Canterbury Tales* as the Tale of the Man of Law.

§ 5

In the spring of 1372 Chaucer's wife Philippa joined the household of John of Gaunt, and from the fact that her master afterwards became the patron of her children,

JOHN OF GAUNT

From the Painting ascribed to Luca Cornelli, in the possession of the Duke of Beaufort

Thomas and Elizabeth, perhaps we may infer that her children and her maids went too. Soon afterwards Chaucer was ordered by the king to proceed overseas on a diplomatic mission. Whatever the causes may have been, he was sent by a commission dated November 12, 1372, to Genoa. Together with two Genoese merchants named Provan and de Mari he was authorized to arrange with the Duke and Council of Genoa for the establishment in England of a trading station of Genoese merchants. Chaucer set out for Italy on December 1, 1372. He returned on the 23rd of May, 1373. In addition to Genoa, he visited Florence on matters probably not altogether unconnected with his royal master's loans from the bankers of that city. Here probably he met, or at least heard with emulation, of an Italian poet, clerk, and scholar some thirty years older than himself—the famous Boccaccio, the great novelist and writer of romances, the first Dante scholar, the first to call back Homer into Tuscany, the creator of the *volgare illustre* and Italian prose. Chaucer must have heard of the *Decameron*, the most famous, and justly famous, collection of stories and fabliaux of the age.

Whether he went to Padua and met Petrarch, as he declares in the prologue to *The Clerk's Tale*—

> I wol yow telle a tale which that I
> Lerned at Padwe of a worthy clerk,
> Fraunceys Petrak, the lauriat poete.

—is not clear from the account for wages and expenses which Chaucer presented on his return, but it was not impossible. Chaucer improved his knowledge of Italian, and almost certainly brought back with him Petrarch's Latin version of Boccaccio's story of Griselda, some of Petrarch's *Sonnets* ; and, of the works of Boccaccio, at least the *Filostrato* and *Teseide*. From these, he proceeded during the next few years to write *The Clerk's Tale, Troilus and Criseyde*, and *The Complaint of Anelida*. Chaucer's political mission appears to have been moderately success-

2

ful. His reward, granted on April 23, 1374, was a patent
entitling him to receive daily from the Chief Butler one
pitcher of wine. This grant was not so absurd as it may
seem. In the first place, it indicated that Chaucer belonged
to the higher rank of household servants. The valets and
squires received beer as their livery : wine definitely put
Chaucer amongst the clerks. Secondly, it had a cash-value.
In April, 1378, Chaucer exchanged his grant of a pitcher of
wine for a new grant under the Privy Seal of a pension of
20 marks a year (£13 6s. 8d.).

Interesting scandal was waiting to greet the ears of
Chaucer on his return to England in the summer of 1373.
Sir Hugh Swynford, the husband of his sister-in-law
Katharine, had died in Aquitaine in 1372, and almost
immediately afterwards the governess of Gaunt's eldest
daughters became his mistress. She was the widowed
mother of a little boy of three who grew up to be Sir
Thomas Swynford, and eventually succeeded to the Roet
property, or at least to part of it, in Hainault. She now
became the mother of John, Henry, Thomas, and Joan,
to whom Gaunt gave the name of Beaufort from one of his
French seigniories. Philippa's sister Katharine became a
despised but influential personage. Gaunt gave her rich
annuities, and manors in Lincolnshire and Nottingham.
She appears to have retired to Lincoln, to emerge, however,
to the scandal of the wives of the nobility when at last,
after the death of Costanza of Castile in 1394, Gaunt married
her in 1396, and made her Duchess of Lancaster. Then
the Beaufort family was legitimized, and Katharine insisted
on her pride of place. She was one of the ladies who
escorted the Princess Isabella of France to London after
her marriage, at Calais, on November 4, 1396, to Richard II.
Philippa Chaucer appears to have remained on visiting
terms with her sister. Evidently she was staying with
her in February, 1386, when, on the nineteenth, together
with Gaunt's heir, Henry, Earl of Derby (afterwards
Henry IV), and the eldest children of Katharine—Sir

Thomas Swynford and John Beaufort—she was admitted to the society of patrons (*fratres et sorores*) of Lincoln Cathedral.

Chaucer's grant of a pitcher of wine terminated his services as an inmate of court. He was now one of the royal clerks and marked for promotion. He must have known what was coming, for on May 10, 1374, he leased from the Corporation of London the house above Aldgate, the eastern gate of the city. It was a roomy house as houses went, consisting of rooms in the two towers connected by a corridor above the gate. True, there were a number of steps to climb around the newels of the towers, and it had no garden, but it had a lovely view down Whitechapel to Stratford atte Bow and across the Hackney Marshes to Epping Forest ; it was also a strong house, and a house with some character—a house that could be recognized. Here for the next twelve years Chaucer resided, and hither no doubt Philippa came periodically to join him, when not employed in her duties at the court of Castile ; perhaps to Chaucer's sorrow, for, like Menenius, he was " one that converses more with the buttock of the night than with the forehead of the morning," and Philippa, like a good housekeeper, was an early riser. There is an interesting divulgement of family secrets in Chaucer's *House of Fame*, ii, 52, where the eagle rouses the poet :

> Me mette " Awak " to me he seyde,
> Right in the same vois and steven
> That useth oon I coude neven ;
> And with that vois, soth for to seyne,
> My minde cam to me ageyn,
> For hit was goodly seyd to me,
> So was hit never wont to be.

Hither no doubt, to grace Chaucer's table, came the silver-gilt cups with which John of Gaunt honoured Philippa.

On June 8, 1374, Chaucer was appointed Controller of the Customs and subsidy of Wools, Hides, and Wool-fells in the port of London, by royal letters patent. The wool-trade was England's great industry in the Middle Ages, and sheep-farming and wool-growing was one of the soundest roads to wealth ; for the busy looms of Ypres and Ghent demanded continually more and more English wool. The customary taxes on the wool exported to Flanders were one of the chief sources of the king's revenue, and in the port of London they were collected by Geoffrey Chaucer. He handed over his taxes to the collectors, who were rich merchants and aldermen of the city, such as Sir Nicholas Brember, William Walworth, Sir John Philipot, and other supporters of the king in the guild-hall. The collectors acted in pairs annually, though Brember and Philipot retained their office from 1378 to 1386, and there was a strong suspicion in the opposition factions that they were not entirely honest. The collectors paid over the customs to the exchequer annually at Michaelmas. Chaucer's duty as controller (*contra-rotulator*) was to keep a " counter-roll "—a duplicate account—of the customable wares passing through the port, and of the taxes received. His patent of appointment prescribed that he should write his official rolls in his own hand, and that he should perform the duties of his office in person and not *per substitutum suum*. And doubtless he sealed his rolls and his receipts with the seal called the cocket, the " other part " of which was the symbol of his office. For this duty he received as salary £10 a year, which, added to his royal pension of £13 6s. 8d., and his Lancastrian pension (from June 13, 1374) of £10, made him a comparatively wealthy professional man, with an aristocratic wife at The Savoy to further his interests—a wife who in her own right enjoyed a royal pension of £6 13s. 4d., and a Lancastrian pension of £10. He wore the king's livery, for which he received moneys from time to time ; and he drank daily the king's good wine. It was originally intended that Chaucer should become at the same time Controller of the Petty Customs of wines, cloths, and other customable wares : the patent amongst the Exchequer Rolls (which contains the note that he took the oath to serve well and faithfully on June 12, 1374) so describes him ; but he had to wait some years for the reversion of this second appointment. Chaucer probably interpreted the conditions of his appointment with the ordinary free interpretation of the Middle Ages. It was not a sinecure : but he appears to have had subordinates capable of managing the Custom House during his five absences on the king's service. At first he carried on his weighing of wools from a hired house ; but in 1383 an official Custom House on the Wool Wharf near the Tower was built by one John Churcheman —a three storied building with weighs on the ground floor, a counting house on the first floor, and rooms above for the clerks. Here Chaucer supervised, when not acting as revenue officer in his boat on the river. Capturing a smuggler was a profitable business. On July 12, 1376, Chaucer obtained from the king a grant of £71 4s. 6d., the price of nearly eight sacks of wool which one John Kent had exported from London to Dordrecht without licence and without paying customs. And there were other profitable additions to his income in the shape of wardships and diplomatic missions. A wardship, which in our age is regarded as a responsibility, was a coveted prize in Chaucer's times. The guardian of a minor was entitled to a percentage of the ward's estate, and the king conferred wardships as a favour. Edmund Staplegate, whose guardian Chaucer became from 1375 to 1377, paid Chaucer £104 for his wardship-dues and marriage-settlement.

In December, 1376, Chaucer went as esquire or secretary to Sir John Burley on a secret mission of the king's for which he received 10 marks. Twice in the spring of 1377 was he absent in France on embassies for which he received the sums of £30 and £26 13s. 4d. The latter mission, according to Froissart, was in charge of Sir Guiscard d'Angoulême, who was Prince Richard's tutor. His associates were Froissart's friend Sir Richard Stury, and " Joffroi Chaucier." Their business was to negotiate a

treaty of peace, and the French ambassadors appear to
have suggested the marriage of Prince Richard to the
Princess Marie of France. On February 17, 1377, when
Chaucer left England, Wycliffe was about to be tried for
heresy in St. Paul's. His trial was prevented by Gaunt,
and on February 20th the London mob rose and besieged
The Savoy. Gaunt heard the news, and fled from Thames
Street, where he was dining with Sir John d'Ypres, to take
refuge in the house of Prince Richard at Kennington.
When Chaucer returned to London from Paris and
Montreuil on June 26th, Edward III was dead, and
Angoulême's pupil reigned in his stead as Richard II.

§ 6

The feud of the city with Gaunt lasted no longer than
the coronation, when all old sores were healed. The new
king confirmed the royal pensions of Chaucer and his wife,
and his advisers continued to employ the Controller of
Customs on diplomatic embassies. Chaucer was probably
in France again in the spring of 1378 with a commission of
ambassadors which was continuing the negotiations sus-
pended by the death of Edward III. In May he set out
for a second time to Italy as esquire to Sir Edward Berkeley
on a mission charged to treat with Bernabo Visconti, Duke
of Milan, and the English knight-adventurer Sir John
Hawkwood, concerning matters related to the war with
France. Exactly what their business was does not transpire. It may have been to forestall the enlistment of
Italian mercenaries by the French. It may have been to
negotiate an alliance, or to borrow more money for the
war. Chaucer left England on May 28th, and returned on
September 19th. To act during his absence, he appointed
as his legal representatives (for his wardships, etc.) his
friends John Gower, the poet, and Richard Forester, who
a few years later leased his house over Aldgate when
Chaucer left it. For this journey he received as payment

of expenses and wages (13s. 4d. per day) £80 13s. 4d.
This was, as far as we know, the last of Chaucer's
missions.

And now occurs a most curious incident in Chaucer's
life. On May 1, 1380, there appeared in the royal chancery
at Westminster a young orphan lady named Cecilia
Chaumpaigne,[1] and, in the presence of witnesses who were
Chaucer's friends—Sir William Beauchamp (the guardian
of John Hastings, Earl of Pembroke, a minor soon to be
betrothed to Gaunt's daughter, Elizabeth of Lancaster),
Sir John Clanvowe the poet, Sir William Neville, and the
Collector of Customs, John Philipot—she released Chaucer
from future liability, both in respect of her abduction and
other possible actions. What does it mean ? At first
sight, one would be tempted to regard Chaucer as one
whose conduct, like that of the " old Person of Philae,"
was exceedingly " dubious and wily." But in the City of
London records there exist recognizances (dated June 30
and July 2, 1380), firstly of Richard Goodchild the cutler
and John Grove the armourer, releasing Chaucer from legal
accountability ; secondly of Cecilia Chaumpaigne, releasing
Goodchild and Grove ; and thirdly of Grove, admitting
liability to Cecilia Chaumpaigne of £10, on promising to
pay it at Michaelmas. These bonds clearly indicate that
others besides Chaucer were engaged in the affair. The
documents can only mean, I think, that Cecilia was the
victim of some Babes-in-the-Wood affair, in which Chaucer
figured as the hero, with the armourer and the cutler as the
two villains of the piece. It may be that Cecilia Chaumpaigne was a ward, and John Grove wished to become her
guardian. In a wardship, as in other matters, possession
was nine points of the law. Chaucer's father had been
similarly abducted by some well-intentioned friends in
1326. By a curious irony Geoffrey Chaucer himself was
appointed one of a commission in May, 1387, to inquire

---

[1] The Chaumpaignes were an old-established London family of Alders-
gate and Cheapside. Cecilia's father, William Chaumpaigne, a saddler,
died before 1379.

into the abduction of Isabella atte Halle, a ward, from the guardianship of Thomas Kershill of Chislehurst. I suggest then that Goodchild and Grove made an attempt to kidnap Cecilia, possibly for a wardship, possibly as security for a debt owed by her brother Robert, or possibly to force her to marry someone. Hence (1) Cecilia's claim against Goodchild and Grove. Secondly, Chaucer frustrated the attempt out of friendship for the Chaumpaignes, and conveyed Cecilia from her home and guardian, thus committing technically the crime of abduction. Hence (2) Cecilia's release of Chaucer from liability " *de raptu meo.*" The matter appears to have been settled by mutual engagements. Goodchild and Grove swore not to take action against Chaucer. Cecilia Chaumpaigne swore not to take action against Goodchild and Grove, and John Grove promised to pay Cecilia £10 in settlement of her claim. Possibly it was for her that Chaucer wrote *The Life of St. Cecile.* Who shall say ? The whole matter is obscure, and seems likely to remain so.

In June, 1381, came the Peasants' Rising. On June 12, the men of Kent and Surrey assembled on Blackheath ; on the thirteenth, the men of Essex crowded around Aldgate until some friendly person opened the gate, and they entered the city in hundreds under Chaucer's house. For three days riot raged in the city ; and Gaunt's palace, The Savoy, was sacked. John of Gaunt was at Berwick-on-Tweed negotiating with the Scots. Costanza and her demoiselles were probably at Hertford, the manor at which she usually resided. Thoroughly alarmed, she summoned her household, and rode north to the Lancastrian castle of Knaresborough—the very castle where, in Gower's tale of Custance, the wicked Donegild changed the letter of the messenger. Whether Philippa Chaucer went too we cannot say. Chaucer remained in London, as we can tell from the fact that he concluded the sale of his father's house in Thames Street to Henry Herbury, a vintner, on June 19th ; and later in the year, on November 28th, he received a bonus of 10 marks in addition to his stipend *pro assiduo labore et diligentia in anno ultimo elapso.*

Meanwhile the marriage of Richard II to Anne of Bohemia, the eldest daughter of the late Kaiser Karl IV, and brother of Wenceslaus, King of Bohemia and future Kaiser of the Holy Roman Empire, was being negotiated. In spite of the land of her origin, French was her natural speech. Negotiations began in 1380 : the contract of marriage was signed in London on May 2, 1381. The Peasants' Rising delayed Anne's coming ; but in the autumn she began her leisurely journey, and, after waiting until a safe-conduct was granted by the King of France, she crossed from Calais to Dover, landing in England on December 18th. The marriage took place in St. Stephen's Chapel, Westminster, on January 14, 1382. Chaucer congratulated the royal pair with *The Parlement of Fowles.* On April 20, 1382, he received the reversion of the second office which Edward III had promised him. Chaucer became Controller of the Petty Customs.

And now begins the busiest period of Chaucer's life. In his leisure moments, he finished *Troilus and Criseyde*, wrote *The House of Fame*, and The Knight's Tale of *Palamon and Arcite.* His business hours were occupied with the affairs of two offices. He obtained a new Custom House for the Wool Wharf ; and threw himself heart and soul into his official work. So busy art thou, he says of himself in *The House of Fame*, ii, 141, that

> of thy verray neighebores,
> That dwellen almost at thy dores,
> Thou herest neither that, ne this.
> For when thy labour doon al is,
> And hast ymaad thy rekeninges
> In stede of reste and newe thinges
> Thou gost hoom to thy hous anoon,
> And, also domb as any stoon,
> Thou sittest at another boke
> Til fully daswed is thy looke,
> And livest thus as an heremite
> Although thine abstinence is lyte.

He obtained a month's leave of absence on November 25, 1384 ; and in February, 1385, begged " qu'il puisee avoir suffisant deputee en l'office de Comptrolour à le Wolkee." Evidently by this time he felt the need of " reste and newe thinges." The fact that in 1385 and 1386 he figures in the Patent Rolls as one of the Justices of the Peace for the county of Kent suggests that he was possessed of an estate in Kent, perhaps near Greenwich ; and in August, 1386, a month after the departure of Gaunt's second expedition to Spain, he was appointed Knight of the Shire for Kent. Yet during that summer he wrote *The complainte of Mars*.

The short Parliament of October, 1386, proved to be the turning-point of Chaucer's career. If Gaunt had been in England, Chaucer might have weathered the storm, but Gaunt was in Portugal, wedding his daughter Philippa to João I, King of Portugal ; and preparing to invade Castile. War weariness, dissatisfaction with high taxation, alarm at the extravagance of court and royal favouritism came to a head when Richard raised his favourite Robert de Vere from Earl of Oxford to Duke of Ireland, and all the factions united to hate Michael De la Pole, Earl of Suffolk—one of Gaunt's retinue, whom Richard II had made Chancellor. The House of Commons refused to grant supplies until a change of government should be made. The Chancellor was impeached, and imprisoned ; and a council of regency, headed by the king's youngest uncle, Thomas of Woodstock, Duke of Gloucester, assumed the government. The first act of the new council was to review the revenues and offices of the Crown, and a commission was appointed to enquire into the workings of the Customs. The result was that Chaucer was dismissed from both Controllerships in December, 1386. With this dismissal we may connect a petition of the House of Commons that no Controller of Customs should hold office, except during the term of his good behaviour.[1]

The facts seem to indicate that Chaucer had grown too

[1] Rotuli Parliamentorum, iii, 250. Records Commission.

KING RICHARD II
From the Painting ascribed to André Beauneveu, in Westminster Abbey

big for his post.   A Kentish squire, a Justice and Knight of
the Shire, he was an absentee, relying on the "suffisant
deputee" at the Customs House ; and in complete ignorance of his impending fall he had removed from Aldgate to
the country.   Aldgate was leased again by Sir Nicholas
Brember, Lord Mayor of the City and Collector of Customs,
on October 5th, to Richard Forster—probably the Richard
Forester who acted as his attorney when Chaucer was
absent on the Italian journey of 1378, possibly his deputy
at the Wool Quay.   Probably the commission of enquiry,
amongst other abuses, objected to the gratuities made to
the Collectors Brember and Philipot of £20 each, and to
Chaucer of 10 marks, which had continued from 1381 until
Chaucer's dismissal.   Indeed Brember continued to take
his until 1388.

§ 7

Chaucer went into retirement hoping for a speedy
reversal of the situation.   Richard II rebelled against the
commission of regency, released the Earl of Suffolk, and
prepared for civil war ; but he failed to arrest the Earl of
Arundel, one of his most powerful opponents, in November,
1387 ; and the forces of the Duke of Ireland were routed
by the Earl of Derby, Gaunt's heir.   Suffolk and Ireland
fled to France, and Richard II found himself again under
the harsh tutelage of his uncle Gloucester.   In February,
1388, the "Merciless" Parliament appealed the Court
faction of treason : the judges were arrested, the ministers
condemned.   The chief ministers—Suffolk, Ireland, the
Archbishop of York, and the Lord Chief Justice—had
escaped ; but Gloucester's wrath wreaked itself on the
smaller men.   Chaucer's Collector, Sir Nicholas Brember
and Sir John Beauchamp, Sir Simon Burley, Thomas Usk,
and others were executed.   Was Chaucer proscribed ?
The queen went on her knees to Gloucester to intercede in
vain for Sir Simon Burley.   Did she also intercede with
success for Chaucer ?   Let Chaucer speak :

Hire name was Alceste the debonayre,
I preye to God that ever falle she fayre ;
For ne hadde confort been of hire presence
I hadde ben ded withouten ony defence
For dred of Love's wordes and his chere.

(*L. G. W.*, A., 179).

That is fiction, but it may envelop a fact ; especially when we consider that Brember was a victim. In the midst of Chaucer's troubles, perhaps as a result of them, Chaucer's wife died in the summer of 1387.

The council of regency was not content with taking away Chaucer's offices, they took away his pensions. On May 1, 1388, he surrendered " at his own request " as the Patent Roll records with delicious irony, the pensions amounting to 40 marks per annum which had originally been granted by Edward III, and they were granted by the king to John Scalby to be drawn from the revenues of the county of Lincoln for future good services. This was Chaucer's blackest time. His wife was dead ; his son Thomas, who had entered the service of the house of Lancaster, was probably absent with Gaunt in Castile and Aquitaine ; his daughter Elizabeth was a nun at Barking. Chaucer stood alone.

But the hoped-for good luck was already speeding on its way. Suddenly on May 3, 1389, Richard II overrode the council of regency, dismissed Gloucester, and personally assumed the reins of government. Lancaster was recalled from Aquitaine, and landed in England in November. But before he arrived, namely, on July 12th, Richard II appointed Chaucer once again to a royal office. He became Clerk of the Works at the Palace of Westminster, the Tower, and of the royal castles, manors, and lodges. It was an honourable post, which William of Wykeham had enjoyed in the reign of Edward III. It was an office comparable in our age to that of Commissioner of H.M. Office of Works. It was, moreover, a better-paid post than the Controllership of Customs : Chaucer's wages were 2s.

per day—no less than £36 10s. a year—and it was something of a sinecure too, for he was allowed to employ an overseer, one Hugh Swayne, to whom he paid 2s. per week ; and by October, 1389, he had appointed other deputies at the Tower, Eltham, and Berkhampstead. At each of the royal palaces and manors were storehouses of tools and building materials, and of that old lumber, consisting of scrap-iron, odds and ends of timber and rubble, which gathers in every builder's yard. Here he would assemble his skilled craftsmen and his impressed labourers, and would set them to work under the direction of his overseers. By April, 1390, Chaucer was so much the master of his office that he was able to shift the burden of Hugh Swayne's wages from his own pocket to the broader shoulders of the royal exchequer. He conducted building operations at Westminster Hall, in the Tower of London, and at St. George's Chapel, Windsor. He erected scaffolds in Smithfield in May, 1390, and again at Michaelmas for that magnificent tournament described by Froissart, presided over by the king and queen, at which sixty knights tilted for two days and the gold crown was awarded to the Count d'Ostrevant.

Under the presidency of his old friend Sir Richard Stury he was appointed in March, 1390, one of a commission to compel the Kentish landowners of the marshy banks of the Thames between Greenwich and Woolwich to repair their embankments and drains. But perhaps Chaucer's best-loved work was not the rebuilding of Westminster Hall, but his repair of the Wool Quay, and the building of new weigh-houses for the Customs Office. Perhaps it was he who recognized the need, and suggested the improvements. In the midst of these new energies he was assaulted and robbed on September 3, 1390, near the " Foul Oak " at Hatcham, in Surrey, by three trailebastons who escaped only to be peached by an accomplice, one Richard Brerelay, who also robbed Chaucer of £10 at Westminster three days later. These knaves robbed Chaucer, according to his own statement, of £20 6s. 8d., and of a horse worth £10 and gear valued at £5. Hatcham, we might observe, was the half-way house on the old Kent Road between Southwark and Eltham or Greenwich. Probably Chaucer was on his way to Eltham Manor to pay his workmen's wages ; and the thieves, knowing his regular movements, lay in wait for him. The esteem in which he was then held by Richard II is indicated in this, that, by the especial grace of the king, he was discharged from the repayment of these " vingt livres de nostre tresor." It was about this time too that the poet Gower in his *Confessio Amantis* (viii, 2941) greeted Chaucer " As mi disciple and mi poete." About this time also Chaucer was appointed under-forester of the Forest of North Petherton by Roger Mortimer, Earl of March, in whose family, by a purchase of lands and manorial rights made in 1357, vested the bailiwick of the royal forests of Petherton, Exmoor, and Selwood. What this meant is obscure ; but it probably signified that Chaucer was entitled as a bailiff to occupy the manor-house of Newton Regis, to hold the local court-leet, and to make the usual exactions of the lord of the manor, and the customary fines for infringements of the laws of the forest. In short, it was a sinecure.

In 1391 Chaucer retired from the Clerkship of Works. The circumstances of his withdrawal are obscure ; but certainly the mandate to hand over his office to John Gedney, dated June 17, 1391, is a friendly document. It is addressed to " dilecto Galfrido Chaucer, nuper Clerico operationum nostrarum," and it concludes : " volumus enim te inde erga nos exonerari." There can be no doubt, I think, that Chaucer was glad to be exonerated. Probably the shock of the robbery, and the dread of the probability of other attacks upon an old man of fifty who was not as nimble as he once was, made him realize that an outdoor occupation with long journeys, to carry the workmen's wages to Eltham and Sheen, was beyond his powers. Probably also the financial side of his office was a greater strain than he could bear. The exchequer assigned him moneys from time to time, drawn from the sheriffs and from the collectors of customs ; but the exchequer was always in sad arrears, and Chaucer lent his office 100 marks of his capital on April 6, 1391, taking an exchequer tally for it ; which was not repaid, without interest, until May 22, 1393—two years after he had retired from the post. It was not until after July, 1392, that Chaucer received the balance of the £20 19s. 1½d. which was owing to him when he handed over. His duties as clerk entailed paying his overseers and recovering their wages from the exchequer, paying his masons, carpenters, gardeners, and labourers out of his current account, besides the purchase of materials, tools, and stores. He was a builder and contractor, involved no doubt in many disputes, and almost certainly without that painfully acquired experience of materials, prices, and local custom which is essential to success in that art.

We may picture Chaucer now in retirement—householder, poet, and still something of a public man—working at the *Treatise on the Astrolabe* for his little son or godson named Lewis, to whom he had given an astrolabe, a little boy about whom nothing more is known ; and devoting all his happy moments of inspiration to the writing of *The Canterbury Tales*. He still resided near Greenwich in Kent. as is apparent from the *Envoy to Scogan*, where, according to notes in three manuscripts, " Greenwich " is indicated by the lines :

> In th' ende of which streme I am dul as dede
> Forgete in solitarie wildernesse.

Residence near Greenwich is also indicated by the fact that on April 6, 1396, Chaucer was appointed a member of a board of Greenwich freeholders empowered to act jointly and severally as the representatives of Gregory Ballard in the matter of the manor of West Coombe, including lands in Deptford, East Greenwich, and Charlton, which he held from Thomas Arundel, Archbishop of York. But in all probability Chaucer also spent some time at Newton Regis, Somerset. He was regarded as a man of standing and of comparative wealth, or he would not have been appointed trustee—or magistrate, for that is practically the modern equivalent—of this large ecclesiastical manor which stretched along the south bank of the Thames from Deptford to Charlton and included two water-mills. He was evidently still in favour at court, or Gregory Ballard, the king's squire and royal butler, would never have appointed him. Chaucer's eldest son, Thomas, was rapidly rising in the service of John of Gaunt. In the latter part of 1394, whilst Gaunt was in Aquitaine, he and one Reginald Curteys [1] received from the Lancastrian exchequer for business transacted £13 6s. 8d., which appears to have been paid to Thomas Chaucer for division between them. And soon afterwards, probably in the following year, he married a rich heiress, Matilda, daughter of Sir John Burghersh, and acquired the manor of Ewelme, near Oxford. On March 20, 1399, Thomas Chaucer received an annuity of £20, payable from the revenues of the borough of Wallingford, near Oxford, in return for the surrender of his Lancastrian offices, which the king had granted to William Scroop, Earl of Wiltshire, when he seized the Duchy of Lancaster immediately after the death of Gaunt in February, 1399.

Chaucer must have been a poorer man after the loss of the salary of his Clerkship of Works. Yet he cannot have been destitute, as has often been suggested. He was agent for two estates. He had powerful friends. He

---

[1] The Receiver's Certificate pays: "à Thomas Chaucier, de noun Reynald Curteys, à luy deuz pur certeines busoignes Mons." The meaning of " de noun " is obscure. Perhaps " trading as," " of the firm of "—or, as Kirk suggests, " in the name of " or " on account of." Reginald Curteys of Wragby was a Liocolnshire squire in the service of Gaunt, who granted him a pension of £5 a year for life in 1383, when he was appointed Collector of Customs for Boston. He appears to have dealt in corn, victualling Calais in 1399 and 1405, and Harfleur in 1416. He remained a friend of Thomas, for he was associated with him in the purchase of Hampshire manors from Roger Forde in 1417. He died 1419. See *Life Records of Chaucer*, Kirk's Forewords, pp. liii–lv.

retired from the clerkship with £20 6s. 8d. owing to him (repaid July 13, 1392), and his exchequer tally worth £66 13s. 4d. (repaid May 22, 1393). On January 9, 1393, Richard II gave him £10 " *pro regardo et bono servicio per ipsum habito isto anno iam presente.*" What those services were does not transpire. Very possibly they were poetic services. Like Dickens, Chaucer appears to have given readings of his poems—only Chaucer's readings were given at court and in high places. This gift was followed on February 28, 1394, by a new pension by royal letters patent of £20 a year. We may be sure that Chaucer's state was no disgrace to Thomas, when he attended his wedding to Matilda Burghersh. Chaucer's close connexion with the family of Lancaster seems to have been maintained. The account-book of Henry, Earl of Derby's Clerk of the Wardrobe for 1395–6, contains an entry which indicates that Chaucer conveyed £10 from Bolingbroke's treasurer to his master. Curiously enough, the amount is that of Gaunt's pension of 1374. Was it now being paid by his son ? Did Chaucer carry the £10 to Bolingbroke only to beg it as his due ? Or was Chaucer acting in some clerical capacity in his service ? The fact is interesting, but the meaning is obscure.

§ 8

The suggestion has been made repeatedly that Chaucer fell on evil days in his old age. The grounds for such a supposition are his *Complaint to his Purse*, and the fact that in 1398 he was sued for debt. He may not have been as rich as he desired to be. Few of us are. He was certainly not as wealthy as his son Thomas ; but he cannot have been anything but comfortably endowed ; and if he were unable to pay his just debts, he was probably only temporarily embarrassed by the poverty of the royal exchequer. He appears, from the records of the exchequer, to have been unable to count upon the regular payment of the promised pension ; and who shall blame him for applying

for advances to the Collectors of Customs when, in 1396
and 1397, the exchequer was unable to pay the sums due
at the proper times ?   He was sued, together with one John
Goodale of Milford (who owed £12 8s.), by the executrix of
Walter Buckholt, for the sum of £14 1s. 11d. in the Easter
term of 1398.   Chaucer failed to appear.   The Sheriff of
Middlesex reported that the defendants had no property
within his jurisdiction, and was ordered to arrest them.
But they were not arrested ; and on May 4th, Chaucer
obtained from the king at Westminster a patent which
protected him, and his men, his lands, goods, and income,
from legal process.

The exchequer was now kind to Chaucer.   He received
the Easter instalment of his pension (£10) on June 4, 1398,
four small loans of half a mark in July and August, the
Michaelmas instalment (£10) on October 28th, and the
instalment for the following Easter in two sums, viz.
£7 16s. 8d. on April 26, 1399, and £2 3s. 4d. on July 9th,
when he also borrowed a mark.   He also applied to the king
and was granted the additional pension of one butt of wine
—the laureate's butt—to be received in the port of London
at the hands of the Chief Butler " pur Dieu, et en œure de
charitee."   Meanwhile the suit of Isabella Buckholt was
pressed against Chaucer and Goodale by her attorney.
In the Trinity term, 1398, their arrest was again ordered ;
which shows that Chaucer, though armed with letters of
protection, had failed to defend the suit ; and in the
Michaelmas term of 1398 the defendants were to appear or
be outlawed.   What does it mean ?   There can be no
doubt that if Chaucer had wished, he could have paid
£14, or at least *promised* to pay.   That he did not must
indicate that he disputed the amount.   As Chaucer
apparently was not outlawed, not arrested, nor otherwise
penalized, and as no further records of this case are known,
the action was probably settled out of court, and Isabella's
attorney instructed to withdraw the suit.

Then followed the Lancastrian revolution.   Richard's

first queen, Anne of Bohemia, had died on June 7, 1394. Two years later, on November 4, 1396, Richard married Isabella of France, a little child of eight, whom he treated as a daughter and idolized as a child. It was purely a political marriage, intended to cement a truce between France and England for twenty-five years ; but it was followed by a complete change in Richard's government. Perhaps he realized that a wise despotism was the best government for an unhappy and discontented age in which the Church was corrupt, the peasants disaffected, and the nobles factious. Certainly he never forgave his uncle Gloucester for his harsh restraint, nor the Lords Appellant for their power. He divided the Lords Appallant by winning Henry, Earl of Derby, and Thomas Mowbray, Earl of Nottingham, to his side, promoting them to the dukedoms of Hereford and Norfolk ; and then arrested Gloucester, Arundel, and Warwick. Gloucester was put to death at Calais by Mowbray. In 1398 the Parliament of Shrewsbury delegated its powers to a council of the king's friends, twelve peers and six commoners ; and Richard II became practically an absolute monarch, forced unfortunately by his extravagance and consequent poverty to sell pardons to the friends of his enemies, and to procure forced loans to fill his exchequer.

Gaunt's son, Henry Bolingbroke, Duke of Hereford, mistrusted the hand that had struck down his uncle Gloucester, and it was on January 30, 1398, in the Parliament of Shrewsbury, that he charged Mowbray with treason. The affair dragged on through the summer of 1398, and at the trial by combat in the lists at Coventry on September 16th the king stopped the duel and banished both the accuser and the accused—Bolingbroke for ten years, Mowbray for life. During Bolingbroke's exile in France, on the death of his father John of Gaunt on February 3, 1399, Richard confiscated the Lancastrian estates and revenues. Thomas Chaucer's interest, as we have seen, went to William Scroop, Earl of Wiltshire, one of the council of eighteen and Lord Treasurer ; and in return he received from the royal exchequer an annuity of £13 6s. 8d. Chaucer who, as we have seen, may actually have been in the service of Bolingbroke in 1395–6 evidently felt keenly both Richard's covetise and extortion, and Bolingbroke's exile. Surely that is the meaning of his ballade entitled *Lack of Steadfastness* :

II

What maketh this world so variable
But lust that folk have in dissensioun ?
For nowadays a man is holde unable
But if he can, by som collusioun,
Don his neighbour wrong or oppressioun.
What causeth this, but wilful wrecchednesse
That al is lost for lak of stedfastnesse ?

III

Trouthe is put down ; Resoun is holden fable ;
Vertu hath now no dominacioun ;
Pitee exiled ; no man is merciable ;
Through covetise is plent discrecioun.
The world hath made a permutacioun
Fro right to wrong, fro trouthe to fikelnesse,
That al is lost, for lak of stedfastnesse.

Envoy.

O prince, desire to be honourable ;
Cherish thy folk, and hate extorcioun !
Suffre no thing that may be reprevable
To thine estate, don in thy regioun.
Shew forth thy swerd of castigacioun.
Dred God ; do law ; love trouthe and worthinesse,
And wed thy folk again to stedfastnesse.

But Bolingbroke's exile was not of long duration. During Richard II's absence in Ireland in the summer of 1399, Bolingbroke eluded the easy restraints of the French

and landed at Ravenspur on Spurn Point, Yorkshire, on
July 14th.

> well furnish'd by the Duke of Bretagne
> With eight tall ships, three thousand men of war.

He was welcomed by other disaffected lords, and, after a
triumphal march to London, was joined by the regent,
his uncle the Duke of York. Their joint forces marched
on Bristol, where William Scroop, Earl of Wiltshire, and
others of Richard's council were captured and beheaded.
They then advanced into Wales to meet Richard II, who
had arrived at Conway Castle from his Irish expedition.
Bolingbroke offered terms. If Richard would restore the
Lancastrian estates and punish the murderers of his uncle
Gloucester, he would crave forgiveness and become his
dutiful subject. Reconciliation was made between the
cousins, and they returned together to London. Here,
however, Richard abdicated, or was persuaded to renounce
his throne, in favour of Bolingbroke. Parliament met on
September 30, 1399, and Richard's abdication was accepted.
Henry Bolingbroke, Duke of Hereford, Earl of Derby,
was crowned as Henry IV on October 13, 1399, and was
supported by the English people and the majority of the
nobles. A conspiracy to restore Richard II, prominent in
which figured John Holland, Duke of Exeter, husband of
Elizabeth of Lancaster, failed at Cirencester on January 7,
1400. Exeter was beheaded at Pleshy on January 15th.
Richard died the death of Gloucester at Pontefract Castle.
Isabella was sent back to France, to marry later her poetic
cousin Charles d'Orleans.

The Chaucers in their comparatively humble way were
whole-hearted supporters of Henry IV. On October 13,
1399, the day of his coronation, the new king granted
Geoffrey Chaucer an annuity of 40 marks (£26 13s. 4d.),
and on October 18th confirmed the late king's grants of
£20 a year and a butt of wine, Chaucer having testified
that the former patents were accidentally lost. Thomas

Chaucer was made Constable of Wallingford Castle, Berks —a useful post, since his annuity of 20 marks was received from the revenues of the town. His pension was confirmed on October 23rd, and on October 26th he was made Steward of the Honour of Wallingford with a salary of £40 a year for life. If, as seems most probable, Chaucer's *Complaint to his Purse* was written at this time, since it was envoyed to the " conqueror of Brutus' Albion," we must date it between September 29, 1399, the last day of Richard II's reign, and October 13, 1399, the date of the patent of Chaucer's new pension.

Soon afterwards Chaucer took up residence in the precincts of the Abbey at Westminster. On December 24, 1399, he leased from the monk who acted as warden of the Lady Chapel a house which stood in the garden behind it. He leased it for fifty-three years at a rent of £2 13s. 4d. a year. It may be that Chaucer removed from Greenwich to live near " the stremes hede of alle honour " ; but more probably he had resolved to devote the last years of his life to the cultivation and practice of religion, like his friend Gower, who a few years earlier—in 1397—had taken an apartment in the priory of St. Mary Overy, Southwark. Wealth had little attraction for Chaucer in his last years. He willingly retired from the struggle for place and power. He had learned his limitations. He now knew that such genius as he had was poetical and literary, not political and administrative. He made this epigram :

> Of al this worlde the large compass
> Hit wol not in mine armes tweyne ;
> Whoso mochel wol embrace,
> Litel therof he shall distreyne.

Here at Westminster, if Shirley is to be believed, he wrote his " balade de bon conseil " or *Truth* :

> Flee fro the prees and dwelle with sothfastnesse,
> Suffice unto thy thing though hit be smal.

He sorrowed for "the enditynges of worldly vanitees" and "many a leccherous lay" which he had written in his unregenerate past—poems which were now copied and scattered beyond recall. He made his peace with Holy Church, and caused his retraction of works "that sounen into sinne" to be appended to his unfinished *Canterbury Tales*. But Chaucer did not long enjoy the sanctity of his retirement. He died, as his monument in Westminster Abbey, where the monks buried him, formerly stated, on October 25, 1400. Of the circumstances of his death we know nothing, nor whether he was a benefactor of the Abbey. But the house at Westminster afterwards passed into the tenancy of Thomas Chaucer, who also followed his father as under-forester of North Petherton. He afterwards became Butler to Henry IV and to Henry V, Knight of the Shire for Oxford, and Speaker of the House of Commons. Thomas Chaucer fought at Agincourt, and died, encumbered with riches, in 1434.

THE CANON AND CHRONOLOGY OF CHAUCER'S WRITINGS

§ I

BEFORE we proceed to consider the works of Chaucer critically, let us pause for a few moments to decide what those works are, and when they were written.

In the first place, no autograph manuscript of any of Chaucer's works has been found. His writings have been handed down to our age in numerous manuscripts of the fifteenth century. Some of these are wholly copies of Chaucer's poems. Others, again, are miscellaneous, containing both genuine and doubtful poems mingled with the writings of poets of the next generation. Sometimes the works of Chaucer were attributed to him by the booksellers and copyists, but oftener they were copied without either title or colophon. In the absence of a traditional method of spelling, each copyist spelled his words much as his inclination prompted ; and naturally made the mistakes of misreading, insertion, and omission, which are inevitable —such is the fallibility of human nature—in the mechanical operation of copying. Some copyists, scorning exactitude, even arrogated to themselves the editorial privilege of altering, and, as they thought, of improving, words and phrases here and there. Hence both the canon and the text of what Chaucer wrote present to modern critics a good many problems which may not be decided definitely and uniformly, and which probably never will be finally agreed upon.

Next, after a century of copied manuscripts, came the introduction of printing into England, and the printed

editions of Chaucer's works. *The Canterbury Tales* were
published by Caxton (1478, 1483), also by Pynson (*c.* 1493,
1526) and by Wynkyn de Worde (1498). Caxton printed
also *The Parlement of Fowles* (1478), *The House of Fame*,
and *Troilus and Criseyde* (1483) ; and Pynson and Wynkyn
de Worde later followed suit. Caxton included with *The
Parlement of Fowles* some of the short minor poems, e.g. the
ballades of *Fortune*, *Truth*, and *Gentilesse*, and part of the
Envoy to Scogan. In yet another volume he printed *The
Complainte of Anelida* and Chaucer's *Complainte to his
Purse*. Another early printer, Julian Notary, published
The Complainte of Mars, *The Complainte of Venus*, and the
Envoy to Buckton (*c.* 1500).

The first collected edition of Chaucer's works was
William Thynne's folio, first published in 1532,[1] reprinted
1542, and *c.* 1550. Thynne's edition is of considerable
interest, and is, moreover, of some importance as a text ;
for example, it is an authority for the text of *The House of
Fame*, and it is the only authority for lines 1–44 of *The
Romaunt of the Rose*; but it added fresh problems for
modern editors by its individual readings, and by
Thynne's unhappy insertion of certain apocryphal works,
which to reject has been one of the conclusions of nineteenth-
century textual criticism. Later followed the editions of
John Stowe (1561), Thomas Speght (1597, 1602, reprinted
1687), and John Urry (1721), who reproduced Thynne's
text more or less carefully ; and each in turn bettered the
instruction of his predecessors in finding fresh poems to
add to the works of Chaucer ; so that in their final form, as,
for instance, in Anderson's *British Poets*, Vol. I (1793), the
" Works of Chaucer " had grown to an enormous size.
The *Canterbury Tales* were followed by the Cook's *Tale of
Gamelyn*—an ancestor of that romance which ultimately
became Shakespeare's comedy *As You Like It*,—also by
the Chaucerian imitations entitled *The Plowman's Tale*,

---

[1] Reproduced as a *Facsimile of the First Folio of Chaucer*, edited by
W. W. Skeat, Oxford, 1905.

*The Merry Aventure of the Pardoner and Tapster at the Inn
at Canterbury,* and The Merchant's *Second Tale of Beryn.*
Chaucer's *Troilus and Criseyde* had as its sequel a sixth
book, to wit, Henryson's *Testament of Fair Creseide. The
Book of the Duchess* had prefixed to it a long poem in
octosyllabic couplets (named by Skeat, " The Isle of
Ladies ") which was terminated by the corrupt text of a
charming little *Ballade of Obeisaunce* ; then followed *The
Book of the Duchess* with the *Envoy to Buckton* as its sequel,
to which was prefixed the note, " This seems an envoy to
the Duke of Lancaster after his loss of Blanch," and the
whole medley had been entitled by Speght *Chaucer's
Dreame. The Legend of Good Women* had as its epilogue a
short poem in the seven-line stanza entitled *A Praise of
Women,* and it was followed later by a poem celebrating
the amazonian prowess of *The IX Ladies Worthie.*
Chaucer's lost work *Origen on the Magdalene* was represented
by a curious devotional poem in the seven-line stanza—
more interlarded with Latin scraps than any of Chaucer's
unquestioned work—called *The Lamentation of Mary
Magdalene.* Other apocryphal works were a translation
(by Sir Richard Ros) of Alain Chartier's poem called *La
Belle Dame sans Mercy* ; also *The Assembly of Ladies* and
a very charming allegory entitled *The Flower and the Leaf*
(both by a poetess whose name is unknown), and *The
Cuckoo and the Nightingale* (by Sir Thomas Clanvowe),
The Complainte of the Black Knight (by John Lydgate),
The Court of Love (by " Philogenet . . . of Cambridge,
clerk "), *The Remedy of Love* (a metrical version of Solomon's
warnings against evil women), and a little bundle of Balades,
etc., mostly spurious, in which Chaucer's *Ballade de visage
sans peinture* (or *Fortune*) appeared as the " Ballade of the
vilage without paintyng."
    One prose work—an imitation of Boëthius's Consolation
of Philosophy entitled *The Testament of Love*—was regarded
as Chaucer's until 1868, when Bradshaw and Furnivall
rejected it.   Finally in 1897 Bradley and Skeat skilfully

showed from an acrostic of the initial letters of the chapters which, when rectified, read MARGARET OF VIRTW HAVE MERCI ON THIN USK, that it must be the work of Thomas Usk, one of the victims of the " Merciless " Parliament in 1388. With this ascription went Usk's autobiographical references to his connexion with the Lord Mayor, John of Northampton, the enemy of the fishmongers —references which had been wrongly applied by biographers to the life of Chaucer.

With the growth of the critical spirit during the eighteenth and nineteenth centuries came the desire for a more satisfactory printed text of Chaucer's works. The honour of first gratifying this desire belongs to Thomas Tyrwhitt, who published an edition of *The Canterbury Tales* in five volumes, octavo (1775–1778), with notes which are still valuable, and a glossary. Tyrwhitt's edition of *The Canterbury Tales* was the standard text until the middle of the nineteenth century, when new texts were prepared by Wright and by Morris. Thomas Wright edited for the Percy Society (1847–1851) an edition of *The Canterbury Tales* based upon MS. Harley 7334 (British Museum), a manuscript which differs considerably in detail from those upon which the text of *The Canterbury Tales* had been and is generally based, and which has undoubtedly undergone some sort of revision, either by Chaucer himself (as Pollard suggested) or more probably by some copyist with a genius for emendation. Richard Morris also followed this manuscript, and, rejecting the older printed texts, went back to manuscripts rather than to Thynne and Speght for his text of the other poems in his edition of Chaucer (Bell, 1866, revised by Skeat for Bohn's Library, 1892).

So far, the labours of the various editors of Chaucer had only served to pile Pelion on the Ossa of confusion, and a reliable text of Chaucer became a just and an immediate necessity. On the one hand there were a number of more or less complete Chaucer manuscripts in the British

Museum, the Bodleian Library, in Cambridge, and scattered in the private libraries of country houses—each manuscript differing to a greater or less degree from the others. On the other hand were the various printed editions of Chaucer's works, some thoroughly unreliable ; others well-intentioned, but imperfect. The need for a standard edition led to the formation of the Chaucer Society in 1868 by Frederick Furnivall and others, and to the publication by the Chaucer Society of reprints of the best manuscripts of Chaucer's works. Eight manuscripts of *The Canterbury Tales* were published between 1868 and 1902, also parallel texts of *Troilus and Crisyde* and the Minor Poems. These reprints of good manuscripts offered a new basis for the preparation of a critical text of Chaucer ; and the Chaucer Society, not content merely with the poems, published also editions of Chaucer's *Boece* (1886) and *The Astrolabe* (1872). The Chaucer Society, moreover, " discovered " the Ellesmere manuscript, which is now generally accepted both as the best text of *The Canterbury Tales* and as the best representation of the spelling and grammar of the author.

The publication of these reprints lightened the clerical labour of later editors, and led to the preparation and publication of the two texts now commonly in use, namely, the " Oxford " edition of *The Works of Chaucer*, edited by Rev. W. W. Skeat (Oxford, 1894), and the " Globe " edition of *The Works of Chaucer*, edited by A. W. Pollard, Heath, Liddell, and McCormick (London, 1899). The texts of these editions differ slightly in word, and considerably in spelling. The editors of the " Globe " edition normalized i and j, u and v. Skeat normalized still more, using i for the short vowel, and y for the long ; and endeavouring (not with complete success) to use a consistent form of spelling for common words. Both texts have their merits ; but neither, unfortunately, can be considered faultless. The " Globe " text is, in the opinion of the present writer, the more reliable ; but Skeat's

glossary is fuller, and therefore more useful. The fact is
that the work of preparing a critical text of Chaucer is
too laborious for one pen, and yet too complicated for more
than one directing mind.

§ 2

What, then, is an editor's task ? The task of an editor
of Chaucer should be, firstly, to decide what Chaucer
actually wrote ; secondly, to restore the original text of
each work from the extant manuscripts (or from early
printed versions where no manuscript authority exists) ;
and thirdly, to print without error his own critical text.
This seems so obvious and so reasonable that it may surprise the reader to learn that it is a comparatively modern
conception of what is an editor's duty to the text.   Thynne,
for example, appears simply to have printed what he
regarded as a good manuscript of each work—a method
which survived as late as the nineteenth century in the
Canterbury Tales of Thomas Wright (Percy Society, 1847–
1851).   Urry revised his text and made it " correct " by
the insertion or suppression of expletives, much in the
same way as Pope improved Shakespeare. It is not
enough for an editor to copy, or to revise by the light of
nature, that which appears to be the best early text ; nor
is a composite text derived from a selection of the most
appropriate variant readings of the various manuscripts
as desirable as a text based on the oldest and most authentic
version, emended where corrupt by the readings of other
reliable manuscripts. And by a " corrupt " passage is
meant not merely a feeble or a tautological reading ; but
a word or phrase which cannot be allowed to stand, either
because it is nonsense in its present form, or because it
deviates clearly and inexplicably from the grammatical or
prosodial use of Chaucer.

The first problem of an editor, then, is to find the most
authentic manuscript of each work by Chaucer, and to
use that as the basis of his text. To do this, he collates

and compares the various extant manuscripts ; and, after rejecting the derivative and corrupt manuscripts, he selects the manuscript (or the group of related manuscripts) which, by its outstanding excellence of spelling, grammar, and metre, represents the earliest and purest copy of Chaucer's original. This is " the best " text. This he uses as the basis of his text. If, now, he should print this text as it stands in the manuscript, it would certainly contain errors—mistakes of letters, words, and lines made in copying,[1] not to mention the omission of lines, or even parts of poems ; and possibly also it would contain certain scribal alterations and additions.[2]

His second problem is therefore to correct the errors and scribal alterations of the manuscript which he has selected as the basis of his text. This correction, or " emendation," as it is called, ought to be restricted to actual corruptions. In the words of Pollard (" Globe " *Chaucer*, p. ix) an editor's task is " to offer an accurate reflection of that manuscript or group of manuscripts which critical investigation has shown to be the best, with only such emendation upon the evidence of other manuscripts as appear(s) absolutely necessary, and with the utmost parsimony of ' conjecture.' " The attractive variant readings of the discarded manuscripts should be regarded usually as unauthoritative scribal alterations. An acceptable emendation should conform to the sense, language, and metre of the context ; and its intrinsic value is increased if it resembles the corruption, and so accounts for the error and explains it.[3]

The difficulty of preparing a critical text of Chaucer's works is greatly complicated by the fact that the manu-

---

[1] Such as : My *sorow* (son3) is turned to pleyning (*Duchess*, 599) ; Your *semy* (semly) voice that ye so *fynal* (fmal) outtwine (*Rosemound*, II) ; etc.

[2] Such as : Ne that a monk whan he is *cloysterless* (reccheless) (*Prologue, C. T.*, 179) ; or, And eek [*suffred*] that Longius his herte pighte (*A. B. C.* 163) ; or, No maner *counseyl* (rede) but at hir loke (*Duchess*, 840), etc.

[3] As in *The Book of the Duchess*, l. 959, where *pure sewing* may be corrected by " pursuing."

scripts are numerous (except of certain minor poems), widely scattered, frequently incomplete, and are mostly late copies of earlier copies. Hence they contain compound errors, and scribal emendations and alterations. The problem is made more difficult by their spelling. The Chaucer manuscripts were written by fifteenth-century copyists, the early printed copies were set up in type by sixteenth-century printers from fifteenth-century manuscripts, and the spelling is consequently in the main that of the English of a period somewhat later than that of Chaucer. Moreover, the spelling of one good manuscript will differ from that of other good manuscripts ; and even in the same manuscript the copyist did not consistently spell the same words in the same way. There are differences in the spelling of long vowels, e.g. stoon, stone ; heved, heed ; seurtee, suretee ; heigh, hy ; and also in words containing i and u, owing to the fact that i and y, u and w were alternative and interchangeable, e.g. fyr, fire, fir ; wif, wyf ; vertu, virtw ; foul, fowl, etc. No version of Chaucer's work whether transcribed, critically emended, or modernized, can ever satisfy every one ; and, in the present state of the text, every student of Chaucer must be to some extent his own textual critic. Fortunately, the variant readings recorded by the editors of the " Oxford " and " Globe " editions, the accessibility of the Ellesmere Facsimile [1] in public libraries, and the reprints of the Chaucer Society,[2] make it possible for a student to check the work of the editor of the printed text which he reads ; and will enable him either to restore a more authentic reading, or to try his skill at the interesting game of emendation.

§ 3

It is part of an editor's task also to see that he admits

---

[1] Reproduced from the Ellesmere Manuscript in facsimile by the Manchester University Press, 1911.
[2] For a full list thereof, see Oxford University Press Catalogue under publications of The Chaucer Society.

to his edition only the authentic works of Chaucer. He should approve not merely poems which seem to be Chaucer's—works written in Chaucerian language and prosody, and perhaps even bearing the marks of his style and personality—but works which are authenticated either by Chaucer or by his contemporaries. It is one of the many merits of the " Oxford " and " Globe " editions that they exclude the poems entitled *The Court of Love, The Complainte of the Black Knight, The Cuckoo and the Nightingale, The Flower and the Leaf,* and *Chaucer's Dreame,* which Tyrwhitt and his immediate successors had regarded as authentic.

How, then, are Chaucer's works authenticated ? What warranty have we that a poem included by an editor amongst Chaucer's works is really genuine ? Chaucer was not in the habit of signing his works, and no autograph manuscripts have survived ; so that the establishment of Chaucer's authorship is a problem of deduction which depends upon evidence of two kinds—on (1) internal evidence, namely, passages in Chaucer's approved works which give the names of his writings ; and on (2) external evidence, such as allusions to Chaucer's authorship of certain poems by contemporaries, and scribal ascriptions of works to Chaucer in manuscripts written by copyists likely to know the truth. Let us deal with each in turn.

1. *Internal Evidence for Chaucer's Writings.*

(i) In his old age Chaucer regretted that ever he had composed works " that sounen into sinne," and at the end of *The Canterbury Tales* he caused to be inserted his " Retracciouns "—a document wherein he expressed contrition for ever having written some works, but in which he commended others. This retraction expresses just that regret which Chaucer may well have felt, when, as an old man, lodged within the monkish precincts of Westminster Abbey, he prepared his soul to make a good end.

Its authenticity is supported by Thomas Gascoigne (d.
1458), Chancellor of the University of Oxford, in a note in
his *Liber Veritatum*,[1] which is still extant in Lincoln
College Library, Oxford : " Chawserus ante mortem suam
saepe clamavit ' Vae mihi ! Vae mihi ! quia revocare nec
destruere jam potero illa quae mala scripsi de malo et
turpissimo amore.' " In this last work, at the end of *The
Canterbury Tales*, Chaucer declares himself to be the writer
of *Troilus*, *The Book of Fame* (House of Fame), *The Book of
the XXV Ladies* (Legend of Good Women), *The Book of
the Duchess*, *The Book of S. Valentine's Day* (Parlement of
Fowles), *The Canterbury Tales*, and *The Book of the Lion*
(lost) ; also of a translation of Boëthius's *De Consolatione
Philosophiae*, and of other books of legends of saints, and
homilies, besides " many a song and many a lecherous lay."

(ii) In the prologue to Group B of *The Canterbury Tales*,
entitled " The wordes of the Hoost to the companye," the
Man of Law is made to attribute to Chaucer tales of lovers,
and he instances two, namely, " Ceys and Alcione " (ll.
62–220 of *The Book of the Duchess*), and a later work which
he calls *The Seintes Legende of Cupide*, which obviously
from the context is none other than *The Legend of Good
Women*.

(iii) In *The Legend of Good Women* we shall find a further
list of works mentioned in the common version of the
Prologue (Text B). The god of Love charges Chaucer with
enmity in that he hinders lovers, and accounts it folly to
serve Love. " Thou needst not deny it," he says, " for
(l. 329) :

> Thou hast translated *The Romaunce of the Rose*,
> That is an heresye ayeins my lawe,
> And makest wise folk fro me withdrawe ;
> And of *Criseyde* thou hast seyd as thee liste,"

which, as line 265 of Text A—

> How that Criseyde Troylus forsook—

---

[1] Selected passages in J. E. Thorold Rogers's *Gascoigne's Theological
Dictionary*, Oxford, 1881.

4

shows, is clearly an allusion to the faithlessness of the heroine of *Troilus and Criseyde*. Whereupon, in Chaucer's fiction, Alcestis defends him on the ground that he had " furthered well your law in his making " (poetry), and instances as loyal works *The House of Fame, The Book of the Duchess* (The Death of Blaunche the Duchess), *The Parlement of Fowles, The Love of Palamon and Arcite of Thebes* (The Knight's Tale ?), a prose translation of Boëthius, *The Life of St. Cecile*, and an early work entitled *Origines upon the Maudeleyne* (Origen's homily on St. Mary Magdalene). She also mentions " balades, roundels," and " virelayes," without indicating their titles. The later version of the Prologue (Text A), found only in the Cambridge MS. Gg, 4, 27, adds to these

> *The Wrechede Engendrynge of Mankynde,*
> As man may in Pope Innocent i-fynde.

(iv) So that by internal evidence alone we may ascribe to Chaucer the following works : *The Canterbury Tales, Troilus and Criseyde, The Legend of Good Women, The Book of the Duchess, The House of Fame, The Parlement of Fowles, Palamon and Arcite* (The Knight's Tale ?), *The Life of St. Cecile* (Second Nun's Tale), a translation of *The Romance of the Rose*, and of Boëthius's *De Consolatione Philosophiae ;* also the lost works, *The Book of the Lion, Origen on the Magdalene*, and *The Wretched Engendering of Mankind*. The only extant work which answers to Chaucer's " Origen " is the poem included in early editions with the title *The Lamentation of Mary Magdalene*, and this is generally rejected on the ground that in style it resembles nothing that Chaucer wrote. *The Wretched Engendering of Mankind* appears to have been a translation of Pope Innocent III's treatise *De Contemptu Mundi, sive De Miseria Conditionis Humanae*, but possibly it was Chaucer's name for the Prologue to *The Man of Law's Tale* (B 99–121), which is taken from the sixteenth chapter of the book in question, and was probably added to the story of Custance together with three or four inserted stanzas (noted in the " Globe " text), when it became the Man of Law's Tale.

2. *External Evidence for Chaucer's Writings.*

(i) In 1393 (?) the French poet Eustache Deschamps sent to Chaucer a book of his poems by the hands of an English knight named Sir Lewis Clifford, together with a ballade [1] in which he hailed Chaucer as the translator into English of *Le Roman de la Rose.*

(ii) John Lydgate, a fifteenth-century English poet, a disciple of Chaucer and a friend of the bookseller, John Shirley, praised Chaucer in the Prologue to *The Fall of Princes* (1431–1438). He acclaimed his " fresh comedies " and his " ful pitous tragedies," and gave a list of his works which adds something to Chaucer's own attributions. " In youth," he says, " he made a translacioun Off a book which called is Trophe [2] In Lombard tunge " . . . and " Gaff it the name off *Troilus and Cresseide.*" He also translated Boëthius's *Consolation (of Philosophy)*, and made for his son Lewis a treatise on *The Astrolabe.*

> He wrot also ful many day agone
> Dante in Inglissh, himself so doth expresse
> The pitous story off Ceix and Alcione,
> And the Deth (eek) of Blaunche the Duchesse,
> And notably dede his bisynesse,
> By gret avys, his wittis to dispose
> To translate the Romaunce off the Rose.

" Dante in English " is a crux. It is usually interpreted as another name for *The House of Fame* ; for, if the list of works named by Lydgate be compared with the lists

---

[1] This ballade is No. CCLXXXV of Deschamp's *Oeuvres* (S.A.T.F., 1878–1903), Vol. II, p. 138 ; also *Oxford Book of French Verse*, 9 ; or Paget Toynbee, *Specimens of Old French*, p. 314 ; or The " Aldine " Chaucer (1845), Vol. I, p. 102.

[2] Lydgate was correct in saying that the original of Chaucer's *Troilus and Criseyde* was written in Italian ; but it was not called *Trophe* (perhaps Lydgate's error for *Troylo*), but *Filostrato.*

given by Chaucer, it will be seen that all the works mentioned by Chaucer are also mentioned by Lydgate with the exception of one poem—*The House of Fame*. It may, however, mean that Chaucer was a translator of Dante, and if so, possibly, but improbably, refers to the *Invocatio ad Mariam* (cf. *Paradiso* xxxiii, 1–21) which appears before the Second Nun's *Life of St. Cecile* (G, ll. 29–50). It will be noticed also that Lydgate states that Chaucer translated *The Romance of the Rose* " by great advice," i.e. at the request of a great man, a statement which tallies with Chaucer's (cf. P.L.G.W., B 366, A 346), that " him was boden " to write *Troilus* and *The Romance of the Rose*. Lydgate proceeds in the Prologue to *The Fall of Princes* to attribute to Chaucer also *The Parlement of Fowles, Origen on the Magdalene, The Book of the Lion, The Complaint of Anelida on False Arcite, The Brooch of Thebes* (*The Complaint of Mars*), *The Legend of Good Women*, and *The Canterbury Tales*, including the tales of Melibeus (Chaucer's Tale), Griselda (The Clerk's Tale), and the Monk's Tragedies. He also wrote, said Lydgate (l. 353),

> Compleyntes, balades, roundeles, virelaies
> Ful delectable to heren and to see.

Lydgate also in another poem, *The Pilgrimage of the Life of Man* (ll. 19755–9), attributed to Chaucer the " noble oryson " translated from Guillaume de Guileville's *Prière à nostre Dame*, and names it " Off Our Lady the A.B.C."

(iii) The copyists of manuscripts ascribed to Chaucer many poems which he certainly never wrote, but there are good reasons for accepting the ascriptions of a copyist named John Shirley (1366 ?–1456), who seems to have made manuscripts of contemporary poetry partly for the purpose of lending them for profit, as well as for sale. Six at least of Shirley's manuscripts still exist, written on paper in the crabbed handwriting of the fifteenth century, the chief of which are MSS. Additional 16165 (British Museum), Trinity R, 3, 20 (Cambridge), Ashmole 59 (Oxford), and Sion College L, 40, 2a/3 ; and four more lost manuscripts are represented by copies, the chief of which is MS. Harley 7333 (British Museum). Shirley ascribed to Chaucer the Complaintes of *Anelida, Mars,* and *Venus,* the Ballades of *Fortune, Truth, Gentilesse, Lack of Steadfastness,* and the so-called *Complaint to his Purse, The Complaint to Pity* including the fragmentary *Complaint to his Lady,* the " devoute prayer to oure lady " known as *Chaucer's A.B.C.,* and the stanza *To Adam, his owne Scriveyne.* Shirley also ascribed to Chaucer (in MSS. Addit. 16165) a *Ballade of a Reeve,* which neither the Oxford nor the Globe editors included in their texts.[1]

(iv) There is good manuscript authority for the *Envoy to Scogan,* which is attributed to Chaucer by MS. Fairfax 16 (Bodleian) and MS. Pepys 2006 (Magd. Coll. Camb.) ; also for the *Envoy to Buckton,* which the only authority (MS. Fairfax 16) authenticates as " the counceyll of Chaucer touchyng Maryage &c. whiche was sente to Bucketon." The poem called *The Former Age* (or *Aetas Prima*) is found in two manuscripts in Cambridge University Library, both of which attribute it to Chaucer. The so-called *Proverbs* were not attributed to Chaucer by Shirley when he copied them in MS. Addit. 16165, but two other manuscripts (Fairfax 16 and Harley 7578) head them " Proverbe of Chaucer." The doubtful ballade *To Rosemounde,* found only in one manuscript, Rawl. Poet, 163 (Bodleian) is followed by the curious colophon " tregentil — — chaucer," on the strength of which Skeat proclaimed it genuine in 1891, and the poem is usually accepted as a specimen of Chaucer's humour. The manuscript is late. It is said to have been copied *c.* 1580. No doubt the scribe thought that Chaucer wrote the poem,—but did he know ? An envoy to a lady,

---

[1] For a reprint and a facsimile, see Brusendorff, *The Chaucer Tradition,* London, 1925, p. 280. We need not regret the omission of this Ballade, for it is not in Chaucer's happiest vein.

called by Skeat *Womanly Noblesse,* occurs in only one manuscript, Additional 34360 (Brit. Mus.), where it is entitled
" Balade that Chauncier made." The manuscript is late,
but it is perhaps a copy of one of Shirley's manuscripts.
The text is somewhat corrupt, but Skeat, who discovered
it in 1894, was probably correct in declaring it to be an
authentic poem.

(v) So that we can determine the canon of Chaucer's
writings as follows, regarding as lost *The Book of the Lion,*
Origen on the Magdalene, and perhaps *The Wretched Engen-*
dering of Mankind. The letters C. L. S. in brackets stand
for the ascriptions of Chaucer, Lydgate, and Shirley
respectively ; where they do not follow the title, the
authenticity of the work depends on anonymous
ascriptions.

ROMANCES AND LEGENDS : *Troilus and Criseyde* (C. L.) ;
Legend of Good Women (C. L.) ; and *The Canterbury Tales*
(C. L.) including *Palamon and Arcite,* and *The Life of St.*
Cecile (C.), *Melibeus, Griselda,* and the Monk's *Tragedies* (L.).

DREAMS AND ALLEGORIES : Translation of *The Romance*
of the Rose (C. L.) ; *The Book of the Duchess,* including *Ceyx*
and Alcione (C. L.) ; *The House of Fame* (C.)—which is
possibly Lydgate's " Dante in English," and *The Parlement*
of Fowles (C. L.).

COMPLAINTES : *To Pity* and *To his Lady* (S.), *Of Anelida*
(L. S.), *Of Mars* (L. S.), *Of Venus* (S.).

MORAL BALLADES : *Of Fortune* (S.), *Truth* (S.), and
Gentilesse (S.).

ENVOYS : *To Adam* (S.), *To Rosemounde, Womanly*
Noblesse (Ballade that Chaucer made), *To Scogan, To*
Buckton, To Richard II (Lack of Steadfastness) (S.), *To*
Henry IV (Complaint to his Purse) (S.).

MISCELLANEOUS : *The A.B.C.* (L. S.), *The Former Age,*
Proverbs, Ballade of a Reeve (S.).

PROSE WORKS : *Boece* (C. L. S.), *The Astrolabe* (L.).

This is the canon of Chaucer's works, namely the writings

declared on credible evidence to be Chaucer's ; but Skeat admitted also three roundels called *Merciless Beauty* which are not ascribed to Chaucer in MS. Pepys 2006, where they follow several genuine poems.   And both Skeat and Heath (Globe edition) admitted the ballade *To Rosemound* as authentic (rightly ?), and yet relegated to an appendix the ballade *Against Women Inconstant* (i.e. " Madame, for your newe-fangelnesse "), the *Complainte d'Amours*, and *A Ballade of Complainte*, because they are not expressly attributed to Chaucer in the manuscripts.   If one goes beyond the verge of manuscript ascription, it is difficult indeed to know where to draw the bound between genuine and spurious works ;   for, despite the too convincing arguments of their academic professors, it is certain—if, indeed, it is not a matter of common knowledge—that the evidences of language and style are slippery and dubious. Therefore, unless fresh manuscripts are discovered which definitely attribute further poems to Chaucer, it seems likely that the canon will be restricted to these two prose works and twenty-five poems.

§ 4

Let us now turn to the chronology of Chaucer's works, which is most difficult to establish, and indeed not yet fully agreed on.   The general order of some of the most important works may be inferred from Chaucer's own statements.

In *The Canterbury Tales*, at the beginning of Group B, the Men of Law is made to allude (l. 61) to *The Legend of Good Women*.   Further, in the Prologue to *The Legend of Good Women* several earlier works are named : *The Romaunt of the Rose, Troilus and Criseyde, The House of Fame, The Book of the Duchess, The Parlement of Fowles, Palamon and Arcite* (The Knight's Tale), the *Boece*, and *The Life of St. Cecile*.   From this it is clear that *Palamon and Arcite* (The Knight's Tale) was written before *The Legend of Good Women*, and the latter before the framework of *The Canterbury Tales.* But which comes first ?—*Troilus and Criseyde* or *The Knight's Tale* ? Remembering Lydgate's statement that Chaucer wrote *Troilus* " in youth," and that *The Knight's Tale* was written in heroic couplets, the metre of *The Legend of Good Women*—Chaucer's latest metrical pattern, we may surely agree that *Troilus and Criseyde* was written first. But it has been pointed out that Chaucer's translation of Boëthius influenced his thought in the composition of *Troilus and Criseyde*, leading him to insert screeds of philosophical moralizing into the romance—especially in Books III and IV. We may therefore reasonably infer that Boëthius was fresh in his memory, and that the *Boece* preceded the *Troilus.* Hence it follows that we can now place in general order these important works : the *Boece, Troilus and Criseyde, The Knight's Tale of Palamon and Arcite, The Legend of Good Women*, and *The Canterbury Tales.*

Actual evidence for the dates of composition of Chaucer's works is unfortunately rare. None of the manuscripts offers any indication of when the works contained in it were composed, and the date of the copyist's handwriting is of course no help. Our only further guides to chronology are inferences which we can draw from the matter of Chaucer's works, and from allusions which he makes ; or secondly, inferences from literary influence. Let us discuss each in turn.

I. *The Internal Evidence of Date.*

(i) *The Book of the Duchess* is clearly enough a poetic tribute to " the goode faire white "—the dead wife of the knight in black. The poem is referred to in the Prologue to *The Legend of Good Women*, and also by Lydgate in his Prologue to *The Fall of Princes*, as " The Dethe of Blaunche the Duchess." Now there was only one English duchess named Blanche in Chaucer's time—Blanche, Duchess of Lancaster, who married Gaunt in 1359 and died on September 12, 1369 : so that we may regard *The Book of the Duchess* as a poem addressed by Chaucer to John of Gaunt shortly after her death and say with comparative certainty that it was written in the winter of 1369–1370.

(ii) Chaucer's *A.B.C.* was first printed by Speght in 1602 with this note : " made, as some say, at the request of Blanche of Lancaster, as a praier for her privat use." This may reproduce a note on a lost manuscript by Shirley, or it may be pure invention ; but, until we have further evidence, there is no insuperable reason why we should not regard the *A.B.C.* as an early work, written before 1369.

(iii) Lydgate tells us in his Prologue to *The Fall of Princes*, and the statement is substantiated in the Prologue to *The Legend of Good Women* (B 366, A 346), that Chaucer was bidden to translate *Le Roman de la Rose* by some important noble. As the quest of the dreamer is for a beautiful red rose, which was (we are told by Camden) the badge of Blanche, Duchess of Lancaster, it is not unreasonable to suggest that this noble patron was John of Gaunt, and to connect the beginning of the translation with Gaunt's marriage to Blanche, which took place in 1359. A long translation such as this could not have been completed in a short time. Chaucer's labour must have endured for years ; if, indeed, it was ever finished : but one indication that he was translating *The Romaunt of the Rose* before he composed *The Book of the Duchess* is the fact that passages in the latter (e.g. ll. 416–433, 616–740) are unquestionably based upon reminiscences of the former.

(iv) In *The House of Fame* Chaucer alludes to his unremitting toil in the Customs House on the Wool Quay (e.g. Bk. ii, ll. 140–150). This would appear to refer to the period 1379–1385, when, as far as transpires, Chaucer could find no good excuse for absenting himself from the office. He also tells us (Bk. i, l. 63) half the date of his dream—" the tenthe day of Decembre "—but unfortunately, like many of our epistolary correspondents, he omits to add the year, so that his date is no guide. But it is not improbable, as Brusendorff (following Imelmann) pointed out,[1] that *The House of Fame* was modelled on Froissart's *Temple d'Onnour*, and that it was written to announce at the end tidings of the betrothal of Richard II to Anne of Bohemia. This would fulfil Chaucer's desire to learn " newe tydynges of Love's folk." Unfortunately the poem was left unfinished, or, less probably, was truncated after Richard's second marriage to Isabella of France in 1396. If *The House of Fame* was written to celebrate the betrothal of Richard II, the date referred to in the poem would be December 10, 1380, when arrangements were being made for an English embassy to negotiate with Bohemian envoys. Otherwise the poem baffles chronology. Its metre would suggest the early period of *The Romaunt of the Rose*, and *The Book of the Duchess*. Its matter would indicate composition during Chaucer's period of Italian influence, after 1373 ; and one would be inclined to date it *c.* 1375.

(v) Following Koch's brilliant theory, it is now generally held that *The Parlement of Fowles* was written to celebrate the marriage of Richard II to Anne of Bohemia, which took place in St. Stephen's, Westminster, on January 14, 1382. And we may infer that the poem was written in the spring of 1382, after the wedding. The formel eagle of the poem represents Anne of Bohemia, daughter of Kaiser Karl IV, and sister of good King Wenceslaus of Bohemia. The three tiercels represent three suitors for her hand— Richard II of England, Friedrich of Meissen, and Wilhelm of Bavaria ; and the grace of one year, which in the poem Nature allows her, represents the unforeseen interval between the beginning of the negotiations and her marriage, which was delayed by the Peasants' Rising.

(vi) In Prologue B of *The Legend of Good Women* (l. 496), Chaucer expressed his intention of presenting the book to the queen. Now Richard's second wife, Isabella, was a

---

[1] See Brusendorff, *The Chaucer Tradition*, O. V. P., 1925, p. 165. Also Imelmann, " Chaucer's Haus der Fama " in *Englische Studien*, xlv, p. 397.

little girl of eight when he married her in 1396, and however precocious she may have been, she could not possibly have found much enjoyment in these doleful stories of Cupid's saints. What she liked, in all probability, were the Prioress's Tale and the Nun's Priest's Tale. The queen of Chaucer's homage therefore was Anne of Bohemia, and the poem was written after her coming to England in 1382, and before her death in 1394, probably c. 1386.

Now the famous Prologue is extant in two versions, text A, found only in MS. Gg, 4, 27 (Cambridge), and text B, the vulgate version of the other manuscripts. Skeat and Pollard regarded text B as an amplification of text A, which they regarded as the earlier version. Lowes has, however, suggested that as a matter of fact text B was the earlier, and text A was an abridgment made later, after the death of Queen Anne. This is unimpeachable, I think ; for if the texts be compared, it will be found that text B is written for and addressed to a living queen (e.g. B 83–96, 296–9, 496) who by a pretty conceit is identified with the Queen of Love (B 213) and the daisy, Cupid's flower (B 321), probably because contemporary French poets were praising the marguerite, and because she wore a petalled coronet adorned with pearls. There are also allusions to two parties at court who associated themselves under the rival names of the Flower and the Leaf, meaning—as the poem long attributed to Chaucer entitled *The Flower and the Leaf* explains—the gay and the serious. It will be found that text A is shorter, and that Chaucer has much abbreviated his eloquent praise of his sovereign lady (cf. A 55–58 with B 50–59, B 83–186) and of the cult associated with her of the Flower and the Leaf. He has, moreover, ceased to call her " my lady sovereyne " (B 94, 275) and " my lady " (B 255, etc.), and instead alludes to her throughout as Alcestis (cf. B 275–81 with A 179–84, B 255 with A 209) using the past tense as if she were dead :

" Hire name was Alceste the debonayre."

It is significant too that the lines (B 496–7) which express Chaucer's intention of presenting his book to the queen are absent from text A. Chaucer also added a long passage (A 261–312) which alludes to himself as an old man ; and refers both to his anti-feminist writings, and to the authority of certain books in the library of Clerk Jankyn of the *Wife of Bath's Prologue*—which seems to indicate revision late in Chaucer's life. There is also a veiled reference to injustice at court (A 324–7) coupled with a veiled plea for justice to petitioners (A 360–4). The inference can only be that text B was written whilst Queen Anne was still alive, but that text A was a revision with both abridgment and addition made after her death in 1394, and probably about the same time as the *Wife of Bath's Prologue* was written.

(vii) The Proem to *The Complaint of Mars* is capable of a twofold meaning. It is based on the classical fable of the secret love of Mars and Venus discovered to the gods by Phœbus the sun-god. It is also a fanciful description of a conjunction of the planets Mars and Venus in Taurus ; or, in other words, of Mars and Venus visible together in the sky about sunrise in April. According to Shirley's note in MS. Trinity R, 3, 20, it may bear still another interpretation. He says that it was written at the request of John of Gaunt, and that it concerned the Duchess of York and the Earl of Huntingdon ; that is, that Venus represents Isabella of Castile, the wife of Gaunt's brother Edmund, and that Mars represents Sir John Holland, who became Earl of Huntingdon in 1387, was for a short time Duke of Exeter. So that the poem may be allegorical. That it is a fable we may rule out. It is not told as a mythological fable, and Vulcan is never mentioned.

The conjunction of Mars and Venus is not a very frequent phenomenon, and to one as interested in the aspects of the heavens as was Chaucer this unusual spectacle might well suggest the making of a poem. If we could find out in what years such conjunctions took place, we might possibly find a clue to the date of the poem. Through the kindness

of my friend Mr. R. Stoneley of Leeds, the following problem was sent to Dr. A. C. D. Crommelin of Greenwich
Observatory : the planets Mars and Venus were in conjunction when the Sun entered Taurus some time between
1370 and 1400 ;—in what years was this possible ?   He
worked out the calculation on the basis of periods of
recurrence, and found that the only possible years were
1383 and 1385, and of these 1383 was improbable because
the planets were so near the sun that it is doubtful whether
they could be seen.   So that the year 1385 was the only
year in which a conjunction of Mars and Venus in Taurus
was likely to impress Chaucer and his fellow star-gazers.[1]

Shirley's note appears to be correct as far as concerns
Sir John Holland, the half-brother of Richard II.   There
is an ironical allusion to " Seynt John " (l. 9) and to his
" crueltee and bost and tyrannye " (l. 37) which fit John
Holland, who was capable of any crime, and equally skilful
in evading the penalty.   He tortured a Carmelite friar at
Salisbury in most peculiar circumstances in May, 1384 ;
and in July, 1385, he slew on Richard's Scottish expedition
the son of the Earl of Stafford, for which he suffered the
loss of his estates and of the royal favour, which he did not
receive again until after his submission to the king in
January, and his reconciliation with Stafford on February 8,
1386.   The suggestion has been made [2] that Chaucer's
Complainte of Mars refers to a *liaison* between Holland
and Isabella of York during his enforced period of retirement, July, 1385, to January, 1386 ; but, as Holland took
sanctuary in Beverley, this is unlikely.   And indeed it
seems probable that Shirley's note, made some forty or
fifty years after the occasion, errs in naming Isabella of
York.   No scandal with Holland is mentioned by any of
the chroniclers, and it is impossible that Chaucer, even at
the request of Gaunt, should publicly reflect on the honour
of York and his wife ; not because he was incapable of

[1] This conflicts with the calculation of Professor Thurein given in Koch,
The Chronology of Chaucer's Writings, Chaucer Society, 1890.
[2] Brusendorff, *The Chaucer Tradition*, p. 267.

such a thing, but because he dare not. In those days honour was satisfied only by blood.

Who then was the lady ?   Immediately after Holland's pardon in January, 1386, he returned to London and fell madly in love with John of Gaunt's second daughter Elizabeth,[1] who had just " come out " at court.   It is this conjunction of Mars and Venus which is referred to in *The Complainte of Mars*.   Elizabeth of Lancaster, one of the children of Gaunt's first wife, Blanche of Lancaster, and brought up by Chaucer's sister-in-law Katharine Swynford, her governess, had been betrothed on June 24, 1380, to John Hastings, Earl of Pembroke, and was then nominally at least the Countess of Pembroke—for in the Middle Ages a betrothal was as binding and as sacred as the ceremony of marriage.   She was at court when Holland emerged from sanctuary, hated for his murder of Stafford's son, and avoided by honest men.   As Chaucer puts it (l. 66) :

> For hit stood so, that ilke tyme, no wight
> Counseyled him, ne seyde him welcome,
> That nigh her wit for sorwe was overcome.

But Holland's ardour and his martial bearing found favour with Elizabeth, in spite of his brutal and unsavoury reputation :

> And she hath taken him in subjeccioun
> And as a maistresse taught him his lessoun,

and finally she was unfaithful to Pembroke.   The affair became known just before Gaunt's departure on his second expedition to Castile.   The first betrothal to Pembroke was annulled, and the marriage to Holland took place immediately.   Holland was appointed Constable of Gaunt's Spanish expedition and the bride aвd bridegroom sailed together for Corunna.   The situation of the poem fits exactly a meeting of Mars and Venus in London, followed

---

[1] Higden's *Polychronicon* (Malverne's supplement), ix, p. 96–7, Rolls Series.   See S. Armitage-Smith, *John of Gaunt*, p. 459, London, 1904.

by a further meeting during the course of the progress of the expedition from London to Plymouth early in April 1386, and the discovery of the affair by Phœbus (Gaunt). Gaunt and Costanza left London for Plymouth on March 25th, but the expedition did not sail until July 7th.

Recollecting the astronomical conjunction of Mars and Venus in 1385, Chaucer turned the inauspicious marriage of his patron's daughter into a fiction which he intended to be apologetic, and yet dignified and poetic, by the quaint fancy with which it is invested. The date of the poem was 1386.[1]

(viii) *The Complainte of Venus* is closely connected with *The Complainte of Mars*. Whomever Mars and Venus represent, they are the same persons in both poems, and *The Complainte of Venus* is another apology for this rash marriage, written after some years. Chaucer makes Venus praise the nobility of Mars :

> In him is bountee, wisdom, governaunce,
> Wel more then any mannes wit can gesse.

True, he gives her cause for jealousy ; but what of that ? —she loves him.

> No fors ! thogh jalousye me tormente,
> Sufficeth me to see him when I may ;
> And therfor certes to myn endyng-day,
> To love him best, ne shal I never repente.

This would fit perfectly the relationship of Sir John Holland, Earl of Huntingdon, and Elizabeth his wife, the " Venus " of *The Complainte of Mars*. Shirley stated correctly in a note in MS. Trinity R. 3, 20 that *The Complainte of Venus* was translated from the French of Sir Otes de Granson, a knight from Savoy in the retinue of John of Gaunt. Granson was in England from 1391 to 1396, and received a pension from the royal exchequer in 1393. Shirley also stated that by Venus was meant

[1] See "Chaucer's Complaintes of Mars and of Venus," in *Review of English Studies*, ii. p. 405.

Isabella, Duchess of York ; but almost certainly he was in error.   If the Venus of *The Complainte of Mars* was Elizabeth of Lancaster, so was the lady of *The Complainte of Venus*:   the two poems stand together.   In the envoy addressed to his " princess," Chaucer speaks of himself as an old man.   He would presumably become acquainted with Granson's poems some time between 1391 and 1396. We may, therefore, date *The Complainte of Venus, c.* 1393.

(ix) The Prologue to *The Canterbury Tales* has been dated by the allusion of Chaucer to the Merchant (l. 276) :

> He wolde the see were kept for any thing
> Bitwixe Middleburgh and Orewelle.

Hales pointed out that (according to Craik's *History of British Commerce*, i, 123) the staple of wool was removed from Calais to Middelburgh during the years 1384 to 1388. If this be true to fact, and if Chaucer intended to refer to his Merchant as an exporter of wool, which is probable, the famous Prologue must have been written between 1384 and 1388, say *c.* 1386.   This is supported by other allusions.   The prologue to *The Clerk's Tale* (l. 38) alludes to the death of " Lynyan," or Giovanni di Legnano, an Italian jurist who died in 1383.   *The Monk's Tale* includes the " tragedy " of Barnabo Visconti, who died in 1385.

(x) The envoy to King Richard II entitled *Lack of Steadfastness* is said by Shirley in a note in MS. Harley 7333 to have been sent by Chaucer " to his soverain lorde kynge Richarde the secounde thane being in his castell of Windesore " ;   and in another note in MS. Trinity R. 3, 20 he says that Chaucer wrote it " in hees laste yeeres."   Only two dates seem to be possible, namely, 1389, when Richard seized the reins of government ;   and 1398, when the parliament of Shrewsbury delegated its powers, and the king became practically an absolute monarch—the period of Bolingbroke's accusation of Mowbray and of their banishment.   Considering Chaucer's openly expressed dissatisfaction with the king's absolute rule, and his statement that pity was exiled (like the son of John of Gaunt), coupled with his earnest warning—almost a reproof—against extortion ; we may agree with Shirley that Chaucer made the poem in his last years, and may date it 1398 or 1399.

(xi) The envoy to King Henry IV entitled *The Complainte of Chaucer to his Purse* may be dated with certainty, at least in its final shape, by the accession of Henry IV in October, 1399.

(xii) The Ballade de Bon Conseyl, usually known as *Truth*, is stated by Shirley in a note in MS. Trinity R. 3, 20 to have been written by Chaucer " on his deeth bedde." This cannot mean that Chaucer wrote the poem in his last moments. It must mean that he wrote it sometime during his last illness. We may, therefore, date the poem 1400.

2. *The Evidence of Literary Influence.*

(i) Since French and Latin were the languages which Chaucer used at school, French and Latin poetry would be likely to influence Chaucer from the outset of his poetic enthusiasm. But Italian was different. Chaucer may have picked up a little of the Genoese dialect from their commercial ambassadors in London, but it is unlikely that Chaucer learned to read and to enjoy Italian poetry until after he had visited Italy, first in 1372 and again in 1378. We must conclude therefore that the poems which reveal direct Italian influence—*Troilus and Criseyde* (based on Boccaccio's *Filostrato*), *The Knight's Tale* (based on Boccaccio's *Teseide*), *The Complainte of Anelida* and *The Parlement of Fowles* (borrowing from *La Teseide*) and *The House of Fame* (influenced by Dante's *Divina Commedia*) —were all without exception written after 1373. This argument applies also to *The Clerk's Tale* which, Chaucer tells us, his Clerk had learned in Italy " of a worthy clerk . . . Fraunceys Petrak, the lauriat poete."

(ii) As has already been stated under the external evidence for Chaucer's writings, the French poet Deschamps

5

once sent Chaucer a volume of his poems. We neither know what poems this volume contained, nor the precise year in which it was sent and received ; but some modern academic investigators of Chaucer's literary borrowings have suggested that the contents of this volume, which they assume contained Deschamps's anti-feminist poem *Le Miroir de Mariage*, influenced some of Chaucer's later work, particularly the *Wife of Bath's Prologue* and *The Merchant's Tale*. It has also been suggested that, in the Prologue to *The Legend of Good Women*, the allusions to the Flower and the Leaf were borrowed from Deschamps's ballades, and that the identification of Alceste with the daisy came also from Deschamps. These hazardous conjectures are very questionable. The date 1393 has been suggested as the date of Clifford's arrival with Deschamps's volume. But to my mind it passes understanding how any one with a feeling for excellence in literature, and even a little knowledge of how poetry is written, can suggest that in 1393, at the height of his powers, Chaucer stooped to pillage not half so excellent a poet. Deschamps after Boccaccio and Dante ? Is it likely ? Chaucer needed no verbal prompting to satirize women. His wife was dead, and satire upon wives was a fashion of the age. In any case, he only repeated what de Meun had said in *Le Roman de la Rose*. As for calling Queen Anne a daisy, it was simply a courtly fashion of the time, just as it was a cockney fashion in the nineteenth century ; and none has yet suggested literary influence for Mr. Harry Lauder's charming little song, " She's ma daisy."

(iii) One example of Chaucer's influence may be appended. Thomas Usk's *Testament of Love* is modelled upon Chaucer's *Boece*, and borrows from *Troilus and Criseyde* in Book I, and from *The House of Fame* in Book II. We can, therefore, assume that Chaucer's *Boece*, *Troilus*, and *The House of Fame* were written and in circulation some time before Usk's execution in March, 1388.

We can now place the octosyllabic poems in order as

follows : *The Romaunt of the Rose* (after 1359), *The Book of the Duchess* (1369), *The House of Fame* (1375 ? or 1381 ?). We can agree that the poems written in heroic couplet are late, and that *The Legend of Good Women* comes after *The Knight's Tale,* and possibly after the Prologue to *The Canterbury Tales,* but certainly before the prologue to *The Man of Law's Tale.* The question now arises : how shall we decide the order in which the poems in Chaucer's seven-line stanza were written ? I think some evidence may be derived from the metre.

The Chaucerian stanza commonly has a pause or *volta* determined by the sense. This rhetorical pause breaks the unity of the stanza, and the second part of the stanza is ordinarily a continuation, an amplification, a contrast, a consequence, or perhaps an explanation of the first part ; or, more rarely, an apostrophe. The traditional place for this stanzaic pause was after the fourth line, making the stanza a quatrain followed by a tercet ; for this was originally a lyrical stanza (ab, ab ; bcc), and the musical form of a melody which could be sung to it was a phrase (ab), repeated (ab), and followed by a coda (bcc)—as in the hymn-tune called " Luther." This traditional form I call the 4 : 3 type of stanza ; and Chaucer's early poems, e.g. *The Man of Law's Tale, The Clerk's Tale,* and *The Complainte to Pity,* have a marked preponderance of stanzas of this type. But Chaucer never restricted himself only to the regular form. Even his earliest poems in this metre contain other types of stanza, such as the 3 : 4 type, viz. a stanza with the pause after the third line, followed by two couplets (aba ; bbcc) ; the 5 : 2 type, a stanza with one couplet after the pause (ababb ; cc) ; and various rare and irregular types such as the 2 : 5, 1 : 6, 6 : 1 types, the stanza with no pause, and the stanza with a pause in the middle of one of the lines. Now a close examination of the metre of certain later poems shows that Chaucer wrote the stanza after a time with greater freedom. *The Parlement of Fowles,* which we have agreed to date 1382, shows no preponderance of stanzas of the 4 : 3 type, but, on the contrary, about equal numbers of 4 : 3, 3 : 4, and 5 : 2 types —indicating that Chaucer had passed from the fairly strict versification of *The Clerk's Tale* to a comparatively free mode of writing the stanza. For the purpose of comparison I add a table of the statistics for each poem (see p. 69). The first group of figures contains the actual numbers of stanzas. The second contains the percentages of types 5 : 2, 4 : 3, 3 : 4, and irregulars respectively.

Judged by this metrical test—which must not be regarded as something absolute, but merely as a rough indication of a trend of development which may at times have been diverted by the nature of the poem or tale—the poems written in the Chaucerian stanza fall into two groups which I have called A and B.[1] It is a characteristic of Group A that the percentage of 4 : 3 stanzas is 40 per cent or more, and that of the 3 : 4 type is usually under 20 per cent. Group B is characterized by greater variety in the position of the pause, and, moreover, the percentages of the 4 : 3 and 3 : 4 types are almost equal. We have suggested 1382 as the date of *The Parlement of Fowles* and 1386 for *The Complainte of Mars*. We have also agreed that it seems likely that *The Clerk's Tale* and *The Complainte of Anelida* were written soon after Chaucer's return from Italy in 1373. The composition of *Troilus and Criseyde* must have extended over some years. When therefore we find that the metre of the first four books is homogeneous, and that the fifth book differs markedly from the first four and agrees with the metre of *The Parlement of Fowles*, which can be dated with comparative certainty, it is reasonable to assume that whilst Books i–iv were written, as Lydgate stated, in Chaucer's youth, Book v is later and was finished about 1382. The break in composition which must have led to this change in style of versification seems to have been the second Italian journey of 1378–1379. So that we can

---

[1] See " A Note on Chaucer's Stanza," in *Review of English Studies*, ii, p. 311.

GROUP A
(Probably 1373–1379)

	Stanzas	Numbers				Percentages			
	Total	5 : 2	4 : 3	3 : 4	Irreg.	5 : 2	4 : 3	3 : 4	Irreg.
Man of Law's Tale ..	147	27	60	37	23	18·3	40·8	25·1	15·7
Clerk's Tale ..	160	26	75	31	28	16·2	46·9	19·3	17·5
Complainte to Pity ..	17	3	8	3	3	17·6	47·1	17·6	17·6
Complainte of Anelida ..	30	7	12	8	3	23·3	40	26·6	10
Troilus and Criseyde, i ..	156	26	75	20	35	16·6	48	13	22·4
Troilus and Criseyde, ii ..	251	48	101	48	54	19·1	40·2	19·1	21·5
Troilus and Criseyde, iii ..	260	59	120	45	36	22·7	46·1	17·3	14
Troilus and Criseyde, iv ..	243	73	105	46	19	30	43·2	18·9	7·8

GROUP B
(Probably 1380–1386)

	Stanzas	Numbers				Percentages			
	Total	5 : 2	4 : 3	3 : 4	Irreg.	5 : 2	4 : 3	3 : 4	Irreg.
Troilus and Criseyde, v ..	267	69	76	74	48	25·8	28·5	27·7	17·9
Parlement of Fowles ..	98	24	28	28	18	24·5	28·6	28·6	18·4
Complainte of Mars ..	22	6	6	6	4	27·2	27·2	27·2	18·2
Life of St. Cecile ..	79	15	24	24	16	18·9	30·4	30·4	20·2
Prioress's Tale ..	34	5	9	9	11	14·7	26·5	26·5	32·3

limit the dates of the poems in Group A to a period extending from 1373 to 1378 or so, and date Group B from about 1380 to 1386. *The Man of Law's Tale* is generally regarded as an early tale which underwent some revision before its inclusion in *The Canterbury Tales*. Revision is indicated by the style of versification of Part iii, which resembles Group B in character, but even allowing for this, the metre as a whole indicates an early date. Very possibly Chaucer wrote it as a compliment to Costanza of Castile, whom Gaunt married as his second wife in 1372.

Lastly, since for the most part the poems in the seven-line stanza were composed before the poems in heroic couplets, it needs follow that *The Man of Law's Tale*, *The Clerk's Tale*, *The Life of St. Cecile*, and perhaps *The Prioress's Tale*, were written before *The Legend of Good Women* and *The Canterbury Tales*. Indeed, in the Prologue to *The Legend of Good Women* Chaucer mentions *The Life of St. Cecile* as a poem already in existence. It is probable that, when the idea of *The Canterbury Tales* suggested itself to Chaucer, he made no attempt to work out the scheme as a whole. He did not begin at the beginning and write steadily through to the end of *The Parson's Tale*. *The Canterbury Tales*, as found in the manuscripts, are fragmentary. They consist of separate portions only partially arranged, and eight or nine of these " groups " or fragments are recognizable by this, that they are unprovided with connecting links. They do not join inevitably to the other " groups," and the order of arrangement is somewhat doubtful. Now the first fragment after the general Prologue begins with *The Knight's Tale* of Palamon and Arcite, and we may conjecture, from the mention of " Palamon and Arcite " in the Prologue to *The Legend of Good Women* that this tale was written comparatively early. The second fragment begins with *The Man of Law's Tale*, which, we may conclude, would be revised by Chaucer for this purpose ; the fifth begins with *The Clerk's Tale*, and the seventh with *The Second Nun's Life of St. Cecile*, both early tales ; so that it would be reasonable to conclude that Chaucer collected his earlier tales, wrote a Prologue for *The Canterbury Tales*, and began to add other tales after each head-tale, hoping at some later time to weld all the fragments into one harmonious unity. If this be true of the tales that we can trace, it seems reasonable to conclude that the head-tale of each group is earlier than those which follow it ; and arguing in this way we may say that not only are *The Knight's Tale*, *The Man of Law's Tale*, *The Clerk's Tale*, and *The Second Nun's Life of St. Cecile* comparatively early tales ; but also that *The Doctor's Tale*, *The Wife of Bath's Prologue* and *Tale*, the unfinished *Squire's Tale*, *The Manciple's Tale*, and (from the fact that it is in the seven-line stanza) *The Prioress's Tale*, are earlier than the tales which follow them.

Summarizing these results we may arrive at the following chronological table, which is the result of deduction, and is not to be regarded as inspired truth.

CHRONOLOGY OF CHAUCER'S WORKS

1. *Early Poems* : 1360–1372.

Romaunt of the Rose (Translation).

The Book of the Duchess, 1369–1370.

The (Man of Law's) *Tale of Custance* (1372 ?).

A.B.C., before 1369.

2. *First Italian Period* : 1373–1379.

The House of Fame.

The (Clerk's) *Tale of Griselda.*

Boece (prose translation).

Troilus and Criseyde, Bks. i–iv.

The Complaintes *To Pity*, and *To his Lady.*

The Complainte of Anelida.

The Former Age.

3. *Second Italian Period* : 1380–1386.

The (Second Nun's) *Life of S.*
      Cecile.
Troilus and Criseyde, Bk. v.   *Envoy to Adam Scriveyn.*
The Parl ment of Fowles, 1382.
The (Knight's) *Tale of Pala-*   *The Complainte of Mars*, 1386.
      mon and Arcite.

4. *First Period of Leisure* : Dec. 1386–July 1389.

Legends of Good Women (with
      Prologue B. ?).
Prologue to the Canterbury
      Tales.

   The Canterbury Tales begun : Group A, *Knights* ; B, *Man
of Law's, Shipman's, Prioress's* ; ? C, *Doctor's* ; E, *Clerk's* ;
G, *Second Nun's Tale.*

5. *Second Period of Leisure* : June 1391–1400.

The Astrolabe.   *The Complainte of Venus.*
Prologue A to *Legends of*
      Good Women (1396 ?).

   The Canterbury Tales continued : Group D, *Wife of Bath's
Prologue* and *Tale* ; E, *Merchant's* ; F, *Squire's Tale*, etc.

                        Envoys *To Buckton* and
                              Scogan.
                        Lack of Steadfastness (1398 ?).
                        Complainte to his Purse (1399).
                        Ballade of Truth (1400).

   Retractions added to *Parson's Tale.*

III

THE SCHOLAR

§ 1

COURTLY, yet imbued with the coarser humour of the middle class from which he sprang ; religious at heart, though unashamed of the rude but virile wit of the natural man ; imaginative with quaint fancy, learned with curious instance, dryly humorous, keenly observant, Chaucer offers to his readers almost every poetic delight that the Middle Ages can provide, from the courtly romance of love and chivalry to the salacious anecdotes of " the devil's disours," from pious orison or saintly legend to a parody of knight-errantry or a jesting envoy. His matter contains the most charming allegory and fiction, his style expresses the most musical eloquence of English medieval poetry.

Chaucer's poetry is still modern enough to be an inspiration. His tradition is living yet, and has influenced poets as diverse in their ideals and in imaginative quality as Shakespeare, Dryden, Wordsworth, Keats, William Morris, and John Masefield ; whereas the style of his greatest contemporaries—the alliterative verse of *The Vision of Piers Plowman, Sir Gawain and the Green Knight*, and *The Geste Historiale of the Destruction of Troy*, or the lucid octosyllables of Gower's *Confessio Amantis*—created no tradition and is no longer a living influence. If these poems be still read, they are studied as philological material, or as landmarks maybe in the history of English literature ; they are not read, as is Chaucer, with comparative ease and with continual delight.

When Chaucer began to write verse, the French language

73

in England was dying, it is true, but it was by no means dead, nor was its fate certain ; and he must have considered and debated with himself whether to write in French or in English. It was still questionable whether English, the language of peasants and churls, the literary medium of obscure clerks and anonymous minstrels, was illustrious and dignified enough for courtly poetry. When Chaucer was a youth, French was the vehicle of education. It was also the language of the law and the polite dialect of the palace. Whilst Chaucer was one of the valets of Edward III, Jean Froissart was a member of Queen Philippa's retinue, engaged in his leisure hours in writing the first draft of his Chronicle and in making verses in French. Later in Chaucer's career his ballades were rivalled by those of John Gower, written in French. In the retinue of John of Gaunt was a certain knight of Savoy, Sir Otes de Granson, another writer of French ballades. English was only permitted in the courts of law after 1363. French, or rather Norman-French as it was spoken and written in England, was the official language of law, which next to philosophy was the most important and influential intellectual activity of the Middle Ages ; and, as law French, it survived its abolition by Cromwell, and lasted until well into the eighteenth century.

In selecting English as his poetic language, Chaucer was hazarding the transitory popularity of the minstrels, and of writers of romances and verse-tales. That he became a tradition and an influence was owing no doubt to the great esteem in which his eloquence and learning were held ; but they would have availed him nothing, had he written in a northern or a western dialect. He owed his popularity also to the fact that the dialect of English which he spoke and wrote was the official English which took the place of French as that language gradually decayed in England during the latter half of the fourteenth century. Chaucer's court-English became the literary language of Hoccleve and Lydgate, Capgrave and Malory, and later, at the end of the fifteenth century, the language of the printers of Westminster and London.

Yet whilst Chaucer's variety and grace of style can hardly fail to impress us, his poetry may at first disappoint us. The poetry of the real middle ages widely differs from the sham medieval of the eighteenth and nineteenth centuries. Chaucer is unlike Scott or Keats : he is not quite like William Morris. He is less lyrical, often less individual ; and we ought not to judge his poetry by comparison with that of modern writers. Chaucer was a narrative and descriptive poet. He excelled in allegory and in fiction, rather than in lyric. He wrote for the court, and he appears to have recited his tales and romances to audiences composed exclusively of nobles and ladies. His poetry is rhythmical and at times eloquent, but it is sentimental rather than passionate, and characterized by good sense rather than by depth or originality of thought. His verses, though they vary in style from colloquial bluntness to dignified eloquence, are always pleasing and clear. One would be tempted to call him a minstrel, were it not that to him poetry was a polite accomplishment—a gentlemanly amusement—not a profession.

And finally, if one asks why the tone and effect of Chaucer's poetry differs from modern poetry, the answer is that Chaucer belonged to another age—almost to another world. Strange to us, if we could go back, would be everything around him. He did not see life through our eyes, nor decide its problems by our judgment. The knowledge which he acquired—from school, from home and from experience—his loyalties, his manners, his faith, were all quite different from ours. In reading Chaucer we must be prepared therefor for poems which do not tally with our preconceived notions of what poetry is or should be. We shall expect to find different costumes and different manners : we must not be surprised if we meet with ideas of love and religion which seem to belong to a world of children, and a philosophy of life that ends before ours begins.

§ 2

How Chaucer resolved to be poet, and what became of his earliest strivings—painstaking imitations of poetic fashion perchance, or momentary *jeux d'esprit*, the product of uncontrollable impulse—are speculations over which, in the absence of the evidence of facts, it is profitable to linger. When he was a page in the household of the Countess of Ulster, he must have become familiar with carole and romance, even if he were ignorant of them before. Probably his first attempts were lyrics, now lost without exception, unless some of them are incorporated in later poems. It may be that the Knight in Black's song in *The Book of the Duchess* is one of these early lyrics :

> Lord, hit maketh myn herte light
> Whan I thenke on that swete wight
> That is so semely on to see ;
> And wisshe to God it might so bee
> That she wolde holde me for hir knight,
> My lady that is so fair and bright.

Possibly some are buried amidst *The Complainte of Faire Anelida* and *The Complainte to his Lady*. Or perhaps he tried his hand at romance. It may be that Chaucer's *Sir Thopas* ridicules one of his early efforts.

But those early poems which have survived Chaucer's judgment and the stern hand of time indicate that the first formative influence was French poetry, which inspired him with its courtly sentiments, and taught him to emulate its metres in English. The determining factor in Chaucer's choice of style must have been his acquaintance with Jean Froissart at the court of Edward III. Froissart owed his place in Queen Philippa's household, from 1361 until her death, to his literary and poetic gifts. His allegorical and learned poetry would appear to Chaucer to convey something infinitely more lofty and polite than the childish fictions and elementary sentiments of the popular English romances ; and his ballades of three stanzas without envoy —a form which Chaucer learned and imitated in his ballades *Of a Reeve*, *To Rosamounde*, and *Gentilesse*— attracted the admiration of the young poet as an elegant vehicle for the neat expression of a sentiment.

One may imagine the tiro approaching his distinguished contemporary in hall some day and asking his advice.

Froissart. So thou wouldst become a poet, Master Geoffrey, *hein* !

Chaucer. Yea, Messire Jean, that is my desire.

Froissart. *Hélas !* It is an ill vocation my friend, sooth to say—a very felon life in these days when a poet, to live at all, must needs be a villain clerk or usher in a household. Hear me, Geoffrey, my friend : return to the tavern of thy father, sell wine, marry, and prepare to enjoy thy father's good estate after him—and verily Fortune shall prevent thee.

Chaucer. Say you so ? You would have me a wine-monger, mixing the liquor of La Rochelle with the fumosity of Lepe, or haggling with Gascons on the quay about a few paltry shillings in the price of a tun ? Nay, Messire Jean, what I demand of Fortune is fame, not purchase. Any man can be a crafty vintner, but I would liefer be a crafty maker.

Froissart. Nay, by St. Julian the good taverner, but a man can purchase fame too dearly ! Think, my friend, of an unbeneficed clerk, an unrequited lover, a *protégé* at the mercy of a patron's whim. Think of one who sings not, as he pretends, for love ; but in effect for his bed and board. Such it is to be a poet in this latter age. Regard me. Thou dost believe, like the rest, that I am renowned and richly rewarded. Take thou my troth that I would gladly forsake all my jolly allegories of Beauté and Amour for the secure benefice of a canonry or even of a bailiwick.

Chaucer. But thou hast told me that Messire Guillaume de Machaut was clerk to the good King of Bohemia, who, God rest his soul, was killed at Crécy. Thou too art clerk to my soveran lady, the good Queen Philippa. These, my friend, are honourable recompenses for poets ; and it such a reward that I desire, rather than to win enough money to lend even to my king, or to sit in solemn livery on the dais of our guildhall.

Froissart. Listen, Geoffrey ! Hath any poet in England ever enjoyed even such poor rewards as these ?

Chaucer. Not that I wot, or, an if they had, it hath passed the memory of man. But why may not I ? That it can be done, thou art a living witness. It shall be done, and I shall do it withal.

Froissart. Go to now, thou art a Bellerophon stung by the breeze of conceit ;—but I honour thee therefore, Geoffrey. Thou hast gaiety and wit, and thy English verses seem to my foreign ear to scan better than most of those which I have listened to in thy chill country. Thou hast a father too who could, an he would, keep thee well supplied with wine ; for wine gladdens the heart, when love-longing would make it heavy. Thou wilt be a poet ? Know then what thou must do. Imitate not me, nor those verses of de Machaut's which I lent thee ; for to imitate is not to make. But go thou rather to the *fontaine amoureuse* from which both de Machaut and I have drunk. If thou wouldst be a poet, translate me *Le Roman de la Rose.*

Chaucer. *Le Romaunt de la Rose ?* But it is too long ! If it took two poets fifty years to write it, how shall one silly clerk translate it soon enough to profit by it ?

Froissart. Nevertheless and notwithstanding, translate it ; or as much of it as thou canst compass. Therein thou wilt find beauty of fiction, and grace of language, antique learning, and the proper sentiments of the modern poet. There, if thou canst but learn its secret, thou wilt find the just metre of fiction and ditty—riming octosyllables. Go then, and make *Le Roman de la Rose* thy *ars poetica.*

Chaucer. Grammercy, Messire Jean. I will essay it. Who knows ? Peradventure some noble may requite me well for it, or at least offer me some preferment.

Froissart. May the good God prosper you ! I congratulate you on your spirit. But remember, Geoffrey, my last word : if poetry be thy profession, think not ever of preferment. Think mostly of thy art. Thou art devoted to one of the nine ladies of Helicon : forget her not. If I mistake not, Thalia is her name.

That is fiction, but it may well represent the truth, however inadequately it may be expressed.

§ 3

Much of Chaucer's early manhood was spent upon his translation of *Le Roman de la Rose,* and as it influenced *The Book of the Duchess,* and to some extent his Complaintes *To Pity* and *To his Lady,* and led him with interest back to one of its philosophical sources—the *De Consolatione Philosophiae* of Boëthius—we may begin our consideration of his poems with *The Romaunt of the Rose,* remembering that it was not written in a month or even in a year. There is no doubt that Chaucer translated *The Romaunt of the Rose* ; for he tells us so in the Prologue to *The Legend of Good Women* :

> Thou hast translated the Romaunce of the Rose
> That is an heresye ayeins my (i.e. Love's) law.

There is unfortunately a doubt whether the Middle English

version of *The Romaunt of the Rose*, which traditionally has been regarded as Chaucer's, is really his ; so that we shall proceed to discuss two questions : what was *Le Roman de la Rose* ? and is *The Romaunt of the Rose* Chaucer's ?

Le Roman de la Rose is one of the great poems of the Middle Ages. It is enormously long, and offers a variety of matters to suit all tastes. Ostensibly it is an allegory of a lover's quest and conflict for his lady, symbolized as a rose ; and as an allegory—the first truly popular secular allegory of the Middle Ages—it created a poetic tradition, and set a fashion which lasted for two hundred years. Really, if read with an index, it is a poetic *summa* of the classical learning and the sentiments of the Middle Ages— the whole matter of the art of love tinged with the philosophy of the schools. Its variety is enhanced by the curious fact that it is not the work of one author. The beginning of the allegory was made by Guillaume de Lorris, who wrote between the years 1237–1240. The middle and end were added forty years later by Jean de Meun, called "Clopinel." Both were clerics, but their minds worked differently. Lorris designed the poem as a poetic transmutation into terms of allegory of the progress of true love, coloured by knightly and idealistic sentiment. Clopinel, with a more philosophic mind, regarded love as the triumph of passion over reason, as a battle in which (as in war) bribery and stratagem are fair play, and also as physical desire designed to fill and replenish the earth, rather than as a spiritual affinity which ennobles, empowers, and refines. Lorris was delicate and sentimental. Clopinel was more vigorous, more learned, but cynical and not afraid of grossness. Both these strains of feeling and outlook influenced Chaucer. He drew freely both from the fiction of Guillaume de Lorris and from the hard-headed argument of Jean de Meun.

The poem opens with a defence of the truth of dreams warranted by

Un auctor qui ot nom Macrobes,

who wrote the vision which befell King Scipio long ago.
Since dreams have significance, says de Lorris, he will
narrate a dream which happened to him

> Ou vintième an de mon age
> Ou point qu'Amors prend le péage.

It happened in May, for lovers love the Spring—

> Moult a dur coeur qui en Mai n'aime
> Quand il ot chanter sous la raime
> As oiseaux les douz chanz piteus.

One sunny May-morning when leaves were fresh and the
sky serene, when the small birds sang on every bough their
amorous lays, the dreamer arose from his bed, dressed
himself, and went forth the town, lacing his wide purfled
sleeves as he walked along the bank of the river.   Soon he
approached a wonderful park enclosed by a lofty crenellated
wall—

> Tout clos de haut mur bataillié
> Portrait dehors et entaillié
> A maintes riches escritures.

He gazed with admiration at the pictured carvings on the
wall.   They were portraits of the vices and the ills of life
—Hate, Ill-breeding, Covetousness, Greed, Envy, Sorrow,
Age, Hypocrisy, and Poverty—displayed on the outside
wall of the place which they might not enter, as the game-
keeper exhibits his trophies and " larns " them to be
" varmin."   The poet describes with vivid word-painting
these villainous characteristics as he walks along the foot
of the wall.

Next he finds a gate at which he makes bold to knock.
After some little delay it was opened from within by a
charming young lady who carried a mirror, and was attired
amongst other things in a rose chaplet and a pair of white
kid gloves.   She was in fact a perfect gentlewoman :

6

Il paroit bien à son atour
Qu 'elle estoit poi embesogniée.
Quand elle s'estoit bien pigniée
Et bien parée et atournée,
Elle avoit faite sa journée.

This leisured beauty was Dame Idleness herself. She informed the dreamer that she was one of the many guests of Sir Delight, the owner of the park, a nobleman who appears to have been interested in bird-life ; one who has planted his glades with oriental trees, and has, moreover, caused the ugly pictures to be graven and painted on his wall. Thereupon, without the formality of waiting to be invited, the dreamer insisted upon enjoying the hospitality of Delight.

Nonchalantly, as if quite accustomed to these impetuous juvenile manners, Idleness led the dreamer through bosky thickets where the small birds warbled their notes so sweetly that they seemed like the alluring songs of the mermaids.

Tant estoit cil chanz douz et biaus
Qu'il ne sembloit pas chant d'oisiaus,
Ainz le peust l'en aesmer
A chant de sereines de mer.

She led him by a little path to the lawn where Delight was entertaining his friends Gladness, Courtesy, the god of Love and his attendant squire Sweet Looks (Douz Regarz) who carried Love's darts, also Riches, Largess, and Youth. Minstrels were there, and acrobats, to sing and play ; and from time to time Delight and his crew assembled on the grass for a frolicsome carole, in one of which, at the invitation of Dame Courtesy, the dreamer flung a leg with the best of them.

After the dance the dreamer strolled away to admire the park ; so also, he noticed, did the god of Love and his squire ; but instead of joining him they followed him. After walking some time he came to a pine tree, beneath which was a clear spring enclosed in a marble pool. It

was, he found, the Well of Love, into which long ago
Narcissus fell when he was admiring his own image in the
water. The dreamer sat down to rest beside the water,
and, as he sat, he leaned and peered into the fountain.
What caught his eye was strangely enough not his own
image, but the reflection of a red rosebush. It bore one
bud which pleased him so much that his sole desire was to
pluck it. The dreamer becomes the lover. Straightway
the god of Love came closer and shot six arrows at him.
Stricken by love, the lover surrendered and became Love's
vassal. Love advises him to hope and to endure.

And now as the lover presses forward to grasp his prize
and pluck the rose, Bel Accueil (Fair Welcome) the son of
Courtesy comes to his assistance. He informs the lover
that Danger, Scandal, Chastity and Shame guard his
coveted Rose, and that winning her is no light task ; he
also obtains for the lover a leaf from the rosebush as a
love-token, which only inflames his love-longing. Whilst
together they plan their capture of the Rose, a hideous
fellow—

> Granz fu et noirs et hérissié,
> S' ot les iauz rouges comme feus
> Le nez froncié, le viz hisdeus,

—who, it seems, is none other than Danger, emerges from
his ambush and puts them to flight.

Hindered from approaching his Rose, whom he now
loves to distraction. the sorrowing lover is approached by
Reason who descends from her ethereal tower to endeavour
to convince the youth of the unreasonableness of love ;
but the lover refuses to hear the voice of the charmer,
charm she never so wisely ; and, spurning Reason, he takes
counsel with his bosom friend (Ami) who gives him this
advice, that if he would win the Rose, he must first
conciliate Danger. Danger, we might observe, stands in
the allegory for feminine self-esteem, and is not as one
might imagine the symbol of *patria potestas* So the lover
approaches Danger and attempts to win his help, but

Danger says he cannot permit the lover to approach the Rose ; for, granted that he would, Chastity would still forbid it. Rebuffed once again, the disconsolate lover is cheered by the intervention of Pity and Franchise who intercede with Danger, and so far prevail with him that he now allows the two that he had chased away, the lover and Bel Accueil, to meet again and together to approach the Rose.

The lover, accompanied by Bel Accueil, approaches the Rose. He is overjoyed, and desires to kiss it. Bel Accueil is shocked and hesitates to allow such impropriety, but Venus intervenes and, overcome by her charms, Bel Accueil yields his consent to the kiss. But no sooner has the lover first kissed the Rose than Scandal publishes the news abroad, and awakens Jealousy, who comes to scold Bel Accueil. This is more than the timid lover can endure. He takes to his heels, and flees, leaving poor Bel Accueil a prisoner in the hands of Jealousy, who imprisons him in a pastle which she builds around the Rose—the castle of propriety, guarded by Scandal, Danger, Fear, and Shame. Here Bel Accueil is to be taught manners by an old governess (La Vieille),

> Qui ne fait nul autre mestier
> Fors espier tant solement
> Qu'il ne se moine folement.

Humiliated and separated from Fair Welcome and the Rose, the lover abandons himself to despair, and the first part of a very charming allegory ends abruptly.

Here *Le Roman de la Rose* as told by Guillaume de Lorris breaks off unfinished (l. 4058), and there can be no doubt that had the poet completed his story, it would have told how Bel Accueil was regained for the lover, and how the Rose was won. Clearly it is an allegory of first love, written, as was almost inevitable, from the standpoint of the man. A lover sees and falls completely in love with a maiden. She welcomes him and even gives him a token, but she lets him see that she must be wooed in order to be won. Her dignity and her modesty prevent unconditional surrender. But pity for the lover's plight overcomes her hesitancy. She welcomes her lover and grants him a kiss. Tale-bearers spread the news and arouse the jealousy of the damsel's parents, who intervene to seclude their precious Rose under the guardianship of a duenna, leaving the disconsolate lover without hope. It was at this point that some forty years later the allegory was continued by Jean de Meun, who expanded the naturally simple *dénouement* by the in-weaving of mythological fables, learned instances, and philosophic discourses, into an involved ending which is four times as long as de Lorris's beginning.

According to de Meun, the lover in his despondency is once again challenged by Reason, who urges the lover to forsake his quest by showing the absurdity of love, the fickleness of happiness, and the glory of personal freedom, which is inevitably the foe of marriage.[1] Reason illustrates her topics by the stories of Appius and Virginia, Nero, and Crœsus ; but even her fables fail to convince the lover, and finally, since he is obdurate in his folly, she abandons him. His bosom friend visits him again and advises him, if he still wishes to win the Rose, to proceed by cunning, rather than by direct assault, and to bribe and deceive the guardians of Fair Welcome and the Rose. The friend discourses learnedly and rather tiresomely upon the hardships of poverty, the former glories of the Golden Age, and the miseries of wedlock, in which few wives are found as virtuous as Penelope or Lucrece. He ends by advising him, if he wishes to succeed with women, never to thwart a woman's will, for women love power and think they know everything.

Tired of his discourse, not without cause, the lover leaves his friend to spy out Fair Welcome's prison, whereupon he

---

[1] In the middle of this argument, the first part of the Chaucerian translation breaks off at line 5810, and only resumes after some 5600 lines.

is met by the god of Love who has come to learn whether
his new vassal has been true to his laws. Love professes
himself satisfied, and promises to besiege the castle of
propriety. With this intent he summons his barons, who
prove to be no other than the guests in the park of Delight
—Honour, Riches, Noblesse, Idleness, Largess, Beauty,
Courage, Pity, Courtesy, Delight, Joy, Desire, Youth,
Patience ; and, in addition, Enforced Abstinence and Guile
(Faux-Semblant). The barons in council agree to storm
Fair Welcome's prison,[1] but they advise Love that it will
be impossible to succeed without the help of False Sem-
blant, who now comes forward, and in lines of biting satire
characterizes himself as the symbol of the way of the
world. Fraud and hypocrisy are found amongst all men,
but especially are they the property of the clergy, and, in
particular, of the friars. His discourse pleases the god of
Love, and he is put in command of the vanguard. Dis-
guised as a friar and a nun, Faux-Semblant and Contrainte-
Abstinence make their way to the castle, and beg a night's
lodging from Slander, who admits them, and listens to their
sermons against backbiting and evil speaking.[2] Slander
professes contrition, but as he penitently kneels to receive
absolution the false mendicants stab him. Faux-Semblant
and his companion then conquer the guards of the castle.
Immediately after them two more of the besiegers enter
—Courtesy and Largess. They receive the submission of
the governess, who consents to permit Fair Welcome to
receive the gift of a chaplet of flowers from the lover. The
governess now embarks upon a long discourse containing
her philosophy of love, in which she tells the stories of
Dido, Phyllis, Oenone, and Medea ; she gives good advice
about table-manners (used later by Chaucer in his description of the Prioress in *The Prologue*) ; and with distinct
cynicism pleads for mutual freedom in matrimony. Finally
she consents to admit the lover to visit Fair Welcome.

---

[1] Here the Chaucerian version resumes, ll. 5811-7696.
[2] Here the Chaucerian version ends.

At last the lover is able to penetrate propriety's strong-hold, and is received by Fair Welcome. Together they go to win the Rose, but Danger, its unconquered and intransi-gent possessor, springs from his lurking place and arouses Fear and Shame. Once more they drive the lover away and overcome his Fair Welcome. The lover now falls back upon the god of Love and his jolly barons, who come to his help, and join in a general assault on the fortress of the Rose ; but the event is so doubtful that Love sends for his last resort, his mother Venus, who hastens in a chariot drawn by eight doves. Meanwhile Nature confesses to Genius her priest that she regrets her creation of man, in a discourse which is not only a defence of her creative power against the monkish views of the ascetic, but also an account of the cosmology of the Universe, and a dis-cussion of the dilemma of fate and free-will. Thereupon Genius preaches to Love and his assembled barons the necessity of obedience to Nature's laws, and denounces those who would forbid men to marry. After this dis-course Venus takes command of the assault, and the fortress surrenders. The lover, led by Bel Accueil, plucks the rose, and with that,

> Explicit li Romans le Rose
> Ou l'art d'Amours est toute enclose.

That was the allegory which Chaucer set himself to translate ; and, as he read it, he might justly have said of it as later Dryden said about him : " Here is God's plenty." It is an allegory presented in the form of a dream ; it offers courtly sentiments, learned fictions, and almost the whole armoury of medieval knowledge. It surpassed and superseded the tradition of the romances. If they told of love and arms, so did it, in terms which could easily be applied to fit the circumstances of all lovers. The dreamer was everyman : the rose was his ideal beloved— the lady of his dreams. That is why the poem was so popular, and that goes to explain why it founded a tradition of allegorical poetry, and was the model for a thousand poems written in the form of a dream, in May, of a meeting, in a park.

It carried Chaucer off his feet. It was the initial formative influence upon his poetic composition, and he never forgot it. Late in life, as we have already mentioned, he went back to it for the mincing propriety of the Lady Prioress. Before that he had imitated from it in *The Book of the Duchess* and *The Parlement of Fowles* the induction of the May-morning dream, and had borrowed the tale of Appius and Virginia, which he introduced into *The Canterbury Tales* as the Doctor's Tale. *Le Roman de la Rose* influenced him in three ways. Its classical and mythological stories—the " tragedies " of Nero and Crœsus, the fable of Mars and Venus, the " legends " of Lucrece, Dido, Phyllis, Oenone, and Medea—sent him back to Ovid's *Metamorphoses* and *Heroides*, to read the legends of mythology and love in their original setting. He found Ovid's pictorial and sensuous descriptions better than the simple tales of de Meun. He retold Ovid's story of Ceyx and Halcyone (*Met.* xi, 410–748), and caught from Ovid's temple of Fame (*Met.* xii, 39) the inspiration for his *House of Fame*. He borrowed the Manciple's tale of Phœbus and his crow from the second book of the *Metamorphoses*. All his Legends of Good Women except that of Cleopatra were taken either from the *Metamorphoses* or the *Heroides*.

Its machinery of the dream sent him back to

Un auctor qui ot nom Macrobes.

He read the Commentary of Macrobius on Cicero's *Somnium Scipionis*, or at least Scipio's dream, as we may see if we turn to the proem of *The Parlement of Fowles*. He wondered whether dreams truly had significance, as we may read in divers places, particularly in the proem to *The House of Fame*; and he appears to have studied Cicero's *De Divinatione*, as appears from *The Nun's Priest's*

Tale where the story of the murdered man in the muck-cart and the anecdote of the dream of Simonides, related by Cicero in his first book, are used as illustrations of the validity of dreams. And finally the sentiments and the philosophy of Jean de Meun attracted him. He liked his description of the former golden age, he agreed with Nature's doctrine of gentility—

> que nus n'est gentis
> S'il n'est as vertus ententis,
> Ne n'est vilains fors par ses vices.
> *Noblesse vient de bon corage.*

And moreover, strange as it may seem, his interest was aroused by Nature's prolix discussion on Necessity, Free-will, and Fate. He discovered that these thoughts and sentiments were simply transferred from Boëthius's Consolation of Philosophy, and thither he turned as to the fountain-head a few years later to study their original. It was due to *Le Roman de la Rose* that Chaucer thought so highly of Boëthius's *De Consolatione Philosophiae* that he was prepared to undertake the long fatigue of translating it. It was owing to his translation of *Le Roman de la Rose*, much more than to the poems of Guillaume de Machaut or of Eustache Deschamps, most of which in all probability he never had an opportunity of reading, that Geoffrey Chaucer became the kind of poet he was in his youth. It influenced him more than any book he ever read.

§ 3

And, now arises the question : is *The Romaunt of the Rose* Chaucer's translation ? The sole manuscript in Glasgow University Library (Hunterian V, 3, 7) makes no ascription to Chaucer, but that scarcely matters, for ll. 1–44 are missing ; and not only is the translation without a colophon, but there is a lacuna between ll. 5810 and 5811. The translation was printed first by Thynne in 1532 from another manuscript which is now lost, and until 1878 it was regarded as Chaucer's work ; but it was rejected in turn by Skeat, Furnivall, and Ten Brink, and recent opinion tends on the whole to say that there are grave reasons for not attributing *The Romaunt of the Rose* to Chaucer. Skeat's argument was linguistic. He accepted a three-fold division of the poem, suggested by Kaluza, and called ll. 1–1705 " fragment A," ll. 1706–5810 " fragment B," and ll. 5811–7698 (the episode of Faux-Semblant) " fragment C." The reasons for this division are that in A the French word *bouton* (bud) is translated by " knoppe," whereas in B it appears as " botoun " : also in B the French *Bel Acuel* appears as " Bialacoil," whereas in C it is translated as " Fayre Welcoming," and there is of course the gap in translation between A B (ll. 1–5810) and C (ll. 5811–7698). Fragment B when examined separately turns out to be a more diffuse translation than either A or C. Furthermore it contains Northern English forms such as sittand, fand, doand, hate (hot) ; its poet rimed -y with -yë, e.g. generaly : vilanye, by : folye, I : jelousye, —which, according to Bradshaw, Chaucer never did ; and some of its rimes are false : such as kepe : eke, shape : make, storm : corn. Skeat's conclusion was that frag-ment A appeared " to be a real portion of Chaucer's own translation," but fragment B was originally written by a more diffuse translator and a less dexterous rhymester " in a Northumbrian dialect," and as for fragment C, though it is " more in Chaucer's style," its authorship is doubtful. Following the redoubtable Skeat, critical opinion has tended cautiously to reject the view that *The Romaunt of the Rose* was Chaucer's. We must either assume that in the earliest period of his poetic career Chaucer made use of northern forms of words, assonance, and rimed -y with -yë, or we must abandon the theory of his authorship. So critics said.

But like the answer to most of the problems of life, the solution is not so easy as one would wish. To begin with :

if *The Romaunt of the Rose* is not Chaucer's, whose is it ? What poet of the fourteenth century was capable of such an, on the whole, excellent piece of work as the English translation of *Le Roman de la Rose* ? There is no candidate for first-class honours except Chaucer. Chaucer says expressly that he translated the poem. No other poet, as far as we know, made the same claim. One cannot summarily reject the traditional opinion that the poem is Chaucer's. And that being so, our endeavour must be to account for the present form of the poem. The poem is fragmentary, that is plain. Part C (ll. 5811–end) is a long fragment, probably of something which once included at least the whole of the Faux-Semblant episode, and there is no overwhelmingly convincing reason why it is not by Chaucer.

The real difficulty lies in the linguistic differences between fragments A and B. We may rule out the suggestion that Chaucer wrote A, and that B is the addition of some frowzy continuator ; for Chaucer said that his translation was a heresy against Love's law, a verdict which may apply to the speeches of Wikked Tunge (ll. 4253–66) or of Reason (ll. 4703–84)—both in fragment B, but hardly to the delightful idealization of fragment A. The solution must be that Chaucer's originals and their copies are lost. If, as Chaucer hinted, the translation was prepared for one of the hidalgos of the period by command, it would never get into general circulation. Our version is corrupt. The first section (ll. 1–1715) follows the French line for line fairly close to the sense, and most critics accept this fragment A as Chaucer's work. Fragment B (ll. 1716–5810) appears to be Chaucer corrupted. It appears to have been copied years afterwards by a Northerner with Chaucer's version either in front of him, or imperfectly recollected in his memory. He not only altered words, such as "bothoun" for "knoppe," and revised at will ; but he expanded the translation with spurious lines and couplets, and gave the language some of the characteristics of his own dialect. If one could assume that the original manuscript was borrowed occasionally by some book-lover from the library of the noble for whom it was written, and that each time a copyist was engaged, our book-lover might conceivably have found himself in possession of several copied fragments, A, B, X, C, Y, Z.

If we may still go on with our theory, let us grant that B was done by some cross-grained Northerner without a particle of editorial scruple and with much poetic vanity—a trait which is not yet extinct—who was not employed again. If such conjecture be legitimate, possibly it explains the origin of our two versions, Thynne's and the Glasgow MS. The original, we will assume, was lost or burnt, or set to baser uses such as jam-covers, toy-drums, or worse ; the copy becomes for similar reasons imperfect, and only A, B, and C remain. These fragments, or a copy, become the manuscript of Thynne's printed version, and another early copy finds its way to Glasgow and there remains. This is pure conjecture, arbitrary conjecture ; none need believe it. I merely suggest it, to indicate something of the change of form and character which *The Romaunt of the Rose* must have undergone, if we cling to the traditional view that Chaucer wrote it. Personally I cling to this view, because I know of none else who could have turned the easy couplets of fragments A and C. The use of Fayre Welcomyng in C, instead of Bialacoil in B, does not prejudice me against the authorship of Chaucer, because I know that the scribe of B, if he were capable of substituting " bothoun " for " knoppe," was quite capable of substituting " Bialacoil " for " Fayre Welcome " or " Fayre Welcoming." No doubt the matter seems unimportant, and unworthy of controversy. Perhaps it is. But two things are clear. The first is that, in its present state, fragment B is not Chaucer's original workmanship. The second is that the translation of *The Romaunt of the Rose* furnished Chaucer with allegory, opinions, satire, and stories which influenced him all his life, and which he never forgot.

§ 4

If, as I have supposed, *The Romaunt of the Rose* was written for Blanche of Lancaster, there may be error in the conjecture ; but there is no doubt that *The Book of the Duchess* commemorates her death, and it must have been written to condole with John of Gaunt soon after September, 1369. *The Book of the Duchess* is written in octosyllabic couplets in the free style of the earlier poem—with weak and feminine endings often, without anacrusis more rarely, and with frequent disregard of word-stress. The form of the poem, like all Chaucer's allegories, is a prologue followed by the narration of a wonderful dream—a form which ultimately was derived from *Le Roman de la Rose*. Chaucer begins by saying that he can not sleep for love-sickness, and the other night to beguile the dark hours he picked up Ovid's *Metamorphoses* and read the fable of Ceyx and Halcyone, which he tells from Book xi, 410. The recollection of the dream brought by Morpheus to Halcyone makes him long for sleep, and he vows that if Morpheus will only give him the gift of sleep, he will reward him with a feather bed and downy pillows. So saying, immediately he fell asleep, and dreamed.

This was his dream. On a bright May morning when the birds sang merrily, he awoke in a rich chamber, the walls of which were painted with scenes from *The Romaunce of the Rose*. He arose, and went out into a forest where the Emperor Octavian was hunting the hart, and curiously enough the trees (ll. 416–433) were exactly like those in *The Romaunce of the Rose* (ll. 1391–1408), even to the squirrels. He finds a young knight clad in mourning, seated under an oak singing a doleful lay, and going up to him asks why he is sad. The Man in Black, paraphrasing a passage from *The Romaunce of the Rose*, tells him that Fortune has played falsely with him at chess, and has taken his queen. He proceeds to tell the story of their courtship and marriage, and this gives Chaucer an opportunity which he seizes of describing the beauty of Blanche's appearance and the goodness of her nature. The dreamer asks the man in black: " Wher is she now ? " and he answers, " She is dead." With that the Emperor returns to

> A long castel with walles white
> By Saint Johan ! on a riche hil

—evidently a punning allusion to Blanche of Lancaster and John of Richmond ; and, as the castle bell tolls the hour of twelve, the dreamer awakes, still holding in his hand the book which he had been reading.

It is a youthful poem, and not highly original. Besides the evident and great debt to *The Romaunce of the Rose*, it is possible that the conception of the knight's complaint for the loss of his lady was suggested by a poem of De Machaut, entitled, *Le Jugement du bon Roy de Behaigne*. In this poem De Machaut pictures a debate between a lady who has lost her husband by death, and a knight whose lady has jilted him. The problem is : whose is the greater loss ? And the final decision is made by De Machaut's master, the King of Bohemia. It may be that Chaucer remembered the lady's complaint whilst picturing his Man in Black. That Chaucer went to De Machaut's *Fontaine Amoureuse* for the story of Ceyx and Halcyone is even less likely. The metre supports not that supposition.

But notwithstanding the literary nature of Chaucer's grief, *The Book of the Duchess* has great charm, and is not altogether devoid of power. The setting of the poem is no mere dreamland garden. The vigour of the hunt, and the play of the hound that fawned on the dreamer give a reality which is almost too lifelike ; and the eloquent yet just praise of the Lady Blanche, by pure description alone, conveys the indescribable charm of a pure and good woman without genius, and without eccentricity or peculiarity. It is true that the doleful story of Ceyx and Halcyone compares ill with Wordsworth's *Laodamia*. It relies for its effect upon simple childish wonder, rather than upon criticism of conduct ; but it has intense pathos, and pathos is difficult to catch in the short and steady swing of the short couplet. We must remember that Chaucer was not yet a fully fledged poet, and this was the longest flight he had hitherto ventured. One can see great promise in the invention of the fiction and in its management. The transition from the story Ceyx and Halcyone to the reverse situation by means of a characteristic jest is admirably managed, and a delicate compliment to Gaunt is conveyed by the implication that if Halcyone died of grief, Gaunt's existence must be a living death. If one must blame as well as praise—and " but " is the critic's favourite word— there is a diffusion about the poem, a tendency to over- whelm movement by endless talking, which denies *The Book of the Duchess* a high place amongst Chaucer's works. This was one of the defects of Jean de Meun which Chaucer had noticed in *Le Roman de la Rose*, and possibly admired. He learned later to keep a tighter hand on his dialogue.

§ 5

It is probable that to this early period belongs the tale of Custance (*The Man of Law's Tale*) which Chaucer translated from the Anglo-French Chronicle of Friar Trivet. Possibly also Chaucer's *A.B.C.*, translated from the French of Guillaume de Guileville, a monk of the Abbey of Chalis, should have been introduced by us before *The Book of the Duchess* ; for, if Speght (1602) is credible, Chaucer wrote it for Blanche, Duchess of Lancaster, " a woman in her religion very devout." But both shall be considered later, since, if indeed they were early works, they underwent revision, and now bear signs of maturity.

The next important formative influence upon Chaucer's mind, and indirectly upon his art, was his translation of Boëthius, to whose *Consolatio Philosophiae* he had been led by his study of *Le Roman de la Rose*. Jean de Meun was an ardent admirer of the philosophy of Boëthius, and tradition associates his name with an early French translation which, according to Liddell, Chaucer used to supplement the inadequacies of his knowledge of Latin. Chaucer translated from a Latin text provided with a gloss or commentary, as his "that is to seyn" and his bracketed interpolations indicate. His interest in the work, an interest strong enough to sustain him through to the distant end, is not surprising. Boëthius occupies a unique position in literature as the last of the Roman philosophers and the first of the medieval theologians. His *De Consolatione Philosophiae* is one of the great books of the world, now unfortunately for the world somewhat obscured in the schools by Cicero ; but if the greatest function of literature be to enrich the mind, Anicius Manlius Severinus Boëthius is the author of a rich and great book. Boëthius was the most learned man of his age : he was also one of its most prominent public men. Born about 480 A.D., the son of a patrician house, he studied in Rome and at Athens, and devoted his life in the old Athenian way to science and philosophy. "The geometry of Euclid, the music of Pythagoras, the arithmetic of Nicomachus, the mechanics of Archimedes, the astronomy of Ptolemy, the theology of Plato, and the logic of Aristotle with the Commentary of Porphyry, were translated and illustrated by the indefatigable pen of the Roman senator." [1] He was also a Christian and one of the doctors of the Church, the author of works on the Trinity, the Catholic Faith, and against the heresies of Eutyches and Nestorius. At the summit of his career of public life as patrician, consul, and master of the offices to Theodoric, the Gothic King of Italy, he was accused, falsely, Gibbon suggests, of inviting Justin the Emperor to come from Constantinople to deliver Italy from the Goths ; and after a long imprisonment at Pavia he was brutally executed in 524.

[1] Gibbon, *Decline and Fall of the Roman Empire*, Ch. xxxix.

It was in confinement in the tower of Pavia, in adversity after high esteem and unbroken good fortune, that Boethius wrote his Consolation, " a golden volume," says Gibbon, " not unworthy of the leisure of Plato or Tully." It consists of five books, each consisting of a series of discourses or essays separated by reflective poems in various metres ; each combining " the various riches of philosophy, poetry, and eloquence." Philosophy visits him, as he lies bewailing his lot, to comfort him and to revive his courage. She teaches him to think with gratitude on his long continued weal, and to derive new hopes from the fickleness of fortune. She teaches him of the blessings that remain, in friends and family, and, above all, in virtue. True blessedness lies not in honours, fame, or power, but in obedience to the celestial will. He had learned the instability of wealth by reason, he had learned its emptiness by experience ; it remained now to suffer adversity with fortitude ; knowing that happiness, which springs from virtue, is independent of earthly place and power. Thus consoled, he explores with Philosophy, the ethereal confines of metaphysics, searching for the idea of perfect goodness, and finding that it is at once perfect happiness (*beatitudo*) and God ; agreeing that evil is a defect of good, and that, since all creation is one, whatever is, is right ; discussing with his divine informant the dilemma of providence or fate, and finding providence mightier than evil, and virtue victorious over adversity ; and finally reconciling, as did Augustine, man's free-will with God's foreknowledge, and the imperfections of creation with the perfect attributes of the Creator.

This was the great but difficult book which Chaucer set himself to translate into English. He made only one attempt, and that perhaps at a later period, to versify the *metra* of Boethius—the first four stanzas of Chaucer's poem *The Former Age* reproduce the description and sentiment of the fifth *metrum* of Book ii. He was content to turn it all, verse and prose alike, into a horny English, vivid

7

enough at times, but lacking both texture and rhythmical swing ; and the curious fact emerges that Chaucer could write with precision, ease and grace, more readily in verse than in prose. By translating *Le Roman de la Rose* Chaucer became a poet : he did not become a great prose writer by translating the *Consolatio Philosophiae*. But he absorbed much of the diffusive precision of its philosophic author, and if he did not become a philosopher, he became a convinced believer in the authority of Boëthius. Indeed, when Chaucer in the course of his poems ventures to philosophize, it is the voice of Boëthius which speaks. We hear it not only in *The Former Age*, as we have said. We catch its tones in the ballades of *Fortune, Gentilesse,* and *Truth*. We hear it in the argument of Thesus in *The Knight's Tale* (ll. 2987–3016), in Criseyde's lament for the instability of happiness (iii, 813), in Pandarus's reflection on " the worste kind of infortune " (iii, 1625), in Troilus's praise of Love (iii, 1744–1771), and in his soliloquy on free-will (iv, 957–1078).

Another effect on Chaucer of the Consolation of Philosophy was to confirm by scholastic authority the notion that men's lives were acted upon in accordance with God's providence by Fortune ; who, like Nature, was personified, if not deified, and entrusted with divine purpose in the scheme of things. The medieval view was that one of the evidences of virtue in the noble soul is indifference to worldly fortune : that whether man's lot is to bear her buffets or to bask in the sunshine of her golden presence, he should lift up both heart and head, and take the bitter with the sweet, like a philosopher and a Christian. This conception of the influence of Fortune upon man's life and destiny profoundly affected the medieval conception of tragedy. To Chaucer and his poetic colleagues, the fall of a prince from high estate owed little or nothing to his character. They had no notion that character is destiny ; that men are the masters of their fates, and make or mar their lives. To them, tragedy was the handiwork of

Fortune, and they found in the pathos of overthrow and the terror of death the mysterious working of divinity. The fall of a prince was to them not only piteous and terrible ; it was, if one may stretch the meaning of a word consecrated to religious usage, holy. Hence it is not surprising that Chaucer had Boëthius in mind when he wrote his *Monk's Tale*, which is a series of tragedies in the medieval sense of the word ; and he appears to have commenced the tragedy of Hercules from one of the *metra* of the *Consolatio* (Book iv, metrum 7).

But perhaps the greatest effect of Chaucer's study of Boëthius was its influence upon his philosophy of life, which was very simple and direct, and indeed amounts to little more than this, that life is short, difficult, and per-plexing, and in this mortal coil the only conduct possible is bravely to face each eventuality as it comes, and to do the right and fitting thing. Chaucer often satirizes churlish conduct. He never laughs at " gentilesse." His conception of nobility—as may be seen in his ballade *Gentilesse* and elsewhere—is based on the *Consolatio* (Book iii, prose 6), and is exactly stated by de Meun in the words " Noblesse vient de bon corage," or as Dan Michel of Northgate has it in his chapter on Noblesse in *The Ayenbite of Inwyt* : " The zothe noblesse comth of the gentyle herte."

IV

THE POET

§ 1

CHAUCER'S first glimpse of the idea of great poetry was derived, as we have seen, from the work of Froissart, De Machaut, and the authors of *Le Roman de la Rose*. In middle life that idea was enlarged when his visits to Italy, first in 1373 and again in 1378, introduced him to the work of Dante, Petrarch and Boccaccio. The mysticism of Dante made little or no appeal to Chaucer's practical mind, though he imitated the invocation to the Virgin from *Paradiso* xxxiii in the prologue to his Life of St. Cecilia. He attempted Dante's *terza rima* in *A Complainte to his Lady* (ll. 15–40) but seemingly made no further practice in this difficult metre ; and it would appear that he parodied or at least was influenced by the triple form of the *Divina Commedia* in his *House of Fame*. But though Chaucer was familiar with Dante's great poem, he was unfitted by temperament to appreciate it to the full. Perhaps its greatest influence upon Chaucer was that it sent him back to Virgil to rediscover in the *Æneid* the romance of Troy and the tragic story of Dido's love which he celebrated in *The House of Fame* and in *The Legend of Good Women*. Petrarch too made little impression on Chaucer. That he was familiar with some of the *Canzoniere* is apparent from his translation of the sonnet beginning " S'amor non è, ch'è dunque quel ch'i'sento ? " in *Troilus and Criseyde*, i, ll. 400–420 ; and it is not impossible that he had read the *Trionfi* ; if, as has been suggested Petrarch's *Trionfo della Fama* influenced *The House of Fame*, with its famous names graven on the rock of ice, like the great ones of the *Trionfo del Tempo*.

But if these great Italian poets were to Chaucer names to conjure with rather than living influences, it is otherwise with Boccaccio. It would be possible to overestimate the enthusiasm which Chaucer must have felt for the art of Boccaccio, but it is easier to disparage the influence which Boccaccio's writings exerted upon Chaucer, and this has been done both by French critics anxious to prove that Chaucer was merely a successor of the *trouvères*, and by Anglo-Saxon scholars who with linguistic loyalty have hesitated to admit that the works on which Chaucer's claim to greatness largely depends—*Troilus and Criseyde* and *The Canterbury Tales*—owed anything but a slight and trivial debt to the genius of Boccaccio. The question of the relationship of Chaucer to Boccaccio is complicated by the fact that Chaucer never alludes to Boccaccio by name, even when he is building upon his foundation and with his timber. He calls him "Lollius" sometimes; but in *Troilus and Criseyde* (i, 394) it is Petrarch whom he calls by that name—unless, as seems probable, he thought that this Italian sonnet was the work of Boccaccio. Whatever may be the truth: whether Chaucer's "Lollius" is a wilful blind, or whether Chaucer possessed some large Italian manuscript containing works of Boccaccio and Petrarch which he regarded as the work of one author (and this seems unlikely); it is certain that Boccaccio's works influenced Chaucer in many ways. His romances, *La Teseide* and *Il Filostrato*, spurred Chaucer to emulate them in *The Knight's Tale* and *Troilus and Criseyde*. His Latin works, *De Claris Mulieribus* and *De Casibus Virorum Illustrium*, provides inspiration for Chaucer's *Legends of Good Women* and *The Monk's Tale*. Possibly the excellence of the richness and variety of the *novelle* in the *Decameron*, or at least their reputation, suggested to Chaucer the notion of stringing together that bundle of romances, legends, fables and *fabliaux* which he called *The Canterbury Tales*.

Boccaccio was a writer after Chaucer's own heart. He

was a man of the world, sharpened and polished by the study of human nature in many cities. He was a sensuous poet with a keen enjoyment of beauty in nature, a scholar with a high regard for romance, a novelist of a hundred tales to suit all tastes. He taught Chaucer what to write about. He taught Chaucer the art of narrative. If Chaucer's earliest ambition was to become an English Froissart or a De Machaut, his later desire was to become the English Boccaccio. Whether Chaucer's favourite stanza owes something to Boccaccio's *ottava rima* cannot be answered with a simple negative. It is true that Chaucer's stanza is a French stanza, the seven-line ballade stanza, a lyrical stanza which in decasyllabic or hendeca-syllabic metre was comparatively rare amongst the French poets, who preferred stanzas of eight lines or more. But granted that Chaucer had already borrowed the stanza from the French for the *Man of Law's Tale* and the *Complainte to Pity* before he went to Italy, which may or may not have been the case, there can be no doubt that when Chaucer began *Troilus and Criseyde* a comparison of his seven-line stanza with Boccaccio's eight-line stanza was inevitable ; and he must have noticed then, if he had not realized it before, that if the fifth line of a stanza of *ottava rima* be omitted, the remaining seven lines have the same metrical pattern as the Chaucerian stanza (ab ab(a)b cc) ; and he could not fail to note the soft cadence of its line of eleven syllables, an effect which he deliberately attempted at times to produce by the use of the " feminine " ending. It is not impossible that Chaucer's seven-line stanza would have remained a metrical experiment, had not the poet seen what magnificent narrative was possible in Boccaccio's *ottava rima*.

Chaucer returned from Italy with an enthusiasm for Italian poetry. And in that he showed good taste. He could comprehend neither the religious vision nor the political fury of Dante, and much of the learning and the rhetoric of Petrarch was beyond him ; but as far as his

appreciation went—we must remember that, speaking
generally, literary taste in England was as yet unde-
veloped ; one story was as good as another, as we may
observe in Gower—and as far as Chaucer was able to
discriminate between the highest qualities in his new-
found masters, he understood and prized a more intense
quality of imagination than he had hitherto experienced ;
a formal and more sustained art of narrative ; realistic
description both of men and women and of natural background ; and, above all, brighter colour, more intense
pathos, and keener satire. It must not, however, be
supposed that Chaucer forgot the instruction which he had
derived from French poetry. He did not. Even if he had
wished to abandon the French style, the taste of the court
would have forbidden it. He still pursued complainte and
allegory, but his diction became polished, and he adorned
his fictions with imagery and learned illustrations gleaned
from his Italian masters. It is in his romances, *Troilus
and Criseyde* and *The Knight's Tale*, and in his " tragedies,"
The Legend of Good Women and *The Monk's Tale*, that
Boccaccio's influence is most apparent. The Clerk's *Tale
of Griselda* comes from the last novel of the *Decameron* ; but
Chaucer translated from Petrarch's Latin version, and not
from the original.

Excepting the tales of the Clerk, the Second Nun, and
the Knight, which shall be considered later, the poems of
Chaucer's period of Italian influence, which extended from
1373 to about 1386, consist of complaintes ; two allegories,
The House of Fame and *The Parlement of Fowles* ; one long
romance. *Troilus and Criseyde* ; and that curiously unequal
poem, half allegory, half legends of the lives of Cupid's
saints and martyrs, called *The Legend of Good Women*.
Let us consider first the complaintes.

§ 2

The poetic " complainte "—an expression of grief and

an appeal for pity—was felt by Chaucer to be a definite form, consisting of a proem or introduction, stating the circumstances in the form of allegory, followed by the motive of the poem, namely, the complaint. In this respect he made an advance upon De Machaut to whom a "complainte," like a "confort," was simply the expression of a given theme ; and the name referred to the matter of the poem rather than to its form. Indeed Chaucer in those allegorical poems of his, *The Book of the Duchess*, and *The Parlement of Fowles*, which De Machaut would have called "dits," differed from his French preceptors in dividing his poem into two parts ; so that it was an easy advance later, when Chaucer took up the verse-tale, to pass from the invention of a proem to the magnificent fictions of his prologues. The formal introduction is most characteristic of Chaucer, and is rare in earlier French poetry.

The form of a complainte may be seen at a glance in Chaucer's *Complainte to Pity* ; where the proem, describing the bier of Pity surrounded in his lady's heart by the personifications of feminine charm, is followed by the complainte, or as it is here called by a legal term "the bill," meaning a written statement of the case for the plaintiff. And Chaucer's complaint is that Pity, who we might note appears in *Le Roman de la Rose* as the personification of feminine tenderness, has allowed Cruelty to usurp her throne ; and takes no heed of the poet, who is slowly dying of unrequited love. It is an expression neither of true love nor of platonic friendship, but of that courtly love of the middle ages which, wherever found, was derived from the Provençal poets of the twelfth century. It took different shapes in different countries. In Italy at its highest it became a form of spiritual worship. A poet's devotion was offered without hope of matrimony or reward to an exalted lady whom he scarcely knew ; and he claimed, in worshipping her purity and tenderness from afar, that his life became more spiritual ; her love was at once a refining fire, and the source of his courtesy, valour, and poetic inspiration. In France, it took a more feudal form. The lover became his lady's vassal. He owed to her the allegiance and reverence which he paid to his liegelord. She became his sovereign lady, and he praised her in song, never mentioning her name publicly, for such courtly love was secret ; but he concealed her identity under some figure or some fictitious name, as for example Chaucer in the prologue to *The Legend of Good Women* conceals the name of his sovereign lady under the figure of the daisy, and under the name Alceste.

Chaucer's love-poems follow the fashion. Probably neither the *Complainte to Pity* nor the other complaintes and ballades of protestation express anything more than a purely conventional feeling of regard, yet their language is almost that of religious devotion.

> Have mercy on me, thou serenous quene,
> That you have sought so tenderly and yore
> Let som streem of your light on me be sene,
> That love and drede you ever lenger the more.

That is from the *Complainte to Pity*, but its tone and its vocabulary is the same as that of the language of religious devotion, as may be seen if it be compared with Chaucer's *A. B. C.* It is not quite so fervent, it is true ; but it differs in degree and not in kind.

Who the lady was, none has yet declared. It cannot have been Philippa Roet, unless Chaucer wrote the poem before 1366. Very possibly it was Queen Philippa or perhaps Blanche of Lancaster ; but the identity of the unapproachable lady scarcely matters. The poem lives by its fancy, and by its studied eloquence coloured with personified abstraction from *Le Roman de la Rose*. It is as artificial as a valentine, and yet has a quaint charm in spite of its assumed seriousness. Possibly the lady to whom the *Complainte to Pity* was addressed received on another occasion Chaucer's so-called *Complainte to his Lady*. This poem follows immediately after the *Complainte to Pity* in the two manuscripts wherein it is found, and also in Stowe's folio of 1561; but the former poem is complete without the *Complainte to his Lady*, and their themes are different. Indeed, strictly speaking, the latter is not a "complainte" in form. It has no proem, and, though the text is defective, or perhaps unfinished, it is clear that it is a sequence of love-poems in various metres, rather like the French form called in Chaucer's time a "lay," and is not one single poem. The matter is the usual tissue of conventional love-poetry. The despairing servant is unable to sleep for love-longing; for his unpitying lady (whom he calls the "Faire Rewthelees") recks not whether he weep or sing. Nevertheless, though she scorn his protestations, he will continue to serve her faithfully and to ask for her grace. It is quite clearly an artificial poem, conveying a series of delicate compliments in the shape of a fictitious declaration of Love. Possibly the key to the lady's name lies hidden under the pseudonym, "Faire Rewthelees the Wise, y-knit unto Good Aventure"; but it has not yet been found.

The form of the poem lacks Chaucer's usual studied perfection. Metrically considered, it is in three unequal parts. The first two stanzas are composed in the seven-line stanza, but clearly they are not a continuation of the *Complainte to Pity*. They enunciate a new method of approach to the lady's heart. They develop a new theme. The third and fourth stanzas, which are incomplete and of unequal length, are written in the *terza rima* of Petrarch's *Trionfi* and Dante's *Divina Commedia*, riming aba, bcb, cdc, etc. They offer the sole early example in English of this metrical pattern, and this fact is not only an authority for the genuineness of the authorship—Chaucer being the only Englishman of his age to imitate Dante—but it is a clue also to the date of composition; for the poem must have been composed after Chaucer's first visit to Italy, and by that time both Queen Philippa and Blanche of Lancaster were in their graves, so that the poem was addressed to neither of them. The final nine stanzas, the second of which is defective, are composed of ten lines riming aabaab, cd dc,—a stanza which is of French origin, if indeed it were not directly imitated from some poem of Froissart or De Machaut.

The defective text of the poem, with which Skeat took daring liberties, is due, in part, at least, to omissions and possibly to errors by the copyists; but it is quite possible that the poem, like *The Complainte of faire Anelida and false Arcite*, was left unfinished by Chaucer. It is also quite possible that this unnamed poem, to which modern editors have given the title " A Compleynt to his Lady," is not one poem at all, but three fragments, which, somehow or other, became welded together in manuscript, and finally were added to the *Complainte to Pity*. The first part (in the seven-line stanza) and the last section (in the ten-line stanza) may have been designed originally for insertion in some narrative poem such as *Troilus and Criseyde* or *The Knight's Tale*. They are conventional in tone, and would fall apt from the lips of either Troilus or Palamon and Arcite. It is not clear whether the section in *terza rima*, which seems at first sight to be linked by rime to the first section, is an independent poem or fragment; but the sentiment sounds less conventional, and the " Fair Ruthless " seems to be a real person, not a fiction. This section therefore may have been addressed to a patroness. But whatever the history of the poem may be, we would not be without the *Complainte to his Lady*. With the exception of Anelida's lament, it is Chaucer's highest endeavour in this artificial mode of courtly love. These poems lack the fire and fancy, and the studied perfection of Petrarch's sonnets, but they represent the same mode of poetry in their pedestrian English way. And whilst no doubt it was very bad for the lady to receive these flattering ministrations to her vanity, it was good for Chaucer to write them. He learned to honour womanhood and to value tenderness. Above all, filled with these sentiments, he forgot to mock or to tease, and learned to reverence. And reverence, whether for age, or for honour, or for beauty, is one of the attributes of a noble heart.

The Complainte of faire Anelida is another unfinished poem, which consists in its imperfect state of a complainte in a romantic setting, elaborated by Chaucer from the medieval romance of Thebes. Chaucer begins his prologue with the triumphal return of Theseus to Athens after his conquest of Scythia and his subsequent marriage to Hippolyta. The sources of these opening stanzas Chaucer tells us :

First folwe I Stace, and after him Corynne.

They are Statius, whose *Thebaid* xii, 519 ff, is drawn upon ; and Bocacccio, from whose *Teseide*—the romance of Theseus—come five of the first ten stanzas. Why Chaucer here calls Boccaccio " Corynne " has never yet been satisfactorily explained. One must presume either that Chaucer was ignorant of the real name of Boccaccio (which is incredible), or that he was unwilling to admit his debt.

His imitation ceases, however, at the tenth stanza, and in the rest of the prologue Chaucer narrates an original fiction of a noble lady, Anelida Queen of Armenia, who went to live in Thebes during the reign of Creon. Here she was wooed by a Theban knight named Arcite—perhaps the Arcite of *The Knight's Tale*—to whom she gave her love. But Arcite forsook Anelida for another lady, who was cold and proud, and granted him no grace. Such is the fickle heart of man, says Chaucer :

For what he may not gete, that wolde he have.

Deserted by Arcite, the disconsolate Anelida composed a complaint, and sent it to him. Thereupon follows Anelida's *Complainte*—the most difficult poem of this kind, technically, that Chaucer ever wrote. The story continues that Anelida promised a sacrifice to Mars, and then suddenly breaks off. What the conclusion would have been, it is impossible to say. Not improbably Arcite would have returned, a sadder and a wiser man, armed with a complementary " complainte." Probably Theseus, whose appearance in the story is difficult to account for, would have come to Thebes at last to conclude the story, as in *The Knight's Tale*; for, as the last book of Statius's *Thebaid* tells us :

> With Creon, which that was of Thebes King,
> He faught, and slough him manly as a knight,
> In pleyn bataille, and putte the folk to flight
> And by assaut he wan the citee after.

The complainte itself is prosodially Chaucer's most brilliant lyric, though in sentiment it is far below the *Complainte to his Lady*. After an introductory stanza, in which Anelida laments that the stab of memory only serves to teach her that to be true in love is to suffer, there follows a two-fold complainte, both halves of which are identical in form. The former expresses Anelida's constancy and her forgiveness : the latter her sorrow and her need. The fifth stanza of each is a long irregular double stanza of sixteen lines riming aaab aaab, bbba bbba ; the first three lines of each group being in tetrameter, and the fourth in pentameter. The other stanzas are regular verses of nine pentameter lines riming aab aab bab, as is also the concluding stanza, in which Anelida in medieval fashion attributes Arcite's unfaithfulness to " destiny or chance." To sweep triumphantly through fourteen stanzas of nine lines or more, each built upon only two riming syllables, is a difficult feat in English ; and the poem, considered in its setting, shows Chaucer already in possession of considerable power of inventing a romantic story, as well as of investing a character with emotion.

Whether the poem has some personal reference to contemporary life, like *The Book of the Duchess*, is unknown.

Probably it has ; but the key is lost, and whom Anelida and Arcite represent we do not know. But, as we have already stated, the *Complaintes of Mars* and *of Venus* appear to refer not to an unknown and otherwise unrecorded love affair between Sir John Holland and Isabella of York (as Shirley suggested) but to the marriage of Si͏ͬ John Holland to Elizabeth of Lancaster—a hasty marriage which surprised and scandalized the good ladies of the period, because Elizabeth was at the time betrothed to the Earl of Pembroke. *The Complainte of Mars* consists of an introduction in the seven-line stanza, told as it were by " a little bird "—the whisperer of secrets—on St. Valentine's Day. The story goes that once upon a time Mars was taken captive by the charms of Venus, but the lovers were discovered by Phœbus, and Venus fled to take refuge with Mercury in " Cyllenius' tower." Hereupon follows the " complainte " of Mars, which is formed of an introductory stanza followed by a sequence of laments in five similar lyrics of three stanzas of nine lines, each riming aab aab bcc. (1) Mars tells the reason of his love. He loves the perfect beauty and gentleness of Venus, and will for ever be her true servant. (2) But to whom shall he tell his distress ? (3) Love is torment. (4) Love is like the famous Brooch of Thebes which brought confusion to its owner ; yet for his torment he will not blame his lady, but him " that wroghte hir." (5) Therefore, knights and ladies, think not harshly of our love, but have sympathy with Venus, and show her some kindness.

Here again, we see Chaucer's growing power of inventing a romantic fiction from materials furnished by his reading. The story of Mars and Venus comes from Ovid's *Metamorphoses*, iv, 170 ff. and the " Brooch of Thebes " from Statius's *Thebaid*, ii, 269 ; but Chaucer is not content to take a story ready-made and to re-tell it. He takes as much of the old story as he wants, and invests it with astronomical significance, making it appear that the fiction refers only to a conjunction of the planets Mars and Venus in the constellation Taurus, an event which happened twice between 1370 and 1400—in the years 1383 and 1385. He omits all reference to Vulcan, the husband of Venus—probably out of deference to young Pembroke, who was the ward of his friend Sir William Beauchamp—though the omission of Vulcan obscures the point of the allusion to the Brooch of Thebes; for, according to the myth, Vulcan made this necklace for the daughter of Mars and Venus and put a curse upon it, in order to be wreaked upon Mars. In Chaucer's hands the poem became, as he intended it to be, an apology for Holland's impetuousness and Elizabeth's pliancy, and as such it is a little masterpiece of sympathetic propaganda, designed both as an apology and as an appeal.

When Chaucer wrote *The Complainte of Mars* it was too early to vindicate the wisdom of Elizabeth of Lancaster's marriage. All he could do was to portray John Holland in as favourable an aspect as he could bring himself to express. But *The Complainte of Venus*, written some years later, is an utterance of such sentiments concerning her marriage as Elizabeth, now the Countess of Huntingdon, may well have felt after proving her husband's constancy and affection. She praises the nobility of her husband, scorns jealousy, and expresses her complete satisfaction by a triple ballade riming ab ab bccb, each group of three stanzas being linked by a refrain; and the whole poem is concluded by a short envoy of ten lines addressed to " Venus," in which Chaucer says that he has had the greatest difficulty in following the metrical pattern, and in preserving the meaning

Of Graunson, flour of hem that make in Fraunce.

The ballades of Sir Otes de Granson were discovered again in 1890,[1] and it was found that three of them, Nos. vi, ix, and x, were clearly the originals from which Chaucer freely translated his *Complainte of Venus*. The title may

See E. Piaget, " Oton de Granson et ses Poésies," in *Romania*, xix.

have been suggested by Shirley the copyist, who recorded in a note in MS. Trinity R, 3, 20 : " Hit is sayde that Graunsome made this last balade for Venus resembled to my lady of York, aunswering The Complaynt of Mars." In many manuscripts the *Complainte of Venus* follows the *Complainte of Mars*, and the two poems are entitled " The Complaynt of Mars and Venus."

Shirley is probably correct in suggesting that the *Venus* is a sequel to the *Mars*. He is correct in stating that Granson wrote the originals, but he must be wrong in suggesting that they were written to express the sentiments of " my lady of York " or indeed of any other lady, since in their original form they are ballades written by a lover about his lady. Shirley is probably wrong in thinking that " Venus " represented Isabella, Duchess of York, who was the sister of Gaunt's wife, Costanza of Castile. Isabella of York died on December 23, 1392, soon after Granson's arrival in England, and history has failed to record any scandal of a love-affair between her and Sir John Holland (Mars). Chaucer must have obtained a copy of some of Granson's ballades ; and, seeing in three of them, if turned into an expression of a good wife's sentiments about her husband, an amende for *The Complainte of Mars*, he translated them freely into English and addressed them probably to Elizabeth of Huntingdon, the daughter of his patron. Besides paying a pretty and sincere compliment to one of the former pupils of Katharine Roet, Chaucer probably wished to praise Sir Otes de Granson, who was in England from 1392 to 1396, and received from Richard II the large annuity of 190 marks. There is more sincerity of feeling in Chaucer's translations, loose though they are, than in Granson's courtly and artificial ballades.

§ 3

Chaucer's *Troilus and Criseyde*, begun about 1376 and finished after revision about 1382, is the only long poem which the poet ever completed to his own satisfaction. It is an enlarged adaptation of Boccaccio's romance *Il Filostrato* (1336) a title which to him meant, as he tells us in the proem, "vinto ed abbatuto da Amore." This poem in *ottava rima* was written by Boccaccio to relieve his disconsolate and apprehensive heart during the absence of his mistress, Maria d'Aquino, whom he called "Fiammetta." Its theme is the shame and thwarted hopes of the jilted lover. It is the tragedy of one who loved too well. Most modern novelists in treating such a subject would make a victim of the woman, and would portray her subjected to the buffetings of misunderstanding, and tortured and harrowed by the most excruciating throes of sensitiveness and shame. But frustrated love was otherwise seen in the Middle Ages, in spite of their honorification of womanhood. To the poets of the age of courtly love, the silent agony of the disconsolate lover seemed a more pitiful sorrow than the shame of the forsaken bride. They saw the affair from the standpoint of the man. They were more interested in Tristram than in Isoulde.

Boccaccio, though in comparison a modern, was no exception ; and the central figure of *Il Filostrato* is Troilo, a young knight and a king's son of Troy who is smitten by love, and makes his immense passion for Griseida the absorbing and overwhelming interest of his life. When by unkind fate Griseida is forced to leave Troy for the Greek camp, where it soon becomes apparent that she lacks his deep sincerity, he is disabled by an agony of grief which drives him desperately to meet death in battle. Boccaccio's *Filostrato* is a sentimental romance. It is also a psychological novel, for Troilo feels the longing and regret which Boccaccio had felt for Fiammetta ; and the reflection of his own sentiments adds depth and vividness to the lyrical quality of the narrative. It is in addition a tragedy —the story of how a brave, simple-minded knight, whose life hitherto had been governed and regulated by the courtly code of his environment, was, almost before he was

8

aware of it, obsessed by a passion greater than he had expected or thought possible, and owing to his inexperience was unable to extricate himself from the consequences.

This was the simple and pitiful romance which Chaucer brought back from Italy, and, recognizing its power, he resolved to adapt it for English gentles. On the one hand it was a mirror of the courtly etiquette of an aristocratic love-affair : on the other it was concerned with an episode in the famous siege of Troy, which was likely to commend it both to the knight and the scholar. It is small marvel then that this tale of love, honour, and arms pleased Chaucer ; and that upon this romance he expended all his art, endeavouring to construct it in five books corresponding to the traditional five acts of drama, each with its proper invocation in the grand style ; endeavouring to portray in every mode possible, except by direct description, the feelings and sentiments of the principal characters ; and enriching his verse with allusions and thoughts gleaned from those poets and philosophers whom he regarded as his masters. In Chaucer's hands, *Troilus and Criseyde* became a tragedy of the power of love. Troilus scorned love : therefore he was stricken by love. His fate is pitiful, but it is just.

It was not a new story. It had been told and retold even before Boccaccio made it his. The love-story of Troilus and Briseide seems first to have been invented for insertion in *Le Roman de Troie* (*c.* 1160) by Benoît de Sainte More, a French poet connected with the court of Henry II of England. This romance was based not on Homer, for Greek studies had lapsed in the Dark Ages and Homer was known only in epitome, but on two Latin prose " histories " —the *Ephemeris belli Troiani* (*c.* 350 A.D.) of Dictys Cretensis, who took the side of the Greeks, and the *De Excidio Troiae Historia* (*c.* 600) of Dares Phrygius, whose sympathies rested with the Trojans. Both books appeared to be translations of early records of the Trojan War ; but though the former may be a Latin translation from the

Greek of a slightly earlier original, both are fictions derived
from Homer, Virgil, and imagination. It was whilst
re-telling in French octosyllabic couplets the romance of
Troy that Benoît inserted in some fifteen hundred lines the
story of Troilus and Briseide. It is a counterpart of the
episode narrated in the first book of the *Iliad*—how Chryses,
the priest of Apollo, wrought a murrain on the Greek host
until Agamemnon restored his daughter Chryseis ; and
how, enraged at the enforced surrender of his mistress,
Agamemnon seized Briseis, the like captive of Achilles.
Benoît's story is very similar. As Agamemnon reft Briseis
from Achilles, leaving him aggrieved and disconsolate, so
in the *Roman de Troie* Diomedes takes Briseide from
Troilus. The chief difference is in the preliminaries of the
event. In Benoît's fiction, Calchas the priest deserted
Troy for the Greek camp when he foresaw that the city
would be taken, leaving behind his daughter Briseis. He
then persuaded the Greeks to exchange her for the captured
Antenor. Briseide was betrothed to Troilus, son of Priam,
King of Troy ; but Diomedes, who brought her to the
Greek camp, fell in love with her. Troilus encountered
Diomedes in battle, and wounded him sore ; whereupon
Briseide was touched with pity for Diomedes, and clave
to him.

Benoît de Sainte More's *Roman de Troie* was freely
translated into Latin prose a century later by an Italian,
Guido delle Colonne, who finished his *Historia Troiana* in
1287. Boccaccio no doubt was familiar with Guido's
history, but he appears to have based his *Filostrato*, as far
as it is the product of literary influence, upon Benoît's
romance. He retold the story from the standpoint of
Troilo, regarding it in terms of his own precarious relationship with Fiammetta. He characterized Griseida as a
widow, no doubt for several reasons. As a married woman,
according to the manners of the Middle Ages, she could
remain honourably alone in Troy, and receive the courtly
protestations of Troilo's love. As a widow, she is as

experienced in the ancient art of love as Troilo is ignorant of its power. He created also a new character, young Pandaro, the cousin of Griseida and the bosom-friend of Troilo, to share their secret and to act as intermediary between the lovers, like Governale in the romance of Sir Tristram. To Boccaccio the romance was an attempt to express the heartbreak of broken vows. A man's whole love is given to a woman who proves unworthy. What is he to do? In intention, *Il Filostrato* was to be both heartsease for his agony of suspense, and a poetic allegory addressed to his lady. If these were the sorrows of Troilo for Griseida, let her realize the passion of Boccaccio for Fiammetta.

> Se tu la vedi ad ascoltarti pia
> Nell' angelico aspetto punto farsi,
> O sospirar della fatica mia,
> Pregala quanto puoi che ritornarsi
> Omai le piaccia, o comandar che via
> Da me l'anima deggia dileguarsi,
> Perocchè dove ch'ella ne deggia ire,
> Me' che tal vita m'è troppo il morire.

Chaucer lacked this deep personal interest in the sorrow of Troilus. One reason why he was attracted by the poem was because he knew that his readers would be interested in the setting. Geoffrey of Monmouth had recorded in his history that the Britons were descendants of Trojan refugees, kinsmen of pious Æneas, and it pleased aristocratic vanity to believe it. Whilst Chaucer was writing *Troilus and Criseyde*, two English poets were transmuting the Troy-books of Benoît and Guido into *The Seege of Troy* and *The Gest Historiale of the Destruction of Troy*. It may be that one of them was the " philosophical Strode," to whom together with " moral Gower" *Troilus and Criseyde* is in the penultimate stanza directed. A few years later John Lydgate was to compose his *Troy Book*. But to Chaucer the story mattered more than the setting. His atmosphere is neither that of Troy nor the Greek camp.

Like all his contemporaries, poets and artists alike, he thought of Ilium in terms of his own age. When he speaks of warriors, temples, houses, and city gates, he means the knights and churches, the timbered houses and battlements which he knew. The code of manners is that of medieval chivalry and courtly love.

Chaucer's *Troilus and Criseyde* is not a translation of *Il Filostrato* : it is an imitation with imaginative additions ; and it contains more of Chaucer's invention than of Boccaccio's. It is probable that Chaucer had read Guido delle Colonne's *Historia Troiana*, and that some of the deviations from Boccaccio's *Filostrato* are due to recollections of Guido's version. Chaucer's main interest was not in the action of the story, which is simple indeed both in motive and in incident ; but in the reactions of the principals of the story to circumstance. Troilus is the central figure. At the outset he is still a boy who scorns love and is ashamed of dalliance. Then, like many another potential lover in medieval romance, he sees Criseyde in the temple, and so, he who had scorned love's ways is stricken by love's malady. But Criseyde, having lost one husband, is in no haste to choose another ; and Troilus is so sensitive of the ridicule of the lovers whom he has scorned that he dares not openly confess that he is one of Love's folk, for fear of shame. Unfortunately for this young mirror of knighthood, who otherwise would have suffered the pangs of calf-love and made a speedy recovery, the governor of his destiny at this crisis happens to be his friend Pandarus, a middle-aged jovial cynic, whose humour is to make the most of life. Why suffer these torments ? he says. Is not your lady my niece ? Let me serve both of you by arranging for you to meet. And so, against his best intentions, which are entirely honourable, Troilus is led into a secret relationship which cannot be divulged without sacrificing Criseyde's reputation and honour ; and that, as *The Complainte of Mars* indicates, was a scandal not to be quenched even by marriage.

Chaucer does not blame Troilus. There is really nothing to blame when one understands. Granted that Troilus was sensitive, inexperienced, and entirely blinded by love the catastrophe follows inevitably. Criseyde has to leave Troy with their love-affair still a secret, where Calchas her father arranges her exchange. Marriage is so obviously impossible that neither of them suggests it. Criseyde protests her love, and departs, saying that she will escape from the Greeks and return. But alas, she finds that to escape is hard, and to return to a doomed city would be folly. So she accepts the love of Diomede, and remains amongst the Greeks. Chaucer treats her very tenderly ; for, after all, harshness would suggest that she was to blame, and that he could not agree to. Her faithlessness was not wilful. It was the consequence of indolence, not of malice. Here she differs from his originals. Boccaccio's Griseida is light, unfaithful, experienced, and incapable of remorse. Chaucer's Criseyde is not a heartless trickster, assuming innocence, as in Benoît's *Roman de Troie* :

> Molt fu amée et molt ameit,
> Meis ses corages li changeit,
> Et si esteit molt amorose.

The effect produced by Chaucer's Criseyde on the reader is that of a woman with little depth of passion who is tricked into a second love before she has forgotten the first—a beauty of tenderness without strength, an innocent without a heart.

Troilus and Criseyde is not a book for the young. It has many flowers of rhetoric and many shrewd touches of humour and of characterization. It is a fiction of very high rank, both for its depth of pathos and its beauty of style ; but it lies too near the heart of youth for youth to grasp its magnitude of passion and pity. The tale is slowly unfolded by means of dialogue and soliloquy, and is told with great and sustained narrative art, enlivened by fresh touches of characterization, often most delicately indicated. Chaucer wrote his seven-line stanza with great mastery as a vehicle of narrative, without feeling apparently the constraint of rime. *Troilus and Criseyde* is the most pitiful and the most psychological of all Chaucer's works. A study in character, the characters are scarcely described, but disclosed rather, by conversation, and by the expression of their sentiments and the analysis of their emotions. Chaucer stands aloof and depicts each in turn, faithfully as he saw them, without favour and without palliation. He could not accept the view that a second love excuses unfaithfulness, but he felt the pity of it. In this respect, the poem stands alone in the English literature of its age, and it is not difficult to understand the popularity which it enjoyed down to Elizabethan times.

§ 4

The House of Fame is written in the octosyllabic metre of *The Romaunt of the Rose* and *The Book of the Duchess*, but the fact that it shows the influence of the *Divina Commedia* proves that it must have been written after 1373. It is in three books, the last of which is twice as long as the first and second, and unfinished. Each begins with an invocation, the first to Morpheus, the second to Venus and the Muses, and the third to Apollo. Quite clearly it was designed as an important poem, but it appears to have outgrown Chaucer's conception, and to have been abandoned because it was impossible to keep it within bounds.

The subject of the poem is the description of the seat of Fame amplified from Ovid's description in *Metamorphoses*, xii, 39–63. High in the middle regions of the sublunar sphere is the House of Fame; its doors and windows stand ever open to admit the sounds of every earthly event: within there is no rest, for the house is full of murmuring noises, and a crowd of suppliants for fame magnifies the rumours in repeating them. Chaucer elaborated this

image in the form of a dream-adventure. He begins with
a proem in which he suggests the supernatural nature of
dreams, invokes the help of the god of sleep, and then
proceeds to narrate a remarkable dream which befell him,
he says, on the tenth day of December. (i) He found
himself in a temple of glass dedicated to Venus, the walls
of which were adorned with the romance of Æneas. He
admired the pictures, and then went out of the temple
into a vast desert where he met a golden eagle descending
from the sky. (ii) The eagle seized him in its talons, and
soared aloft with him half-dead with fear. It told him
that as a reward for making " bookes, songes, or dytees "
in reverence of love, and also because his inspiration is
deadened by his " rekeninges," Jupiter has commanded the
eagle to bear him aloft to the House of Fame, where he
shall hear

> Of Love's folke mo tidinges,
> Both sothe sawes and lesinges
> And mo loves newe begonne.

The eagle carried him aloft to the foot of the rock on
which the hall stands, and bade him enter. (iii) The
House of Fame stands on a rock of ice engraved· with the
name of those who have achieved fame. On the north
side they are still fresh and clear, but on the side by which
Chaucer approached they were melted by the sun. The
house itself is made of beryl, and in every niche stand the
images of minstrels and poets. Within the hall, which is
lined with solid gold, Fame sits on a ruby throne ; and on
an avenue of pillars leading from the dais to the doors
stand statues of the great poets—Statius, Homer, Dares,
Dictys, " Lollius," Guido delle Colonne, Geoffrey (of
Monmouth ?), Virgil, Ovid, Lucan and Claudian. As
Chaucer watched the scene, crowds of suppliants approached, and asked for renown in return for their good
works, their nobility, desert, generosity, sanctity, idleness,
treachery or wickedness. Fame's answers are despotic

and capricious. Æolus, her trumpeter, dismissed them
with a blast of laud or slander as she devised. In the
midst of this travesty of fair-play, Chaucer turned to speak
to one who asked if he came to receive renown. He told
him that he came for no such reason, but to learn some
new tidings of love ; and though the place is wonderful,
he had not found what he expected. The stranger then
led him to a maze of basketwork, full of noise and rumour,
where he saw the eagle again still waiting for him. He
entered, and heard a great noise in one corner, where
rumours of love-affairs were told. Here he saw " a man of
greet auctoritee "—and the poem ends unfinished.

On the one hand it is a dream-poem in the style of De
Machaut, like *The Book of the Duchess* ; on the other hand
it is a vision influenced by Chaucer's acquaintance with the
Divina Commedia. Like it, *The House of Fame* is divided
into three books, each of which begins with an invocation ;
and the last in particular seems to be an imitation of
Dante's commencement of the *Paradiso.* Chaucer is
guided by Jove's eagle, as Dante was led by Virgil, and
scholars have pointed out minor similarities.[1] The poem
bears little if any trace of the influence of Petrarch's
Trionfo della Fama, which, though it is composed in three
books, is simply a catalogue of famous names. The
relation to tradition is clear : *The House of Fame* is a
dream-vision ; and as such it is probable that Chaucer
intended it to bear some allegorical meaning, but what
that meaning was is unfortunately not clear.

That the poem is an allegory of Chaucer's experience—a
symbol of his escape from the temple of Venus into the
wilderness, and his flight thence with the aid of the eagle
of ambition up to the temple of Fame—is possible, but
considering the nature of the allegory of his other dream-
fantasies, hardly credible. It is more probable that *The
House of Fame* was written, as a poet laureate's effusions

---

[1] See A. Rambeau, " Chaucer's House of Fame in seinem verhältniss
zu Dante's Divina Commedia," *Englische Studien*, iii, 209, 1880.

should be written, definitely to celebrate and signalize some event. And it has been suggested (first by Imelmann and later by Brusendorff) that the poem was intended to celebrate the betrothal of Richard II and Anne of Bohemia, in much the same way as Froissart's poem *Le Temple d'Onnour* was written to publish in the form of allegory the news of some important betrothal or marriage. Curiously enough, December was a crucial month in Richard's love-affair. It was on December 12, 1380, that commissioners were appointed to treat with the Bohemians for the hand of Anne. It was on December 18, 1381, that Anne arrived at Dover. If *The House of Fame* be an occasional poem, it is highly probable that the new tidings of love's folk which Chaucer was to learn in the house of rumour were the tidings of Richard's approaching marriage ; but if so, why is the poem incomplete ?

On the other hand, as the allegory is anything but obvious, it may be that *The House of Fame* is descriptive purely and simply, and that it was designed originally as a prologue to the Legends of Good Women. The emphasis given in Book i to the unhappy loves of Dido and the heroines of Ovid's *Heroides*—Phyllis, Oenone, Medea and the rest—seems to indicate that the tidings of love's folk were intended to be mournful rather than glad. And it may be that at the end of the poem the " man of greet auctoritee " was intended to instruct Chaucer to signalize the fame

> Of goode wymmen, maydenes and wives,
> That weren trew in loving al hire lives,
> And telle of false men that hem betrayen.

The very fact that the poem lacks significance stamps it as one of Chaucer's well-intentioned failures. Its form is lopsided and top-heavy. It seems clear that Chaucer was coming to the climax when he entered the wicker labyrinth of rumour and met the man of authority ; but by that time he was ready for a fourth book. It is obvious that in Book iii he forgot to use the brake. If Chaucer's intention was to write what Lydgate called "Dante in English," he failed. His nature was unsuited to a Dantesque subject. He was too humorous, too fanciful, and incapable of combining wonder with awe. There is much admirable descriptive writing, but it leads to nowhere ; and this may well be because Chaucer began the poem early in octosyllabic couplets under the spell of *Le Roman de la Rose*, whence was derived the introductory discussion of dreams, and added to it from time to time without any more definite intention than the hope that at some future time it might be useful as an occasional poem. Book i shows his interest in Virgil's *Æneid* and in Ovid's *Heroides*. Book ii shows that he had been reading Dante and Boëthius. Book iii shows him interested in the Trojan lore of "Lollius"

> And Guido eek de Columpnis

which he was using for *Troilus and Criseyde*. If *The House of Fame* lacks unity, it must be because, as we have suggested, it was the product of many spells, and not of one powerful inspiration and motive. It was probably written at intervals between 1368 and 1379.

§ 5

But if we cannot highly appreciate *The House of Fame*, it is otherwise with *The Parlement of Fowles*. The fiction is so charming, the fancy and humour with which it is invested are so delightful, that its excellence needs neither interpreter nor guide. Yet its wealth of poetry is not the spontaneous outflow of natural feelings. It is as if Chaucer had said : " Here will I give the lie to this nonsense about inspiration." Whatever his motive may have been—and it is generally believed that Chaucer wrote the poem on occasion to celebrate the recent marriage of his sovereign lord King Richard to Anne of Bohemia—that motive drove him to literary sources for material. *The Parlement of Fowles* is a medley of borrowings. It is as artificial and as uninspired as a journalist's panegyric. Yet it is more gay and fanciful than anything that Chaucer ever wrote, and a lasting proof that the poet who cannot write a good occasional poem upon a given theme has still much to learn, not only about diction and prosody, but about the skilful manipulation of materials.

The order of the dream-allegory required a proem accounting for the dream. He had invoked Morpheus in *The Book of the Duchess* and *The House of Fame*; and that trick had lost its novelty. But he carried in his mind the wonderful dream of Scipio as he had read it in Macrobius's *Commentarium in Somnium Scipionis*—a commentary and text of a fragment of the sixth book of Cicero's *De Republica* by a neoplatonist of the fifth century;—how the hero of the third Punic war whilst accepting the hospitality of Masinissa, King of Numidia, dreamed that he was visited by Scipio Africanus Major, who explained to him the nature of the heavenly spheres. And had not Claudian in the beginning of his *Panegyric on the Sixth Consulship of Honorius* observed that

> The wery hunter sleping in his bed
> To wode ayein his minde goth anoon,
> The juge dremeth how his plees ben sped,
> The carter dremeth how his cart is goon ;–
> The riche, of gold ; the knight fight with his foon,
> The sike met he drinketh of the tonne,
> The lover met he hath his lady wonne.

Here was his dream. He had been reading

> Tullius of the Dreem of Scipioun,
> —Of which Macrobie roghte not a lite—

and what more reasonable than that Africanus should appear to him also ; and so, invoking the planet Venus, he begins his dream.

The dream was designed to symbolize the wooing of a lady by three lords, and the way Chaucer chose to represent this was suggested by the popular belief that on St. Valentine's Day the birds choose their mates. The tradition of *Le Roman de la Rose* prescribed a park as the setting for such a dream, and Chaucer complied therewith. The inscriptions on its gate are reminiscent of the famous lines on the gate of Dante's Inferno :

> Per me si va nella città dolente ;
> per me si va nell' eterno dolore ;
> per me si va tra la perduta gente.

But there are two of them : one indicating the lover's acceptance, the other symbolizing his rejection by his lady. The park itself, the home of Venus, where stands her temple, and where Cupid forges his arrows, was closely imitated from Boccaccio's *Teseide*, vii, 51-66. And the manner of the gathering of birds on St. Valentine's Day was influenced, as Chaucer says, by the description of Nature, " the vicaire of the almighty Lord," surrounded by the fowl of her creation, which had been made by " Aleyn, in the Pleynt of Kynde." In his *De Planctu Naturae*, Alanus de Insulis, a Cistercian, and Bishop of Auxerre late in the twelfth century, had written in imitation of the proses and metres of Boëthius a satire on the unnatural manners and morals of the world. His celestial visitant was Dame Nature ; and he had described her as dressed in a garment adorned with the whole multitude of birds. Chaucer had, as he tells us, this passage in mind when he describes the assembly of the birds. But he elaborated it, and, bringing the birds to life, he made them speak in a parliament presided over by Nature.

This was his dream. Africanus led him through the gate into the park of love where he sees this parliament of Nature and her birds. Nature declared that the noblest should choose first, and immediately three tiercel eagles demanded the shy formel eagle which Nature held on her wrist. The other birds grumbled at the dispute and its consequent delay, and Nature called for a jury composed of representatives of birds of each class to make a decision. Each gives his opinion. The falcon, for the birds of prey, suggests a tournament. The goose, for the waterfowl, recommends the wooers to seek elsewhere. The dove, for the seed-fowl, pleads for constancy in rejected lovers. The cockoo, for worm-eating birds, advises them not to marry. Since the jury is unable to agree, Nature allows the formel to make her choice, advising her that reason counsels the choice of the royal tiercel. Whereupon the formel asks a year's delay for reflection, which is granted. Nature then mates the other birds, and before they fly away they sing a roundel in praise of summer.

The Parlement of Fowles shows that, in spite of his Italian instructors, Chaucer still found pleasure in the tradition of the French dream-poem derived from *Le Roman de la Rose*. But he no longer worked in the traditional octosyllabic couplet. In Italian fashion he employed a stanza, the seven-line stanza of *Troilus and Criseyde*. There is perhaps some incongruity in the introduction of Africanus, but once Chaucer is launched into the dream both the description of the park and the narrative of the parliament are most pleasing and most spirited. And Chaucer's own invention, the fiction of the parliament of fowls, is delightful in its fancy and its humour. The birds are never anything but birds, but with characteristic humour he makes them think like human types. The falcon speaks like a gentleman, conventional and dignified. The goose is the expounder of that grotesque logic which flourishes amongst the uneducated. The turtle-dove is the sentimental exponent of that blind constancy which Cervantes ridiculed in *Don Quixote*, and which the duck, a man of common sense, finds equally unreasonable in the fourteenth century. We have here a foretaste of the characterization of the *Canterbury Tales*, that dramatic instinct for fastening upon the essential humour of a person without isolating it from the ordinary appearance, which is one of Chaucer's outstanding excellences as a poet. He borrowed much, as we have shown, but he transformed what he took, and welded it into something fresh !

> For out of olde feldes, as men seith
> Cometh al this newe corn from yeer to yere ;
> And out of olde bokes, in good feith,
> Cometh al this newe science that men lere.

That is his defence, and it suffices ; for the gaiety, the love of nature, and the delightful fantasy of the allegory—the qualities that really matter—are Chaucer's own original contributions.

§ 6

If Chaucer found *The Legend of Good Women*—or, as he calls it in the link to the Man of Law's Tale, " The Legend of Cupid's Saints "—so dull in its uniformity of pathos that he was unable to finish it, a modern reader can hardly be blamed if he also finds it somewhat lacking in variety. The poem consists of a prologue followed by the tragic stories of ten famous women who died for love ; but it seems probable—since in the retraction at the end of *The Canterbury Tales* the poem is alluded to as " The Book of the XXV Ladies," and also because (in Prologue B, 1. 283) the queen who appears is accompanied by nineteen other ladies—that the poem was designed originally to contain twenty or twenty-five of these legends. And the allusion to the queen of the Prologue as " Alceste " seems to indicate that the climax of the poem was to have been the legend of Alcestis who gave her life for Admetus. The theme of the poem is the long-suffering faithfulness of good women ; and the form of the legend seems to have been suggested by the collections of lives of the saints, and similar pious stories for religious edification—perhaps indeed by the famous *Legenda Aurea*, a thirteenth-century collection from which Chaucer translated his *Life of St.*

Cecilia. The " incipit " and " explicit legenda " which stand at the beginning and end of each legend are an imitation of the rubrics which are found in the lives of the saints.

Yet *The Legend of Good Women* is not a parody. It is a serious work conditioned by two forces ; by medieval honour of womanhood which is best exemplified in courtly love-poetry, and by the growing interest in antiquity— already apparent in the general esteem in which Ovid was held in the fourteenth century, in Chaucer's respect for Virgil and Statius, and in the classical turn given to romance by the matter of Troy and Thebes—which was to lead at last to that revival of art and letters under the influence of classical authority in the fifteenth and sixteenth centuries, known as the Renaissance. In the fourteenth century the classical stories, which had been forgotten or almost forgotten during the centuries between the passing of the old civilization and the completion of the new, came back once again with the fragrance of romance, and were received with delight. The pagan gods were no longer regarded by the gentle reader as devils in disguise, but as rather interesting examples of superstition possessed of a dignity and beauty which somehow cleric and monk had hitherto failed to recognize. And the stories of the demigods and heroes of Greece and Rome, their adventures, their numerous love-affairs, and above all, the strange manner of their deaths, charmed and thrilled an age sated with monkish legend and with the familiar marvels of medieval romance. Boccaccio had obeyed his instinct and at the same time gratified his readers by relating classical myth and story in his Latin works *De Genealogia Deorum, De Claris Mulieribus,* and *De Casibus Virorum Illustrium.* They were a revival of the antique epitome, and at the same time an approach towards the modern classical dictionary ; but they satisfied a literary need, and whilst they instructed his readers in the matter of antiquity, they delighted them with the novelty and the pathos of tragical history. Chaucer evidently admired these tragical stories of the heroines and heroes ; for *The Legend of Good Women* is a poetic imitation of *De Claris Mulieribus*, and The Monk's Tale seems to have been suggested by *De Casibus Virorum Illustrium*, a most popular book, which was later translated into the seven-line stanza by John Lydgate as *The Fall of Princes*.

Taking from Boccaccio the idea of the celebration of great heroines of antiquity who had been faithful unto death, Chaucer made it his own by suggesting that he did it as a penance for *The Romaunt of the Rose* and *Troilus and Criseyde*. It was to be " a glorious Legende

> Of goode wymmen, maidenes and wives,
> That weren trewe in loving al hire lives."

Therefore it became a book of love's martyrs, or, as Lydgate described it, " a legend of perfite holiness," in that cult of womanly tenderness which the aristocratic love-poetry of the later Middle Ages produced. In the same passage in *The Fall of Princes* Lydgate says that Chaucer wrote the poem " at the request of the Queen." This is not impossible, but the fact that Chaucer never completed the poem suggests that Lydgate's statement is a deduction from the allegory of the prologue, and not literal truth.

Chaucer wrote only nine of these legends, and of these the last appears to be unfinished. They are (1) Cleopatra, who refused to survive Antony, (2) Thisbe, who similarly refused to be separated by death from Pyramus, (3) Dido, forsaken by Æneas, (4) Hypsipyle and Medea, forsaken by Jason, (5) Lucretia, the victim of Tarquinius, (6) Ariadne, forsaken by Theseus, (7) Philomela, the victim of Tereus, (8) Phyllis, forsaken by Demophoon, and (9) Hypermnestra, who refused to slay her husband Lyno (Lynceus) at her father's command. They were all well-known stories, just the kind of romantic love-story that readers of Ovid were familiar with, and indeed some seven or eight of them were introduced by Gower into his *Confessio Amantis*. Chaucer

9

is quite frank in admitting that he is simply retelling Ovid's tales ; and besides the *Metamorphoses* he employed the *Heroides*—a collection of fictitious epistles in verse addressed to their lovers by these and other heroines of antiquity— as he takes care to indicate. Indeed Ovid, in his *Heroides*, had uttered the cry of pity and dismay which Chaucer strove to reproduce in his legends. With greater imagina- tive sympathy, Ovid produced his effect by means of intimate letters, whereas Chaucer relied upon narrative ; but in no work of Chaucer is the influence of Ovid so appar- ent as in *The Legend of Good Women*. If Boccaccio showed that these flowers of antiquity could be grown in a medieval garden, Ovid provided Chaucer with the seed. It is possible that some of these legends were written before Chaucer turned to *The Knight's Tale* ; and if so, it is quite likely that Chaucer's heroic couplets were intended to produce the effect of the elegiacs of Ovid's *Heroides*.

Having once begun his task, Chaucer seems to have forsaken Ovid both for additional details and for new legends. The sources of the legends have been industri- ously traced by scholars ; and whilst such knowledge does not make the poems more attractive, it is not without interest. All the legends, excepting those of Ariadne, Philomela, and Phyllis, which are consecutive, are to be found in Boccaccio's *De Claris Mulieribus*. Philomela comes from Ovid's *Metamorphoses*, vi ; Phyllis from *Heroides*, ii ; and Ariadne from both sources (*Met.*, viii, *Her.*, x). Thisbe was taken from *Metamorphoses*, iv ; and Lucretia from Ovid's *Fasti*, ii. Dido was retold from Virgil's *Æneid*, but Chaucer was familiar with her epistle in *Heroides*, vii. The legend of Hypsipyle and Medea, we are told, was borrowed from the *Historia Troiana* of Guido delle Colonne, though Chaucer knew Ovid's *Metamorphoses* vii ; and *Heroides*, vi and xii. Hypermnestra was based on *Heroides*, xiv ; but the names of the persons in the story are those given in Boccaccio's version in *De Genealogia Deorum*, ii, 22. Finally, the legend of Cleopatra has baffled the

detectives of plagiarism, and they are driven back upon
Florus's *Epitome Rerum Romanarum*, iv. 11, in addition to
the account given by Boccaccio in his *De Claris Mulieribus*,
ch. 86. The fact is, we do wrong to think of Chaucer
working industriously with a Latin version in front of him.
He had read widely, and he probably relied largely upon
memory, which in those days, considering the scarcity of
books, was generally far more developed than it is amongst
educated people to-day. It may well be that all the
legends are simply the product of memory enlivened by
imagination, though Chaucer may have revived his memory
by reading a favourite story again in the nearest accessible
version. But that Chaucer burrowed in half a dozen books,
taking a few lines here and a few lines there—*credat Judæus
Apella !*

Chaucer's verse is interesting in these legends because
this is one of his earliest poems written in heroic couplets,
and probably some of the legends were written before the
prologue. The verse shows Chaucer completely the master
of his new metre. It runs smoothly, and overflows the
limits of the second rime of the couplet. There is no
apparent attempt to regard the couplet as a stanza,
complete in itself. The narratives are vigorous, and any
dullness must truthfully be imputed to the matter of the
legends, rather than to their style. Indeed there is a certain
dignity, and a general air of rhetorical artifice which is
absent from *The Canterbury Tales*, and one feels quite
definitely that Chaucer was here pitting himself against
Ovid ; and that as long as the inspiration lasted, he took
his task very seriously—witness the description of the sea-
fight in Cleopatra, and the rhetorical questions in Thisbe.
And some of the legends still have power to charm. Medieval
writers at times produced a pathos bred of simplicity by
directness which comes to us in our turmoil of complexity
and challenge with a wonderful charm—Marie de France's
Lai le Fresne for example, or *Aucassin et Nicolette*, and *La
Châtelaine de Vergi*, or again Boccaccio's stories of Griselda,

and of Isabella and the pot of basil.   It is this note of grief
visualized, rather than felt and understood, that sings like
the thin tinkling of an old spinet from these old-world
legends, and gives them at their best, in Ariadne or in
Thisbe, a far-away pathos which touches whilst it scarcely
affects the heart.

But the pride of *The Legend of Good Women* is Chaucer's
Prologue, a variation upon the favourite theme of the
May-morning dream.   Text B, the version of all the
manuscripts save one, begins with a profession of Chaucer's
love of books and flowers, and especially of the daisy.   To
praise the daisy he invokes the aid of courtly poets who
have already reaped this crop and left only little to glean ;
and he proceeds to identify the daisy with his " lady
sovereyne."   Here Chaucer is following a French fashion
of addressing the lady worshipped by the poet-lover as
" Marguerite," the pearl of purity, beauty and nobility.
He had in mind such poems as Guillaume de Machaut's
Dit de la Marguerite, and Froissart's *Dittié de la Flour de la
Margherite*.   The latter may indeed have suggested to
Chaucer his myth of the metamorphosis of Queen Alcestis
into the daisy ; for, after honouring the daisy, and blessing
the day when he began to serve this queen of beauty and
goodness, Froissart says that Jove caused it to spring
from the tears shed by a maid named Iris as they fell on
the grave where her husband Zephyr lay buried.   Mercury
found the daisy-flowers and sent them as a chaplet for his
beloved Ceres, whereupon it was found that the flower had
the virtue of causing its votaries to be beloved.

This is Chaucer's dream.

On May Day, he tells us, he went out to greet the daisy and
to admire the birds, and when evening came on he returned
home and slept in a little summer-house which he had.
There he dreamed that in the meadow which he had visited
there appeared to him the God of Love and his Queen,
whose crown

> Made hire like a daysie for to sene.

CHAUCER READING TO THE COURT OF RICHARD II
Frontispiece to " Troilus and Criseyde," MS. 61, Corpus Christi College, Cambridge

He praised his lady in a ballade for her beauty, and continues to thank her for her protection :

> For nadde comfort ben of hire presence
> I hadde ben dede, withouten any defence,
> For drede of Loves wordes and his chere.

Behind Love and his Queen followed nineteen ladies and a host of women who sang a song of praise to the daisy ; and Chaucer kneeled down and did his obeisance to the flower. After the song, the court sat down in order of rank, and the God of Love proceeded to rebuke Chaucer for writing *Troilus and Criseyde* and for translating *The Romance of the Rose.* The Queen defended Chaucer, and begged the God of Love to be just, and to consider how well he had served the cause of love in his works, of which she gives a list. She says she is " Alceste, whilom Queen of Thrace," and she promises that her poet shall amend his ways by making a glorious Legend of Good Women—his penance being to speak well of love. She commands him to give the book when it is finished to the Queen at Eltham or at Shene. The God of Love is inclined to regard this as a light penance, and he asks whether Chaucer has not a book which tells how Alcestis was changed into the daisy ? Chaucer replies that he has, and that he now knows why he so loves the flower. The God of Love then commands him to tell this legend of Alceste

> Whan thou hast other smale ymade before,

and desires that he will begin with the legend of Cleopatra. Thereupon Chaucer took his pen and his book, and began the poem.

Text A of the prologue, the reading of the Cambridge MS. Gg 4, 27 differs slightly in diction. Also it omits the passage identifying the daisy with Chaucer's sovereign lady (B 83–96), it omits the command to present the finished poem to the Queen (B 496–7), and other short passages which praise the daisy and allude to the Queen. It contains, moreover, an addition (A 258–313) which humorously suggests that Chaucer is old and in his dotage, and inquires :

> Why noldist thow as wel a seyd goodnes
> Of wemen, as thow hast seyd wekednes ?

In Text A the Queen of Love is identified from the beginning with Alceste. Quite clearly one of these versions must be a revision of the other. The question is, which was written first ? Whilst Koch, Skeat, and Pollard regarded Text A as the earlier and Text B as the later version, modern opinion tends to follow Ten Brink in regarding Text B as the earlier draft, written whilst Queen Anne was still alive, and Text A as a later revision made after her death, though not all will accept Lowes's contention that Text A is practically a cento from Deschamps's *Lay de Franchise* and some of his ballades.[1] All that is certain is that Text B must have been written between 1385—when Chaucer removed from Aldgate to a house in the neighbourhood of Greenwich which was presumably furnished with a garden and the " litel herber " of which he speaks—and 1394, when Anne of Bohemia died.

If the allegory of Text B means anything, it must mean, as Lydgate suggested, that Chaucer wrote the legends by royal command. The field of birds and flowers which the poet visited on the first of May is probably the court, and the God of Love and Alceste represent Richard II and Queen Anne. The prologue is a pretty compliment to Chaucer's sovereign lady, who is represented as the pearl of flowers, and as Alceste, noblest amongst all faithful women. The God of Love, who if the allegory holds, is Richard II, is pictured in a less favourable light ; and the veiled allusions to his headstrong irascibility and his readiness to listen to slandering tales, if not to his injustice and cruelty, are daring criticisms of his conduct which would

---

[1] See *Publications of the Modern Language Association of America* xix, p. 593.

be incomprehensible, did we not also know Chaucer as the author of the ballade entitled *Lack of Steadfastness*. But how much of the prologue is allegory and how much is simply fiction it is impossible to say. The prologue to *The Legend of Good Women* has been prized as one of Chaucer's most intimate and personal utterances. It certainly has a freshness of description and colour, and a stately processional march which Chaucer never attempted, save in *The Parlement of Fowles*. But whereas, formerly, readers took Chaucer's confession that he loved to go out in May to pick daisies as literally as they accepted his praise of books, one cannot now accept his eulogy of the beauty of the daisy as anything more than a veiled form of compliment to his sovereign lady, the Queen. Nevertheless the opening of the prologue is in Chaucer's finest style, and, in spite of the fact that it is conventional, his genuine love of the flowers of May and its birds refreshes the heart like the memory of the vernal airs of early summer. The entry of the court is most effectively described, but after that point the dream seems to lose its coherence. Chaucer's ruthless revision of his dialogue seems to indicate that he for one was not completely satisfied with it, and before he could complete either the prologue or the legends to his own critical satisfaction, his inspiration was banished from his mind by the new and enthralling interest of *The Canterbury Tales*.

V

THE NOVELIST

§ 1

W HAT happy inspiration suggested Chaucer's
greatest work, and whether it was a flash of
emulation or of unqualified originality, it is impossible now to say; but there is no doubt that before
the idea of *The Canterbury Tales* commended itself to him,
and before he wrote the prologue, Chaucer had already
written the tales of Custance and of Griselde, the Life of
St. Cecilia, and the romance of Palamon and Arcite.
Possibly also he was midway in the " tragedies " which he
later associated with the Monk.

That *The Canterbury Tales* were suggested by a real
pilgrimage in which Chaucer had taken part seems to me so
unlikely that there would be no need to refer to it, but for
the fact that it has been assumed by some scholars, who
have made gallant attempts to discover its date, both from
the records of Chaucer's life, and from the indications of
time alluded to in the poem. But the pilgrimage is clearly
imaginary. The pilgrims are types, selected partly for the
contrast of their particular humours, and partly to fit the
variety of the tales to be told. The pilgrimage itself is
scarcely described. Chaucer cared little about the route,
or the purpose, or the wonderful shrine. The " fore-
word " made in the Tabard Inn between the Host and
the pilgrims :

> That ech of yow, to shorte with your weye
> In this viage, shal telle tales tweye,—
> To Caunterbury ward, I mene it so,
> And homward he shal tellen other two,

is obviously imaginary ; for if Chaucer really went on a pilgrimage to Canterbury in any year after 1385, it is unlikely that he went back from Greenwich to Southwark in order to set out, when he was already half a stage on the way.

The pilgrimage was simply a fiction designed to account for the tales, which, after all, were composed not by the various pilgrims, but by Chaucer. One of the excellences of *The Canterbury Tales* is their variety. The medieval reader was familiar with homogeneous collections of fables, such as Marie de France's *Ysopet* ; or of moral anecdotes, such as the *Gesta Romanorum* ; or of homilies, or legends of the saints. Chaucer's *Legend of Good Women* had been designed as an assembly of stories all of the same pathetic kind. But variety and contrast, such as are found in *The Canterbury Tales*, were so rare before Chaucer that one is almost tempted to hail the fiction of the pilgrimage as a happy stroke of genius. This may be so ; yet I think not.

The recitation of tales and fabliaux was one of the recognized arts of entertainment ; and in the Middle Ages minstrels and disours regularly plied their art in the halls of nobles and rich merchants, on the routes of the pilgrimages, and wherever men and women assembled in a holiday mood. Some of these romantic or satirical tales were written down and have survived to our day. For the most part they were versified in the octosyllabic couplet, and they were designed to be recited or to be read aloud. But in Italy in Chaucer's age, owing to the existence of a reading public—a rich and leisured class with sufficient education to find delight in reading such stories—these tales, or *novelle* as they called them, took literary shape in prose. Books were made of them. It was a favourite device to collect a hundred of them offering all kinds of variety from. grave to gay and from classical to modern subjects, as in the *Cento Novelle Antiche*, and in Boccaccio's *Decameron.*

Gower's *Confessio Amantis* and Chaucer's *Canterbury Tales* are examples of the same literary tendency in

England ; and as Gower praised Chaucer " as my disciple and my poet," it has been suggested that Chaucer imitated Gower. But Gower's English poem consists of a prologue and a series of verse-tales illustrating and reproving the seven deadly sins, which, in its uniformity of metre (the octosyllabic couplet) and in its unity of subject and theme, bears a closer resemblance to Chaucer's *Legend of Good Women* than to *The Canterbury Tales*. In the prologue (not the preface) to Book i of the *Confessio Amantis*, Gower also dreams that on a May morning, wandering in a " swote grene plaine," he met the King of Love and his Queen, and curiously enough, as in Chaucer's prologue to *The Legend of Good Women*, the King of Love is wroth, and the Queen gracious. But if *The Canterbury Tales* were written possibly in emulation of Gower's *Confessio Amantis*, they were certainly not an imitation. Unlike Gower, Chaucer collected tales of all kinds, even some which are not consistent with common notions of either honour or honesty ; and Chaucer's great prologue to *The Canterbury Tales* is no allegorical dream-proem in the French style, but something quite new, namely, a realistic introduction in the Italian manner.

There can be little doubt that Chaucer's variety, his love of trickery as a motive, his " tragedies," his realistic setting, and above all the excellence of his art of narrative, are due to Italian influence. If Chaucer wrote *The Canterbury Tales* knowing only such elementary endeavours as *The Seven Wise Masters* and the *Confessio Amantis*, he is the greatest novelist that England has ever produced. But this assumption of Chaucer's ignorance is incredible and impossible. It is true that in *The Legend of Good Women* he had arrived at the form of a prologue followed by a series of tales, but he was yet in bondage to the idea of the medieval French dream-poem. How otherwise than by granting Italian influence can we account for the tremendous achievement of *The Canterbury Tales* ? I do not suggest that Chaucer possessed a manuscript of the

Decameron. There is no evidence of that. Only two or three of his tales closely resemble *novelle* of Boccaccio; and, moreover, if Chaucer had seriously intended to imitate Boccaccio, he would have written in prose. But that Chaucer had never heard of the famous *Decameron* of Boccaccio, the most famous work of the Italian whom he most admired, nay, that he had not seen a copy of it when he was in Italy, I cannot bring myself to believe. He *must* have read some of these short, pointed *novelle*, with their varied scenes and characters, and their abundance of farcical and satirical humour; and, consciously or unconsciously, he must have noticed that although the collection gained an added interest from its realistic setting—ten ladies and gentlemen take shelter from the plague which was ravaging Florence in 1348, in a country villa, and there pass ten days in telling tales—yet the Pampineas and Pamphiluses are all alike in their genteel piety and indecency; and their stories are no expression of their character, because they have no individuality to express. They have no amiable eccentricities, no predominating humour, or ruling passion.

If Chaucer knew the *Decameron*, he improved upon it. The characters of the setting of his *Canterbury Tales* have all the charm of variety. Chaucer somehow realized the artistic value of contrast. Not only does he bring gentle and simple into proximity, but he portrays the antipathy of the Miller for the Reeve, and of the Friar for the Summoner. And he makes his pilgrims live with that reality of almost independent existence, so characteristic of the best English fiction, which in its love of the personality of the individual shrinks from the pure abstraction of the type. Yet it may be that, besides the *Decameron*, Chaucer knew other collections of *novelle*. It has recently been pointed out that there is a close similarity between the plan of *The Canterbury Tales* and that of Sercambi's *Novelle*.[1] In the latter, a company of representative

[1] See H. B. Hinckley, *Notes on Chaucer*, 1907, p. 2.

Italians, cleric and lay, travel about the country on a pilgrimage to avoid an outbreak of the plague in Lucca in 1374. They gather in a church before setting out, and elect a leader, who suggests that they shall brighten their journey with songs, tales, and discourses. Sercambi is appointed story-teller to the company, and his *novelle* are joined by links of narrative which tell of happenings by the way, and the comments of the pilgrims upon the tales. This is almost too good to be true. Close as is the similarity of the framework of these two collections of stories, it is probable that the resemblance is pure coincidence ; unless we may assume that, on his way from Genoa to Florence in 1373, Chaucer passed through Lucca and met Giovanni Sercambi. But this is to assume that even in 1373 Sercambi had devised the scheme of his *Novelle*, and the more one thinks of the matter, the more it appears horrent with improbabilities. Was Chaucer, for instance, so familiar with Italian when he first set foot in Italy ? Nevertheless, the suggestion is fascinating.

It was some time between 1384 and 1388 whilst the staple of wool was at Middelburgh—probably in 1387—that the idea of collecting his verse-tales into a fictional setting, and of adding others to the number of one hundred and twenty, first took definite shape. Chaucer then composed the prologue, and began to add tales and connecting links to those which he had already written. The fiction of a pilgrimage was not new in allegorical poetry. Chaucer knew De Guileville's *Pèlerinage de la Vie Humaine*, from which he had translated the prayer known as the *A.B.C.* Perhaps also he had come across one of the many manuscripts of *The Vision of Piers the Plowman*, and realized the homely vigour and humour of the pilgrimage to seek Truth. Chaucer's prologue is similar in intention to the prologue of *Piers Plowman*. Both attempt to describe representatives of the age, but whereas Langland saw in his vision types of chapmen, minstrels, beggars, rogues, and friars, etc., Chaucer described individuals with

characteristic peculiarities such as the Prioress's manners,
or the Cook's mormal. Chaucer is more vivid, because he
alone of the English poets of his age had discovered the
interest of the realistic method of description. Like
Boccaccio he made his setting realistic, not allegorical.
Like Sercambi he made it a pilgrimage. The prologue,
unlike his earlier prologue to *The Legend of Good Women*,
though fiction, is not fantasy. It is based on observation
and memory of the bands of pilgrims whom he had seen on
the Old Kent Road, bound for the shrine of England's
most popular saint, St. Thomas of Canterbury. And, in
the connecting links between the tales, the pilgrims are
sketched almost as clearly in dialogue as they are in the
prologue by description.

We have contrasted the variety of Chaucer's tales with
the sameness of Gower's legends. Chaucer produced this
effect in many ways. He provides as the imaginary
narrators of his tales men and women of well-marked
individuality, and of different vocations and tastes, and
he suits the tales to their character. He does not bind
himself to one form of verse, or even to verse alone. He
does not stint himself to one subject, or to one group of
associated topics, but like Boccaccio he ranges over the
whole of the themes of the medieval *novelle*—love, tragedy,
virtue, trickery, vice. He does not adhere to one literary
form, such as the legend or the fable, but attempts the
utmost variety of fiction possible to a poet of his age.
He pursues romance in the tales of the Knight and the
Squire—and mocks it in his own tale of Sir Thopas. His
stories show the utmost variety. There is the legend of
Appius and Virginia told by the Doctor. There are the
sentimental tales of the Clerk and the Man of Law. There
are the Breton lays of love and magic told by the Franklin
and the Wife of Bath. There is the moral supernatural of
the Friar and of the Pardoner. There is the classical
folk-tale of the Manciple, and the beast-fable of the Nun's
Priest. And lastly there are the racy and licentious

fabliaux of the lower orders.   The Prioress and the Second Nun tell legends of the saints.   The Monk narrates his medieval " tragedies."   Moral prose discourse finds representatives in the Parson's tale and in Chaucer's tale of Melibeus.   And lastly, a new and interesting realism makes its first appearance in England in the tales of the Cook—unfinished, alas!—and of the Canon's Yeoman.

With the exception of these two realistic and original tales and of his parody, Sir Thopas, the tales and moral discourses were collected from the common stock of the age.   Chaucer preferred to narrate proved tales of recognized interest.   His art was devoted to story-telling, rather than to the invention of new plots and new themes. There is a danger in this, of course—the danger of slavishly following the original, and of trusting to poetic description and sentiment to compensate for lack of knowledge of human nature and for imaginative sympathy.   As a rule Chaucer avoided the dullness of mere repetition.   He borrowed the subject-matter of the story, but narrated it in his own way, emphasizing the details on which his fancy dwelt.   Often he was compelled to retain original stupidities, such as, for instance, the character of Walter in the Clerk's tale, but his understanding of human nature led him as a rule either to civilize them or excuse them ; and usually also he infused a theme into his story to add to or to strengthen its significance.   Yet one cannot point to any early development in his art.   Sometimes he translated his original, adding a little from his imagination ; sometimes he imitated, re-telling the story with suppression or amplification of character and incident.   It would be natural to suppose that he passed from the elementary stage of translation to the more advanced method of free imitation ; yet whilst the Clerk's tale of Griselda (1374 ?) is a free translation and the Knight's tale of Palamon and Arcite (1385 ?) is an adaptation, the order is reversed in the case of the Man of Law's tale of Custance (1372 ?) and he Life of St. Cecilia (1383 ?).   At first he seems to have translated, imitated, or invented as the mood suggests. But some of his later tales in the heroic couplet show a power of reconstruction which almost amounts to originality. The Pardoner's tale far surpasses in dramatic power any known original, and its local colour appears to be drawn from observation. The Nun's Priest's tale is an old fable transformed into a tale which of its kind has never been bettered. The Canon's Yeoman's tale lacks plot, but it shows Chaucer in his latest phase as a novelist attempting absolute originality ; and the unfinished Cook's tale, perhaps the last of all, promises an original sketch of Cockney humours which seems to anticipate and to rival Dickens.

§ 2

There are something like seventy known manuscripts of *The Canterbury Tales*, of which eight have been printed by the Chaucer Society. These eight are the Ellesmere, Cambridge University Library Gg 4, 27, Hengwrt 154, Corpus Christi College (Oxford), Petworth, and Lansdowne 851 manuscripts, which form the Six-Text Edition of the Chaucer Society ; and the separate volumes containing reprints of MSS. Harley 7334 and Cambridge University Library Dd 4, 24. The Ellesmere MS. has also been reproduced in facsimile by the Manchester University Press. The genealogy of these manuscripts is uncertain. Though classification has been attempted by Skeat, Koch, Zupitza, Miss Hammond, and Brusendorff, the results have been disputed. The Ellesmere MS. has usually been taken by modern editors as the basis of their texts, but Pollard has urged that MS. Harley 7334 with its individual readings " represent(s) Chaucer's own ' second thoughts,' " and Hinckley has called attention to the merits of the Hengwrt MS.

The rubrics introducing the tales differ in different manuscripts, and are therefore scribal insertions ; but Chaucer's retraction is found at the end of all complete manuscripts and must therefore be regarded as genuine, though for some reason it was omitted by all early editors from Pynson to Urry. The order of the tales varies in different manuscripts, and in some the unfinished Cook's Tale is followed by *The Tale of Gamelyn*, a romance written in a rude ballad-metre, which is almost certainly not by Chaucer, but which he may have kept in the manuscript-volume containing the general prologue and the Knight's Tale, intending to narrate it later in the person of the Yeoman. But though the order of the tales varies somewhat, all the manuscripts commence with the Prologue, Knight's, Miller's, Reeve's and Cook's Tales, and end with the tales of the Manciple and Parson ; and it is found that the intervening tales, though differing in position, follow usually in definite groups.

A solution for this peculiarity was found by Wright in 1847. In the introduction to his edition of *The Canterbury Tales*, he suggested that Chaucer's original manuscript was in several books, and that as no indication of the order of these books was given, the copyists naturally made some confusion : " I am inclined to believe," he said, " that Chaucer not only left his grand poem in an unfinished state, but that he left it in detached portions only partially arranged, and that it was reduced to its present form after his death." Accordingly Wright divided it into eight groups, following the arrangement of the best manuscripts, namely, Elles., Heng., Dd., and Harley 7335 ; and of Tyrwhitt's edition (1775). His groups are as follows. Each group is self-contained, and unprovided with a link connecting it to the next :

1. Prologue, Tales of Knight, Miller, Reeve, Cook (unfinished).
2. Man of Law's Tale, and connecting links.
3. Prologues and Tales of the Wife of Bath, Friar, Summoner.
4. Prologues and Tales of the Clerk, Merchant, Squire, Franklin.

5. Doctor's Tale, link, Pardoner's Tale.
6. Shipman's Tale, Tales and links of the Prioress, Chaucer, Monk, Nun's Priest.
7. Second Nun's Tale, link, Canon's Yeoman's Tale.
8. Prologues and Tales of the Manciple and Parson.

It is worth noting that the famous MS. Harley 7334 places group 7 before group 5, whilst other manuscripts are much more erratic in their order, especially of the Tales in group 4.

In 1868 Furnivall and Bradshaw subdivided and rearranged this grouping. Bradshaw split group 4 into its four components; and connected groups 2 and 6, following the arrangement of one manuscript (Selden B 14) where the Shipman's prologue follows the Man of Law's tale, the order being 1 3 4 2 6 7 5 8. Furnivall assumed, wrongly I think, that *The Canterbury Tales* recorded a real pilgrimage in which Chaucer had taken part; and his endeavour therefore was to rearrange the tales in chronological order according to the allusions to time and place. It happens that, in the prologue to Reeve's tale, Deptford and Greenwich are mentioned. The Wife of Bath's tale is prefaced by words between the Summoner and the Friar in which Sittingbourne is spoken of as not far ahead. The Host tells the Monk, in calling for his tale :

Lo ! Rouchestre stant heer faste by !

The pilgrims overtook the Canon and his Yeoman at Boughton-under-Blee ; and the Host calls on the Manciple for his tale near a farm named Bob Up-and-Down, not far from Canterbury. As Rochester is half-way to Canterbury, and would be arrived at before Sittingbourne and Boughton, Furnivall accepted Bradshaw's arrangement of groups 2 and 6 ; because if group 6 be moved up to follow group 2, Rochester then is mentioned before Sittingbourne. He suggested also that the pilgrimage might be supposed to last for three and a half or four days, and rearranged the groups in nine divisions for the Six-Text edition of the Chaucer Society, as follows :

> Day 1. A. Prologue, Tales of Knight, Miller, Reeve, Cook (unfinished).
> Day 2. B. Man of Law's Tale and links, Shipman, Prioress, Chaucer, Monk, Nun's Priest.
> Day 3. C. Doctor's Tale, link, Pardoner's Tale.
> D. Prologues and Tales of the Wife of Bath, Friar, Summoner.
> E. Prologues and Tales of the Clerk and Merchant.
> Day 4. F. Squire's Tale (unfinished), Franklin's prologue and Tale.
> G. Second Nun's Tale, link, Canon's Yeoman's Tale.
> H. Prologue and Tale of the Manciple.
> I. Prologue and Tale of the Parson.

It will be seen that Furnivall's group A corresponds to Wright's group 1; B = 2 + 6, C = 5, D = 3, E + F = 4, G = 7, H + I = 8. The reason for beginning a new day with the Squire's Tale is that the Squire says (l. 73) that " it is prime," so that evidently the tale was supposed to be told in the early morning.

Furnivall's arrangement was followed by Skeat and Pollard, and as his numbering of the verses has been used by all recent scholars and is now well established, it is likely to remain. But it is well to remember that Chaucer's order for the tales, if ever he had one, is lost ; and that Furnivall's arrangement, though highly ingenious, is quite artificial. The probability is that the arrangement of the Ellesmere group of manuscripts is authentic, and that Chaucer's allusions to place and time were haphazard from the beginning. Had he lived to complete and to revise the work, it may be that these inconsistencies would have been removed.

§ 3

The plan of the *Canterbury Tales* is that Chaucer imagines himself setting out from the Tabard Inn, Southwark, in company with the Host of the Tabard and twenty-nine other pilgrims on a journey to the shrine of Thomas à Becket at Canterbury. The Host suggests that to enliven the long journey, which was done on horseback and took three or four days, each of the pilgrims should tell two stories on the road thither, and two on the return journey ; and that the teller of the best tales should be entertained to supper.

> Here in this place, sittinge by this post,
> Whan that we come agayn fro Caunterbury.

The plan is accepted, and the pilgrims set out. On the way they overtake at Boughton a Canon and his Yeoman, and the latter joins the company. But Chaucer evidently modified the original plan, which had proved too ambitious ; and from the prologue to the last tale, the Parson's Tale, it is clear that that was intended.

> To knytte up al this feste, and make an end.

So that in its amended form the plan, if completed, would have consisted of a Prologue followed by thirty-three tales —thirty by the Host and the pilgrims, two by Chaucer, and one by the Canon's Yeoman. Of these Chaucer wrote twenty-four, including his own two tales and that of the Canon's Yeoman ; but the tales of the Monk, the Cook, and the Squire are unfinished.

The pilgrimage was a happy inspiration. It provided Chaucer with a representative group of characters from all classes, on whom could be fathered stories of every type. It was certain to make an immediate appeal to his audience, for pilgrimages were popular amongst all ranks of society ; and of the four chief English shrines, Our Lady of Walsingham, St. Edward the Confessor in Westminster, St.

Cuthbert of Durham, and St. Thomas of Canterbury, St. Thomas was the most popular of all, partly because he had championed the Church against the Crown, partly because in popular credence prayers and offerings made at his shrine could influence a saint who had power to heal the sick. From his shrine pilgrims returned, after making their vows and supplications, wearing a medal as the badge of their service, which bore an image of the saint and this inscription: " Optimus egrorum medicus fit Thomas." Chaucer little thought that in centuries to come his pilgrimage would seem romantic. To him it was as commonplace as an excursion of a society of antiquaries to visit in a motor char-à-banc some ancient church.

There was a Knight, an experienced and distinguished captain, who was as gentle as he was honourable. With him travelled his son, a merry young Squire, already a member of the profession of arms, and as accomplished in the social arts as in war. And a Yeoman, a woodman clad in green, carrying a great bow and a sheaf of peacock arrows—a sort of Robin Hood, in fact—attended them as their servant. These went to return thanks for the safe return of the Knight from his voyage. There was a Prioress, a lady of rank and refinement, who was not without some traces of affectation and worldliness. She was accompanied, as befitted her station, by her secretary and three priests. Beside them rode a Monk and a Friar. The Monk was an overseer of a monastic grange, a gentleman-farmer who was more at home in the hunting-field than in the cloister. He dressed well, loved good meat, and cared nothing for the opinion of those earnest souls who urged that hunting men were not good men, and that a monk who left his cloister lost his piety. " And," says Chaucer with downright candour, " I seyde his opinioun was good." But he was also a lover of literature, for he it was who related the tragedies of famous men. The Friar was a pleasant worldly-wise rogue, welcome amongst the richer people of his district, to whom he gave easy

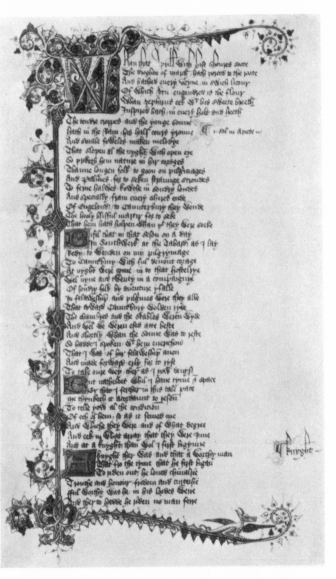

FIRST PAGE OF THE PROLOGUE TO "THE CANTERBURY TALES"
From the Ellesmere MS.

penances. He was the most accomplished beggar in his friary, and the most popular, for he was always courteous ; he could fiddle and sing, and he always had a small gift, such as a knife or a pin, for young housewives.

Representing the learned professions there were a Clerk of Oxford, a Sergeant or Barrister, and a Doctor of Medicine. The Clerk was a university don, a poor scholar whose life was devoted to the study of philosophy. The Sergeant equally learned in his own sphere of study, the law, was shrewd to further his own wealth and interests. He had sat as a judge in the assizes, and as a barrister he had received many fees and robes. The Doctor was a " verray parfit praktisour." He combined the inherited wisdom of the ancient physicians with the practice of astrological magic. Unlike the Clerk, he too was shrewd, as his magnificent gown indicated. What he gained by practising in time of plague he hoarded, knowing full well that " gold in physik is a cordial." Representing the middle classes there were a Merchant, a Franklin or yeoman farmer, and five guildsmen—a Haberdasher, a Carpenter, a Weaver, a Dyer, and a Tapissier or decorator—accompanied by their Cook. The Merchant wore a beaver hat of Flemish shape, for he was engaged in shipping wool from the Orwell to Middelburgh. He always had an eye to profit, and took care not to exchange the foreign money which he received in payment for his goods at a loss. The Franklin was " Epicurus' owene son." Though old and with a white beard, he loved good food and plenty. " It snewed in his hous of mete and drinke." He was a Justice of the Peace, and had beem Knight of the Shire, and Sheriff. The five guildsmen appear to have been wealthy members, not only of their own craft-guilds—which made them freemen of their city—but also of a merchant-guild, for they all wore the same magnificent uniform. But they were dull fellows without a characteristic humour, and Chaucer says very little about them.

There was a Shipman or Skipper from the West Country,

wearing a short serge frock that reached only to the knees. Half a pirate he was. Many a draught of wine had he stolen from the tun, coming from Bordeaux, whilst the merchants slept. In sea-fights if he won, he threw his prisoners overboard. But he was a good sailor, and he knew every harbour from Gothland to Cape Finisterre. Another character from the West was the Wife of Bath. Middle-aged like the Prioress, she was utterly lacking in reticence and refinement. She was strong and bold and self-important. By trade she was a clothmaker, and she was prosperous, as her massive head-dress and her scarlet hose indicated. She had had five husbands, and had shown all that the grey mare is the better horse. In her old age, a loquacious old age full of reminiscences of her old love-affairs, her hobby was travel. She had been on pilgrimages to Rome, Boulogne, Cologne, and to St. James of Compostella. On the way she laughed and jested like a man, and when the jests grew even too gross for her indelicate ears, she pleaded a deaf ear ; and that, says Chaucer, was a pity. In face she was rosy and fair, and her front teeth, which she showed when she laughed, were separated—a sign that she was born to travel. And yet, says Chaucer, " she was a worthy womman al hir lyve."

There was a poor Parson, a gentle earnest soul who devoted his life to his parish, which was a large one. He never let rain or storm interfere with his visiting, and he practised what he preached. " If a priest be foul," he used to say, "whom can we trust ? " So instead of finding a substitute and running after chantries and chaplaincies, he remained amongst his flock and strove by his teaching and example " to drawen folk to hevene by fairnesse." With him was his brother, a Plowman, a true labourer, simplicity, wisdom and strength personified. He lived in peace with all men, paid his just dues, and helped others to the best of his ability. He might have been, in fact, Piers Plowman himself. And lastly there was a group of jolly rascals, a Reeve or Steward, a Miller, a Summoner (or

Archdeacon's constable), a Pardoner (a seller of indulgences), a Manciple, and the Host of the Tabard Inn.
The Miller was a herculean ruffian who was equally skilled
in stealing corn and in playing the bagpipes, which indeed
he sounded down the Borough High Street and along the
Old Kent Road. The Manciple, or housekeeper to one of
the Temple Inns of Court, had nothing to learn as regards
worldly wisdom from his legal employers. The Reeve, a
Norfolk man, was steward of a large estate. By trade
he was a carpenter, but his skill in farming and in keeping
accounts had led him to his high position, and his shrewd-
ness had enriched him. He was strong and active, and his
bailiffs and farm-labourers " were adrad of him as of the
deeth "—they feared him as they feared the plague. The
Summoner and the Pardoner were both knaves. The
Summoner was red in the face and pimpled, a loathsome
fellow. He would frighten sinners with his " Questio quid
juris," and then hint that a bribe might withhold the
Archdeacon's curse. Those who paid him well found him
ready to excuse them. He was a wag too. He rode with
a garland on his head, and carried a great cake instead of
a shield. But the Pardoner was even more shameless.
He carried false relics which he used to deceive the credulous ; and when he preached, his sole object was " to winne
silver." His profession was the selling of papal indulgences,
and by this means he earned more than twice as much as
the honest parish priest. Finally there was the Host, a
bold and merry fellow with twinkling eyes. Though by
no means the highest in rank, he won the pilgrims to his
plan by the weight of his personality ; and he it was who
called for the tales. Perhaps he was a friend of Chaucer's
and drawn from life, for in the prologue to the Cook's tale
Roger the Cook calls him Harry Bailly ; and curiously
enough there was an innkeeper named Henry Bailiff of
Southwark in Chaucer's day, and a Henry Bailly, who
seems to be the same person, represented Southwark in
Parliament in 1376 and 1378.

It is a truly representative band of fourteenth-century Englishmen, not, alas, complete, for it lacks members of the highest and lowest classes ; but typical it is of arms, the church, the learned professions, agriculture, manufacture, shipping, and trade. And it is pictured with wonderful skill. There is nothing like it in contemporary literature. For the first time a poet attempted the portraiture of types with individual characteristics. Think of the lay figures of the *Decameron*. Think of the generalized personifications of *Piers Plowman*. Think of the faint allegorical figures of the prologues to *The Legend of Good Women* and the *Confessio Amantis* ! Compared with any of them the prologue to *The Canterbury Tales* is alive with humanity. And better still, the portraits of the pilgrims are not all drawn in the same way. It is true that Chaucer endeavoured to picture individuals with an outstanding peculiarity—a physical trait like the Miller's wart, a humour like the Franklin's love of rich dishes, or a passion like the Knight's love of prowess and troth ; but the portraits differ in kind, as well as in degree. Some of the portraits are idealized—viewed in the radiance of the light that never was. The Knight, for instance, is not a real man ; he is an ideal. It is true that the realistic method of description is used to give him bars to his medals, but the list of his victories tells us all we know about him as a man. Apart from his battles, he is simply the ideal of knighthood. Similarly the Parson and the Clerk of Oxford are not real beings : they are the perfection of the ideas of the parish priest and of the scholar, and far too perfect to be flesh and blood. The portrait of the poor Parson is a veritable triumph, for Chaucer has made a good man attractive for his own sake without the spice of an eccentricity or a weakness ; and that is the hardest task in the whole art of fiction. Some of the portraits are generalized from observation of their class. Lawyers are learned and shrewd—hence the Sergeant-at-Law. Rich farmers live on the fat of the land—hence the Franklin.

The Merchant is just one amongst many of the same sort, as Chaucer's " but sooth to seyn I n'ot how men him calle " indicates. Other portraits are so realistic that they must have been drawn from life. The Host, if he be not Master Henry Bailly, is one of the fraternity supplied with victual by Chaucer's father. The Shipman is an old acquaintance of the Vintner's wharf. The Miller appears to be an individual, he differs so markedly from type. Finally the portraits of the ecclesiastics are remarkable, and well worthy of attention. There is a striking contrast between the humility of the Parson, the worldly gentility of the Prioress and Monk, and the rascality of the Friar, Summoner, and Pardoner. Whether it be intentional or not—and who can doubt its significance ?—it is a striking illustration of the growth of anti-papal and anti-monastic sentiment in Chaucer's age.

§ 4

And now, having described the pilgrims, and unanimous in our opinion that the prologue is one of the greatest triumphs of descriptive verse in literature, let us criticize their tales.

The Knight's Tale has pride of place, probably because Chaucer thought it first in beauty and in power. Its theme is honour amongst friends. Its subject is the rivalry of Palamon and Arcite for Emily, and how it ended. Its climax is the right generous renunciation of Emily by Arcite ; and it was no doubt for this very incident that the pilgrims found it " a noble storie." But is not this nobility too lofty for real life ? A real rival would have said : " I would rather see her in her grave than married to you." It was because Arcite could feel jealousy and rage against his friend and rival, and still remain a friend, that Chaucer regarded him as the symbol of honour and ideal friendship.

The story is not original. It is an abridged version of

Boccaccio's *Teseide* with descriptive additions; and though the Knight's Tale is the longest of *The Canterbury Tales*, it is only one quarter the length of Boccaccio's romance. Chaucer compressed *La Teseide*, reducing Books i and ii to thirty lines, omitting the account of the war with the Amazons, and keeping Theseus and Hippolyte in the background. He altered the plot somewhat by making Palamon see Emily first, which gives him a better claim to her hand; and he added Arcite's soliloquy in the forest, which rouses Palamon's jealousy to ire and so gives a better motive for the duel. It is a defect of the tale, taken over from Boccaccio's romance, that the characterization is indefinite. Palamon and Arcite are as like as Rosencranz and Guildenstern. There is little to choose between the passionate sentiment of Palamon and the sentimental passion of Arcite. An attempt is made to differentiate the twin squires by their gods, Palamon prays to Venus, Arcite invokes Mars; but it hardly succeeds. Emily, the occasion of their passion, speaks only once; and that is to express in her prayer to Diana her desire to remain a maid and to walk in the wild woods alone. She is purity and tenderness personified, not a real princess. Theseus, the ruling figure of the plot who governs the issue of the conflict, is a dominating personality, as befits the part he has to play. His genial cynicism and his opinions are evidently Chaucer's own. But partly because it is an early tale, and partly because Chaucer received no help from Boccaccio, the characterization lacks individuality and conviction. There is more life in the descriptions of Lygurge and Emetreus than in all the thoughts and sentiments of the chief characters. In fact the style of the tale is pictorial, and not analytic like the earlier *Troilus and Criseyde*; and if it succeeds, it is by the magnificence of Chaucer's descriptive passages.

Not the least interest of the tale is its medieval treatment of a classical subject. It is Boccaccio's addition to the romance of Thebes, which was developed, not from

Sophocles, but from the *Thebaid* of Statius. *La Teseide* is an indication of a fresh interest in the ancient world. Boccaccio, and after him Chaucer, turned from the subjects of Arthur and Charlemagne to find romance in Troy and Thebes. Yet neither had a real sense of historical perspective. They thought of the past in terms of their own age, as did all the medieval writers who took it as their setting. But it is surely an additional charm, a winsome quaintness, that the Knight's Tale is as medieval in its picture of ancient Greek life as, let us say, the *Idylls of the King* are modern in their portrayal of the early medieval.

After this idealistic romance follow three realistic and merry tales. The drunken Miller, who insists on supplanting the Host's next choice, the Monk, tells a tale of trickery. The plot is most skilfully contrived from two merry jests—(1) How a lover got rid of a husband temporarily, a subject which had been treated by Boccaccio in his *Decameron* iii, 4, though not so inventively nor so wittily as by Chaucer; and (2) How a lover got rid of a rival. Later versions of each of these plots, and of the two combined, have been found in German and in Italian; but no original of Chaucer's tale is known. Whether he invented it, as seems probable, or not, Chaucer's narrative of the tale is masterly. It is neatly told in long verse-paragraphs or sections—which never lose sight of Nicholas's final cry, " Help, water, water, help ! " echoed by the sound of John's blow with the axe—and which are admirably varied by description and dialogue. If tales of the tricks of women to deceive their husbands be a suitable subject for poetry—and such trickery is the theme of the seventh day of the *Decameron*, Chaucer's apology that the Miller was a churl is unnecessary. The Miller's tale in skill surpasses them all. Granted the attractiveness of Alisoun, the simplicity of John her husband, and the cunning of Nicholas, the tale is as convincing as it is naughty.

The Reeve's Tale is equally brilliant and even more salacious. Its point is that the Miller had told a story against a carpenter, and so the Reeve, who was a slender, choleric fellow, told this tale of which a miller is the butt. There is a similar tale in the *Decameron* ix, 6 ; and two French fabliaux are recorded in the *Originals and Analogues* published by the Chaucer Society, one of which, " Le meunier et les deux clers," is very like Chaucer's Reeve's Tale. But Chaucer, wherever he found the story, localized the setting at Trumpington, not far from Cambridge, as a parallel to the scene of the Miller's tale ; and made the two clerks speak the northern dialect. His descriptions throughout are brief and vivid, and the narrative moves swiftly to the surprise of the climax and the rough-and-tumble ending. The Cook's Tale, which follows, promises well. It was to be a London tale—" a litel jape that fil in oure citee." It begins with a portrait of a gay and unprincipled apprentice, and then stops suddenly. This was probably the end of the first section of Chaucer's original manuscript.

§ 5

Group B opens with an indication of time. It is about ten o'clock in the morning on the eighteenth of April, a clear indication of another day. The Sergeant-at-Law is called upon for a tale, and he complies with a story which Chaucer had versified early in his career from the prose Chronicle in Anglo-Norman of Nicholas Trivet, an English Dominican who flourished in the first half of the fourteenth century. The legend of Constance is a pious tale which illustrates the virtue of constancy. Constance undergoes a multitude of trials, but she never wavers in her faithful-ness to God and to her husband. This was not especially suitable for the Sergeant, and so Chaucer revised the tale, adding a prologue which makes it an example of the " hate-ful harm " of poverty—a condition which the Man of Law much disliked—and three apostrophes, to sudden grief (ll. 421–427), to drunkenness (ll. 771–777), and to lechery (ll. 925–931), all of which he borrowed from the *De*

Contemptu Mundi of Pope Innocent III. Possibly the tale was unfinished when Chaucer again took it in hand for *The Canterbury Tales* : the versification of the third part is much freer than that of parts i and ii. The Man of Law's Tale follows Trivet's narrative closely as far as incident is concerned, but the reflective passages, the sentiments and the dialogue, are Chaucer's own. He dearly loved a pathetic story, and it was the sentimental nature of the trials of Constance rather than her eventful life which attracted his interest, as his additions to the narrative show. Chaucer's condemnation of the Sultan's mother for urging that " Cold water shal nat greve us but a lite," the gradual investiture of Constance with the sanctity of a martyr, especially the touches by which he portrays her tenderness to her child ; and the joy of the reunion with Alla at the end of the story, are masterstrokes of imaginative sympathy and sentiment.

In Chaucer's hands the story assumed the characteristic piety and wonder of the *Golden Legend*. Custance was an ideal type of womanhood, purity, tenderness, faith and constancy personified—an uncanonized saint. Yet originally the tale of the persecuted princess was a folk-tale which illustrated the mad malignity of mothers-in-law, and two tales of this sort were blended in Friar Nicholas's history of Constaunce. The one was the story of how the marriage of the daughter of the Emperor Constantine to a Saracen prince was marred by his evil old mother. The other was evidently a variant of the Saxon saga of Cyne-thryth or Queen Drida, told in the twelfth-century *Vitae duorum Offarum*, attributed to Matthew Paris, a monk of St. Albans. And indeed variants on the subject of the persecuted princess who married a king, and then by the wicked plotting of her mother-in-law was set adrift in an open boat, and only at last, after many adventures, was reunited to her loving husband, were amongst the most popular of medieval tales. This story is to be found in the contemporary English romance of *Emaré*, in the French romance of *La Belle Hélène de Constantinople*, in the Italian *novella* of Dionigia, in Sir Giovanni Fiorentino's *Il Pecorone* x, 1, and in twenty more romances and in fifty folk-tales.[1] Despite the patent absurdity of Trivet's history, and the repetition of the incident of the abandonment of the heroine to the mercy of the waves, Chaucer found in the legend the romance of Mohammedan and heathen devilry, the pathos of innocence maligned and tortured, and an illustration of a doctrine dear to Milton and Coleridge, namely, the protective power under providence of feminine virtue. As a story, the Man of Law's Tale is simply an improbable string of incidents. In Chaucer's hands it became a commentary on a portrait of virtue and quiet constancy. The tale of Constance was also told by Gower in his *Confessio Amantis* ii. He too borrowed it from Trivet, and used it as an illustration of the sin of envy. If there is any doubt about the excellence of Chaucer's pathos, let the critical reader turn to Gower's version and, in spite of the fact that comparisons are odious, let him judge Chaucer by the merits of his friend.

There is some doubt as to which tale should follow the Man of Law's. The answer turns on the person indicated in line 1179, who comes forward to tell the next tale. Only one manuscript (Selden B 14) names the Shipman. The best manuscripts, including the Ellesmere, omit the link MS. Harley 7334 alludes to the Summoner ; whilst most manuscripts name the Squire, and continue with the Squire's Tale. Chaucer's original scheme must have been modified, and perhaps was not finally arranged ; for the Shipman's Tale, the first tale of Wright's group 6 (otherwise known to the textual critics as B²) is not a very appropriate story for a piratical skipper, and the feminine point of view suggested by ll. 1202–1208 would seem to indicate that the story was originally intended for the Wife of Bath, or for some female pilgrim whose portrait does not

[1] See A. B. Gough, *The Constance Saga*, Berlin, 1902 ; and Edith Rickert, *The Romance of Emaré*, E. E. T. S., 1906.

appear in the prologue as we know it. The Shipman's
Tale is a tale of trickery, the story of how a woman who
deceived her husband was in turn cheated by her lover ;
the implication being that she well deserved it for making
a trade of love. The same story, but in an Italian setting
and with a German, not a monk, as the cavalier, had been
told by Boccaccio in his *Decameron* viii, 1. Those who
deny that Chaucer knew the *Decameron* allege a French
fabliau as the original of both tales ; but unfortunately
none has so far produced an early French story which is
in the remotest degree like them.

On the other hand, the tale which follows was designed
to be told either by the Prioress or by her chaplain, as the
" quod she " of line 1771 clearly shows. The Prioress's
Tale is a sentimental legend of a little choir-boy, devoted
to the cult of the Mother of God, who was martyred by
Jews for singing " O alma redemptoris mater." Such
tales, all ending in the miracle of his discovery, were
common in the Middle Ages, when Jewries and hate of their
inhabitants were widespread, and they persisted in Russia
until the nineteenth century. But the scene was never
indigenous. Chaucer's Jewry was in Asia. A similar
tale in the *Miracles of Our Lady* (Vernon MS.) has Paris as
its scene. A French version makes the miracle happen,
" en la contree d'angleterre," and a fifteenth-century Latin
version by Friar Alphonsus of Lyons in his *Fortalitium Fidei*
(1459) sets the scene in Lincoln, a city which was evidently
in Chaucer's mind as his allusion to " yonge Hugh of
Lyncoln, slayn also With cursed Jewes " shows. The
" miracle," as Chaucer calls it, is very apt from the lips of
the tender-hearted Prioress, and reveals not only her
pitying nature, but her acquaintance with the legends
of the saints. Like the story of Custance, the tale is
narrated in stanzas, and is probably one cf the latest
examples of Chaucer's work in the seven-line stanza.
Chaucer loved a pathetic tale, and he does not forget to
insist on the piety and precocity of the " litel clergeoun,"

and on the fact that his mother was a widow. It reveals that there was a tender and credulous side to the nature of the author of the Shipman's Tale ; and that, as his *A.B.C.* also shows, he was devoted to the cult of the Virgin-Mother. His anti-semitic feeling was common to the age. Jews were banished from England from 1290 until Cromwell rescinded the edict, and it is probable that the legends associated with William of Norwich and Hugh of Lincoln, similar boy-martyrs, arose during the anti-Jewish outbreaks in the reign of Edward I. Whilst we cannot now share Chaucer's credulity, we can still appreciate something of the pathos and wonder which he experienced in writing the legend.

Chaucer often pokes fun at the clergy, but he never jibes at the miraculous absurdities of pious legend. On the other hand the absurdities of the popular romances of his age—the hurdy-gurdy alternation of its 886, 886 metre, its incoherent narratives of trite incidents, the commonplace similes and the tricks of the minstrel to retain the attention of his audience—these romantic absurdities and impossibilities tickled him as the incongruities of Gothic romance amused Jane Austen ; and the result was a nonsense-romance, Sir Thopas. So close is Chaucer's Tale of Sir Thopas to the traditional style of the minstrels that dull critics have regarded it as a serious poem. But it is pure raillery, and its sparkling humour and mordant criticism can be best appreciated after reading the romances which Chaucer mentions—

> Of Horn Child, and of Ypotys,
> Of Bevis and of Sir Guy,
> Of Sir Libiaus, ard Pleindamour.

Guy of Warwick or Bevis of Hampton will serve ; but perhaps the best for our purpose will be Sir Eglamour of Artois in S. O. Halliwell's *Thornton Romances* (Camden Society, 1844). Sir Eglamour—that valiant knight—does two battles with giants and one with a dragon for the hand of Princess Christabel, only to find on returning that (like Constance) she has been put to sea with her little son in an open boat ; whereupon Eglamour goes on a pilgrimage to the Holy Land for fifteen years. Meanwhile the little son, Degrabelle, is carried off by a griffin and deposited in the Holy Land, where he grows up unknown to his father. Christabel arrives in Egypt, and is well received ; but owing to political necessity she is just about to be married to Degrabelle, when Sir Eglamour arrives at the wedding tournament, defeats Degrabelle, and claims his wife again. Degrabelle marries a princess of Sidon ; and they all go back to Artois, where Christabel's wicked father, on seeing them approach, falls from a tower and breaks his neck, so that Sir Eglamour gains a kingdom as well as a wife and child.   It is such romantic absurdity that Chaucer mocks and burlesques.   Sir Thopas, like Launfal and Ywaine, must have a fairy bride. He goes out to do knightly prowess, but his " fair bearing " consists chiefly in drawing " aback full faste " to go in search of his fine armour.   He rides in the fair forest, and pricketh in all directions, but the wilderness is as tame as his exertions. The style of the tale is an admirable parody of the style of the minstrels. Chaucer hits off their metres and their " fits," their hack- neyed literary phrases and their vapidity, as to the manner born ; and his constant effects of anticlimax and bathos provide a laugh in almost every line.

The conclusion of Sir Thopas is intentionally hindered by the intervention of the Host, and Chaucer proceeds to remedy his tale in rime-doggerel with " a litel thing in prose "—the Tale of Melibeus.   It is an allegory of instruc- tion for those who are wronged.   It is also a portrait of a prudent woman. The daughter of Melibeus has been assaulted and injured by his enemies.   The problem is : What shall he do ? He takes counsel with his friends, and they resolve by a majority vote to wage war against the wrongdoers. But Prudence his wife comes forward, and after vindicating the wisdom and virtue of women, advises

11

Melibeus to make peace with his adversaries, which he does, after they have admitted their fault and asked for pardon. What Melibeus would have done if his enemies had remained rebellious and unmanageable, this monkish story does not suggest. It is a feeble tract, coloured by a quaker-like hatred of war and a strong admiration for feminine wisdom, which, in its love of prudence, comes preciously near exalting expediency over right. Chaucer translated it from Jean de Meun's *Livre de Melibee et de dame Prudence*, which was a French adaptation of the *Liber Consolationis et Consilii* by Albertano of Brescia, a lawyer who lived in the thirteenth century. It would be interesting to know whether this be an early work, translated soon after Chaucer's release from captivity, and before the chastening fires of his marriage with Philippa led to the sadder and wiser, though perhaps less understanding, jocularity of *The Wife of Bath's Prologue* and the *Envoy to Buckton*. Its appearance amongst *The Canterbury Tales* seems to indicate that the strain and loss in blood and treasure due to the Hundred Years' War with France had caused the prudence and pacifism of this allegory to appeal to others beside Chaucer.

The tale which follows is a set of variations upon a single theme, like *The Legend of Good Women*, only in this instance the theme is the falls of princes. The Monk calls them " tragedies," which he defines as follows :

> Tragedie is to seyn a certeyn storie,
> As olde bokes maken us memorie,
> Of him that stood in greet prosperitee
> And is yfallen out of heigh degree
> Into miserie.

The Monk's Tale then is a set of tragedies—a series of legends long and short, recounting the wretched deaths or at least the fall of the great. The idea was no doubt taken by Chaucer from Boccaccio's *De Casibus Virorum Illustrium*, the title of which book he borrowed, and called his

poem " The Monkes Tale de Casibus Virorum Illustrium."
Boccaccio's intention was to proclaim in the evident
uncertainty of fortune the need for humility in princes,
and to say in effect : " Be wise now, ye that are judges in
the earth." He begins with a prologue in which, during
a dream in his study, mighty princes pass before him, and
tell the story of their downfall. Chaucer omits a prologue,
but begins by expressing the same intention :

> Let no man truste on blind prosperitee ;
> Be war by thise ensamples newe and olde.

The late is written in stanzas of eight lines, in a common
French ballade stanza riming abab, bcbc, which he also
used for his *A.B.C.* ; but there is no regularity of length to
the tragedies. The heroes are drawn from the Bible,
ancient history, Ovid, Boccaccio, Dante ; and, in the case
of three—Pedro of Spain, Petro of Cyprus, and Barnabo
Visconti of Milan—from contemporary history. Barnabo's
death in 1385 is one of the historical allusions which serve
to date *The Canterbury Tales*. One of these tragedies
—that of the only woman, Zenobia Queen of Palmyra—
follows the account narrated by Boccaccio in his *De Claris
Mulieribus* ; but, curiously enough, Chaucer alludes to
Petrarch as his original. If anyone wishes to read the
details of her battles, he says :

> Lat him unto my maister Petrak go.

Once more we must ask: Was this a wilful blind? Or
did Chaucer really think that the works of Boccaccio were
written by Petrak-Lollius ?

Any romantic interest which these doleful instances may
ever have had is now entirely lost. Our sympathies are
with the Knight, who stinted the Monk of his remaining
eighty-three " tragedies," and said :

> Swich talking is not worth a boterflye,
> For therinne is ther no desport ne game.

Yet in their age these stories must have been regarded with admiration, if not with affection ; for Chaucer's disciple John Lydgate wrote a similar longer book, *The Fall of Princes*, based on Laurence de Premierfait's translation of Boccaccio's *De Casibus Virorum Illustrium* as *Des Cas des Nobles Hommes et Femmes* ; and the tragical history survived until Elizabethan times, and was undertaken by Sackville, Spenser, and Drayton.

Last in this group comes the excellent tale of the Nun's Priest. It is a striking illustration of the amazing versatility of Chaucer that he could stoop to make such a masterpiece of this fable, worthy of the anthropomorphic view of the animal kingdom of Uncle Remus himself. The tale is told with the utmost vigour and with great skill ; the fox's trick to persuade the cock to shut his eyes, and the cock's trick to make the fox open his muzzle, being used by Chaucer to point a double moral. It begins slowly, with appropriate description of the setting, followed by the dialogue between Chauntecleer and Pertelote, into which Chaucer infuses not only a good deal of gentle satire, but a good deal of quaint lore, and of curious learning about dreams which comes ultimately from Cicero, *De Divinatione*. It describes with mingled wit and learning the capture of the cock by the fox, and then moves ever more swiftly to its comic ending. The chase after the fox is one of Chaucer's happiest bits of description. It is idle to look for an earlier version of Chaucer's Nun's Priest's Tale. It is original, if any of his tales are his own. The matter perhaps is as old as uncivilized man's tales about beasts and birds. But it first made its appearance as a fable in the *Ysopet* of Marie de France (*ca.* 1175), where its moral is that fools " Parolent quant deivent cesser, et teisent quant devreint parler." A version of the story also had been told in the French *Roman de Renart* and again in the German *Reinhart Fuchs*. There is no lack of fables of the cock and fox. But Chaucer neither translated nor imitated. He took the old story which somewhere he had

heard or read, and told it again with the utmost freedom,
making it a theme on which to display both his learning
and wit, and to exercise his vein of satire. He changed
the point of view, making Chauntecleer, not Reynard, the
hero of the fable ; and in his hands it became not only a
triumph of cunning over vanity, and cunning countered by
trickery, but a lively comedy of husband and wife and
robber-baron in the guise of cock, hen, and fox—a comedy
in the knight's meaning of the word :

> As whan a man hath ben in poure estaat,
> And climbeth up and wexeth fortunat
> And there abideth in prosperitee.

It is hard to say which one admires more : the vigour and
wit of the verse, or the mock-heroic dignity of its style.
It is still the jolliest fable in the English language.

§ 6

Group C, which consists of the tales of the Doctor and
the Pardoner, contains no indications of time and place,
and its true position is doubtful.

The Doctor's Tale of Appius and Virginia comes from
de Meun's part of *Le Roman de la Rose*, where it occurs just
after the point at which what has survived of Chaucer's
version breaks off. It is not a translation. De Meun's
seventy lines are expanded to a tale which is told rather
as a legend of a martyr than as an example of injustice
followed by retribution. Chaucer was not familiar with
Livy's original of the story. The tragedy of Virginius and
the political aspect of the story Chaucer left unemphasized ;
and he follows de Meun in naming the false witness of
Appius as " Claudius." It is a story which contains the
potentiality of tragedy. Sheridan Knowles made it the
tragedy of *Virginius*. But Chaucer saw only its pathos
and its moral, and consequently his characterization is
slight. Lines 72–100 would seem to indicate that Chaucer's

interest in the story was stimulated firstly by the scandal which attached to Katharine Roet's ward Elizabeth of Lancaster in 1386, and secondly by the inquiry into the abduction of Isabella atte Halle in 1387, which he was commissioned to attend.

The Pardoner's Tale, which follows, is much more vigorous and powerful. His prologue, like that of the Wife of Bath, is an addition to the characterization of the descriptive portrait given in the general prologue. The Pardoner, whose occupation was to collect alms in return for papal indulgences which claimed to remit the punishment due to sin, lays bare the tricks of his craft, and reveals himself as a practised rogue. It is a prologue which, in its satire of the artfulness of begging friars and of popular belief in the efficacy of relics, is strikingly paralleled by the tale of Friar Cipolla in the *Decameron*, vi, 10. The Pardoner admits his avarice, and illustrates his method of collecting money from the faithful by the sale of relics and pardons. His tale is one of the anecdotes which he employs in his sermons to emphasize his constant theme " Radix malorum est Cupiditas " ; and he interlards it with warnings against gluttony, drunkenness, and swearing. The actual tale, isolated from the half-drunken confidences of the Pardoner, is Chaucer's most dramatic story. The proximity of the " privee theef " Death, the mysterious and ominous appearance of the old man, the swift and tense acts of the three riotous fellows, and their awful yet inevitable end, make it a tale of mystery and horror of the highest kind, a tale which belongs at once to no age and to every age.

Where Chaucer discovered it is a mystery. The nearest known analogue to the Pardoner's Tale is the tale of the Hermit who found great Treasure, which occurs in an edition of the *Cento Novelle Antiche* printed in 1572. Other earlier editions of " Il Novellino " contain a similar story (No. lxxxiii) in which the treasure is found by Christ and his disciples, and is made the occasion of a lesson upon the

doctrine that love of money is the root of all evil. The
disciples pass by, and the treasure is later found by two
men who kill each other by knife and poison as in the
Pardoner's tale. On their return, Christ points the moral
to his disciples. Indeed, the story appears to have come
from the East, where it was told as an apocryphal story of
Our Lord ; for, as Clouston has shown,[1] numerous analogues exist in Mohammedan lands with Jesus as the
hermit-teacher ; and it is analogous to other apocryphal
stories—such as that of the dead dog with the white teeth
—in which something met with by the way is made an
object-lesson to the disciples by Our Lord. It seems
probable that Chaucer heard the tale in Italy, but he
elaborated an apocryphal anecdote into a dramatic story,
and amplified it with the bold yet masterly satirical
portrait of the Pardoner. The Pardoner's tale is a little
masterpiece in the grim and gruesome.

§ 7

Group D opens with the confession of the Wife of Bath
in the form of a prologue to her tale. It is a sermon
against monkish celibacy uttered by a hearty and witty
old soul who has ruled five husbands by suiting her methods
to the man. Chaucer makes the medieval distinction
between clergy (including the regulars) and laity, and his
conclusion is that whilst

Virginitee is greet perfecccoun,

it is impracticable and foolish for those who carry on the
secular duties of the world. This he elaborates from the
woman's point of view, together with the popular notion
that husbands are henpecked for the good of their souls,
by recounting the Wife of Bath's rich and multifarious
experiences in wedlock. The Wife of Bath's prologue is
frank and at times coarse, but its humour is unmistakable ;

[1] *Originals and Analogues*, Chaucer Society, p. 417.

and as a piece of self-revealing characterization it is admirable.

The subject-matter is drawn from experience and observation, but perhaps the prototype of the Wife of Bath is the old governess (La Vieille) in *Le Roman de la Rose* ; and with quaint humour Chaucer makes her fifth husband a young clerk who had read learned treatises on marriage to her, so that she is able to attack the clerical arguments in favour of asceticism of Jerome's *Epistola adversus Jovinianum* (which quotes Theophrastus, *De Nuptiis*) and of Walter Mapes's *Epistola Valerii ad Rufinum de non ducenda uxore.* She also illustrates her discourse with examples from Valerius Maximus. Her learning is perhaps improbable, but its point is that

> it is an impossible
> That any clerk wol speken good of wives,
> But if (unless) it be of holy Seintes lives.

We need not assume that Chaucer was disappointed by Deschamps's *Miroir de Mariage.* He does not allude to it, and, in spite of Lowes's argument,[1] he may never have seen it. Chaucer sheds none of the venom of the disciples of Abstinence-Contrainte. He laughs at the wiles of women, but he does not disparage the sex. With him wedlock is not a matter of sour grapes. Speaking as the happy warrior, he sees in marriage, firstly, the normal state of man, not to be regarded as a fall from purity, as the clerics falsely held ; and secondly, a progress from love to respect—a conflict of wills which terminates in compatibility as a rule by the victory of the unsearchable cunning of the spouse.

The Wife of Bath's Tale which follows is an illustration of the question : " What thing is it that women most desiren ? " And her answer is, " Women desiren haven sovereintee." It is a very charming lay of enchantment and love which Chaucer associated with the Arthurian

[1] See Lowes in *Modern Philology*, viii, pp. 165 and 305.

legend. In it he developed his favourite doctrine of gentilesse—"that he is gentil that doth gentil dedis"—a belief that is easy to utter to-day, but which was not so readily accepted by an aristocratic audience in the feudal age. The tale is a variant of a theme dear to the Middle Ages—an enforced marriage to a loathsome being who turns out to be enchanted,—Grimm's story " The Frog-Prince " is an example. Gower tells a similar story in his *Confessio Amantis*, i, of Florent, nephew of the Emperor, who is forced to marry an old hag who turns out to be an enchanted princess and the daughter of the King of Sicily. Chaucer may have learned the tale from Gower ; or he may have heard something more nearly approaching his version from a minstrel, for the story is the subject of two ballads in the Percy folio manuscript, and the knight is Sir Gawain. But he makes the tale his own by telling it as a fairy-tale, a very appropriate form for the old Wife of Bath, and by making it an apologue of her philosophy of marriage ; and he tells it in most characteristic fashion with touches of humour and learning. The dialogue in particular is most excellently done.

One would expect as a reply to the Wife of Bath the Clerk's tale of Griselda, but instead of replying immediately the Clerk reserves his judgment like a good scholar, and the Friar and the Summoner fall to grips. Each tells a tale maligning the profession of the other. The Friar's Tale is an anecdote with a point directed against heartless greed. Chaucer may perhaps have heard it as a tale told against lawyers. But he expanded it with characterization and dialogue into one of the best of his merry tales—a jolly excursion into the never-never land of diablerie. He begins with the reason for the Summoner's nefarious promenades —the Archdeacon—and then passes on to give a detailed account of the Summoner's wiles, into which with masterly ease he manages to convey the impression that the Summoner is so hardened and determined in his trickery that, compared with him, the devil is a country bumpkin.

It is in strict conformity with the design of this excellent bit of satire that there is no out-harrow and welladay when the devil seizes the Summoner. The Summoner is ever curious to learn new wiles, and is eager to learn more of hell.

> Han ye a figure thanne determinat
> In helle, there ye been in your estaat ?

he asks the devil ; and to him the devil's final word was a consolation.

> Thou shalt with me to helle yet to-night
> Where thou shalt knowen of oure privetee
> More than a maister of divinitee.

The Summoner's Tale is another expanded anecdote, but it lacks the pith and point of the Friar's excellent *exemplum*. It is just one of the many coarse and merry tales of the Middle Ages, used as a vehicle of satire against the friars. It became a tale by the additions which Chaucer made to the central incident—the character of the begging friar, who drove the cat from the settle " and sette him softe adoun "—the most realistic dialogue between the friar, Thomas and his wife—the discourse against ire—and the geometrical consolation which the friar received at the hall. Chaucer gave the tale a setting in Holderness, and told it as circumstantially as a true history ; but in spite of its excellent realism it fails to convince. It is not its improbability that is the obstacle. The Friar's Tale is even more improbable, yet it succeeds. It is not the digression on the sin of anger. The Wife of Bath's Tale is half digression, and we feel it no drawback. The fault is that to temper the intolerable coarseness of the climax, Chaucer carried on the tale too long, and belabours the friar more than he deserved. Jenkin's suggestion of the cartwheel is unsavoury and unnecessary. In construction this is Chaucer's weakest tale.

§ 8

Group E continues the discussion of the state of marriage introduced by the Wife of Bath. The Clerk tells the tale of Griselda's patience, and disarms criticism by his blunt advice to wives at the end : the Merchant begins with an ironical discourse in praise of wives, and proceeds to reveal his cynicism in the tale of January and May.

The Clerk's Tale was originally written not long after Chaucer's return from Italy in 1373. It is a fairly close verse-translation of Petrarch's story of Griseldis, which he had written in Latin prose from Boccaccio's *novella* in *Decameron*, x, 10. Chaucer admits his debt in the prologue which he added to the tale when later he inserted it amongst *The Canterbury Tales*, and the inference must be that he heard Petrarch read his " Mythologia de obedientia et fide uxoria," and perhaps even received from him a copy, when in Italy on the king's business in 1373. Petrarch died in 1374, and he appears to have composed his " Griseldis " in the early summer of 1373. The fact that Petrarch greatly admired this story was no doubt a recommendation ; but as it is a pathetic tale, like the Man of Law's Tale of Custance, and not only a better story but a true one to boot, there can be no doubt that Chaucer found genuine delight and true pathos in the wifely obedience of the patient Griselde. Like Petrarch, he told the tale not so much to urge wives to imitate her patience, as to rouse both men and women to bear their lot with fortitude, and

> Receiven al in gree that God us sent.

Notwithstanding its undoubted pathos, the story no longer charms as it once did. The character of Walter is difficult to understand in an age when nobles can scarcely command their subjects hastily to marry them, much less to vow wifely obedience into the bargain. One can understand his reluctance to marry, one can even believe in his whimsical trial of Griselde's fidelity : but what one does find difficult to account for is his charm. He must have been an attractive gentleman, or Griselde restored to him would reap no reward for her virtue ; but what did she see in him to love ? The character of Griselde is still the personification of meekness and devotion, and her relationship to the legends of the saints and martyrs is perhaps more noticeable than it was in Chaucer's age ; but with the passing of the medieval scandalous tales against the wantonness and cunning of women has gone the need for vindicating of the name of wife in this illustration of the apostolic doctrine : " Wives be in subjection to your husbands."

Chaucer was comparatively young and sentimental when he wrote this tale. Later in life when he adapted the story for *The Canterbury Tales,* remembering the Wife of Bath (l. 1170), he added eight stanzas after the moral conclusion of Petrarch's story—or rather, two stanzas which connect the tale to six stanzas in a new metre riming ab ab cb, all six having the same rimes. This envoy to the Clerk's Tale contains Chaucer's own criticism of the impossibility and the sentimentality of Petrarch's story, and his personal recommendation of the theory and practice of the Wife of Bath. The Clerk had told a story of wifely patience and obedience, but Griselde is merely an ideal of the old-fashioned days. From which it is manifest that he had been unable to use his story of Griselde in Group D as a reply to the Wife of Bath's Tale He had tried, but he had found Griselde unconvincing, and the Wife of Bath right ; if the truth must be frankly confessed : " Women desiren haven sovereintee." And in this addition to the story he completely lost sight of Petrarch's higher theme of stoical fortitude.

This contrast between the ideal and the real is continued in the Merchant's Tale. The Merchant is unhappily married, as he tells the pilgrims in his prologue, and his tale is a cynical attack on the cunning and unfaithfulness of wives. The story of January and May and the incident

of the pear-tree is an old and lewd example of the ready wit
of woman. A blind husband receives his sight in answer
to prayer, only to discover his wife's infidelity ; whereupon
she excuses herself by saying that, all unwillingly, she had
acted in accordance with a divine command in order that
her husband's sight might be restored. One version of
this story is to be found in the *Fables* of Adolphus
and another in the *Comoedia Lydiae* of Matthieu de
Vendôme. These and other analogues are to be found in
the *Originals and Analogues* published by the Chaucer
Society.

Chaucer took this old anecdote and added to it the
supernatural humour of Pluto and Proserpina, whom he
makes, following a learned superstition of the Middle Ages,
king and queen of faerie. This was an excellent touch,
for it gave a fresh interest to the old story, as well as a
ready means of accounting for the miraculous restoration
of January's sight. But his chief addition to the original
story was the long introduction, almost a counterpart to
the prologue of the Wife of Bath, in which with wonderful
and sustained irony he pictures January's rosy ideal of
matrimony, the polite complaisance of Placebo, and the
guarded warning of Justinus. Except for a few lines which
appear to be reminiscent of the *Liber Consolationis* of
Albertano of Brescia—a book which Chaucer possessed, for
he had translated it as his tale of Melibeus—this introductory portion of the tale (E 1245–2056) is original, and is
moreover one of the keenest of all Chaucer's jests on
" thilke blisful lyf That is bitwixe an husbonde and his
wyf." The picture of the ideal drawn by an aged innocent
is almost too ironic. Chaucer goes out of his way to
profane the most reasonable and the most sacred of
human contracts ; if ever he uttered a heresy against the
law of love, it is here. He realized the noblest aspect
of marriage and the perfection of a good wife ; but he
deliberately made use of them to characterize the dis-
gusting imbecility of an old bachelor in his dotage. It is

blasphemous and unpardonable ; and yet notwithstanding its bitterness, and in spite of its vileness, the Merchant's Tale has undeniable power. It is most skilfully constructed. Its characterization is convincing ; and its intellectual qualities—its polite irony and cynical wit—make it the supreme example in Chaucer and perhaps in English literature of *l'esprit gaulois*. It is a story worthy of Lafontaine or Voltaire. Boccaccio treated the same subject in his *Decameron*, vii, 9, but his *novella* of the enchanted pear-tree is an old wife's tale beside Chaucer's Merchant's Tale.

§ 9

The first tale of Group F, which probably was intended to follow Group E without a break, as manuscripts of the Ellesmere family have it, is the unfinished Tale of the Squire. The Squire's Tale is a romantic excursion in the realm of magic, arms and love. Perhaps it was Chaucer's attempt to rival the wonders of the contemporary romance of *Sir Gawain and the Green Knight* ; for the opening incident (F 76–106) resembles the arrival of the Green Knight at Arthur's hall. It offers a profusion of matter— a magic horse, a magic sword, a magic mirror, and a ring that enabled Canace to understand the language of the enchanted falcon. What the end would have been, none can say. No original or analogue of the romance is known, and Chaucer's usual skill in construction seems to have deserted him at the sight of such romantic profusion. Perhaps the tale was intended to characterize the vivacious fancy of the Squire, and was designed as a series of episodes. Certainly the plan of the tale does not conform to the canon which Chaucer enunciated in line 401.

> The knotte why that every tale is told
> —If it be tarried til that lust be cold
> Of hem that han it afterherkned yore,—
> The savour passeth ever lenger the more
> For fulsomnesse of his prolixitee.

And though Spenser essayed a continuation of the story of Canace and the magic ring, he forgot Cambyuskan and the unhappy formel. Spenser's conclusion of the tale is found in *The Faery Queene*, iv, 2–3 ; but it is not Chaucer's. Chaucer's end, as he tells us (ll. 651–670), was to restore the falcon to her lover. It was also to include the wedding of Algarsif to Theodera, and the winning of Canace by Cambalo. In fact, if Chaucer had finished the story, it would have been as long as a book of the *Faery Queen*, and as coherent.

The Franklin's Tale, which follows, is at once a picture of a perfect marriage and a riddle in comparative liberality. Chaucer claims that it was originally a Breton lay—a short verse-romance of love and wonder—and we need not doubt his statement. Boccaccio told the same story in his *Decameron*, x, 5, from which it is obvious that either both authors derived it from the same original, or that Chaucer borrowed the story from Boccaccio. It was an excellent story to read aloud because the question at the end—" Lordinges, which was the moste free ? "—provoked lively debate in the audience. There is something to be said for the generosity of all the four characters, Arveragus, Dorigen, Aurelius and the magician ; and no doubt Chaucer, when reading, had an appropriate joke to suit each of them.

But Chaucer amplified the story by a statement explaining why the marriage of Arveragus and Dorigen was so happy. According to Chaucer's version, Arveragus renounced all but the title of lord and master and allowed Dorigen to have her own way, in order " to live in ese " ; for :

> Love wol nat been constreined by maistrie.
> Whan maistrie comth, the god of love anon
> Beeteth his winges and farewel, he is gon.
> Love is a thing as any spirit free ;
> Women of kinde (by nature) desiren libertee.

Therefore ye husbands, have patience with your wives,

says Chaucer, patience will win the day when rigour fails. This is Chaucer's own opinion and his last word on the vexed question of how to be happy though married. It is wisdom born of experience. It rejects the shrewishness of the Wife of Bath, the raillery of the Clerk of Oxford, and the cynicism of the Merchant, and suggests a working compromise in favour of the weaker sex. It is a wise solution, which shows that the other opinions on marriage were deliberate jests. The Franklin's Tale is not particularly appropriate to the Epicurean old country gentleman described in the general prologue, but it sets a very pretty problem, and except for one flaw—Dorigen's complaint to Fortune, a learned addition taken from Jerome's *Epistola adversus Jovinianum*, ch. 41–46, which Chaucer had read for the Wife of Bath's prologue—it is a very charming little tale.

§ 10

Lastly we have Group G—the tales of the Prioress's " chapeleyne " and the Canon's Yeoman,—and Group H— the Manciple's Tale and the concluding sermon of the Parson.

The Second Nun's Tale is an earlier work inserted without a proper prologue amongst *The Canterbury Tales*. It is mentioned as " The Life of St. Cecile " in the prologue to *The Legend of Good Women* ; and the personal allusions in lines 62 and 78 show that when it was written, Chaucer had in mind no other narrator than himself. It was written when Chaucer had nothing to do, and no inspiration, as the first four stanzas on idleness suggest ; and he translated it as he tells us (ll. 22–26) from " the Legende " to occupy his time. By the legend he meant one of the many versions of the *Legenda Aurea*, a vast collection of lives of the saints compiled late in the thirteenth century by Jacob de Voragine, Archbishop of Genoa. This great book circulated in manuscript all over western Europe, and took slightly different forms as it was copied in different countries. By "translacioun" Chaucer meant free versification whilst keeping closely to the incidents of the Latin prose before him. The Life of St. Cecilia is a typical legend of a virgin-martyr, comparable to the lives of St. Catharine and St. Juliana; and perhaps its greatest merit is that it enables us to realize something of the ideals and the credence of the age of faith. The life, which begins with the quaint interpretation of the name Cecilia, is prefaced by an invocation to the Virgin-Mother not unlike lines B 1657–77 of the Prioress's Tale, which together with the *A.B.C.* reveal one aspect of Chaucer's religion. This invocation bears a slight resemblance to the opening lines of Dante's *Paradiso*, xxxiii, 1–21; but as the sentiments expressed are common to the medieval worship of the Mother of God, it is doubtful whether Chaucer stood in need of literary inspiration for his prayer.

After the Life of St. Cecile follows the description of the arrival, near Boughton, of a Canon and his Yeoman. They practise alchemy, it appears; and when the Canon has departed for shame of discovery, the Yeoman is easily prevailed upon to tell his confessions. The Canon's Yeoman's Tale is in two parts. The former is a spirited description of the science and art of those medieval philosophers who experimented in the transmutation of metals and sought for "the philosophres stoon." The latter is an anecdote of how a canon by alchemy cheated a credulous priest of forty pounds. It is a spirited and rather cynical tale, packed with learning, which never loses sight of the overworked yeoman at the bellows. It is also an example of Chaucer's originality in making a realistic incident serve as a satire on pretentiousness and greed. The doctrines of the alchemists quite evidently roused Chaucer's sturdy common sense: "ye shal nat winne a mite on that chaffare," he says.

> Philosophres speken so mistily
> In this craft, that men can nat come thereby.

12

And in conclusion, he adduces Arnoldus de Villanova and " a disciple of Plato " in support of his opinion.

The Manciple's Tale is introduced by a prologue which indicates that the pilgrims are now half-way between Boughton and Canterbury. The Host calls on the Cook for another tale, but, as that gentleman had clashed cymbals in Naxos and was now both sleepy and sick, the lot falls to the Manciple. The Manciple's Tale is one of those old tales which illustrate the fact that men hate the lips which tell them an awkward truth. The original is Ovid's tale of Phœbus and the raven in *Metamorphoses*, ii, 531–632. Chaucer retells it as a fable, with the moral :

> Wherso thou come, amonges hye or low,
> Kepe wel thy tonge, and thenk upon the crow.

It is a spirited little tale which Chaucer may have learned from Gower, who tells it in his *Confessio Amantis*, iii. As usual, Chaucer made it his own by the individual style of his narrative, and by his own characteristic sentiments. The comparison of the bird and the cat (ll. 163–182) is excellent.

The Parson's Tale, as its prologue indicates, was written as the conclusion of *The Canterbury Tales* ; and from its final paragraph, the " retraccioun," it would seem that it belongs to the end of Chaucer's life, when, under the influence of the pious monks of Westminster, he was attempting to outweigh his " enditinges of worldly vani- tees " by " homelies and moralitee." It must have been written in a library, for it is a compilation, as its formal and logical structure, and its quotations from the fathers show. Its style is too easy and vivacious for a translation. Sentences such as : " The fool lookinge of the fool woman and of the fool man, that sleeth, right as the basilicok sleeth folk by the venom of his sighte " ; or " Man sholde loven his wyf by discrecioun, paciently and atemprely," have the true Chaucerian character. Yet the matter of the Parson's Tale is not original. It was the common property of the scholastic theologians of the age. Chaucer must have heard it in a hundred sermons, and read it in a score of books. It is a devotional treatise on penitence designed for the wayfaring man. Its chief interest is the light it throws upon Chaucer's mind. It reveals Chaucer as a devout schoolman, the author of a logical presentation of the way of salvation—a sort of religious Euclid, poles asunder from the *Imitation of Christ*—a scholastic handbook of the religion of good works, reduced to a system for the benefit of the confessional.

It has frequently been stated, following the opinion expressed by Richard Morris in his preface to Dan Michel's *Ayenbite of Inwyt*, that Chaucer's Parson's Tale is an adaptation of some chapters of the French treatise which Dan Michel of Northgate translated, namely *Le Somme des Vices et des Vertues* by Frère Lorens. It is true that both classify and describe the seven deadly sins, but there the resemblance ends. Chaucer's book is quite different in form. The Parson's Tale, like a good sermon and omnis Gallia, is divided into three parts—contrition, confession, and satisfaction. It is in the second part that the examination of the seven deadly sins is introduced, and, unlike Frère Lorens, Chaucer follows the description of each sin by an account of the contrary virtue or " remedy." According to Miss Petersen, Chaucer's section on penitence was derived from a version of Raymund de Pennaforte's *Summa Casuum Penitentiae*, and his treatise on the seven deadly sins from a version of Guilelmus Peraldus's *Tractatus de Viciis*. It may be so. But who shall say ? Why look for " sources " in a sermon ? The Parson's Tale is Chaucer's answer to the question of the jailer of Philippi, and the answer is the work of a man who believed and accepted the system of the Church of the Middle Ages.

The Parson's Tale is Chaucer's last word, and it reveals him as a sound churchman. Yet *The Canterbury Tales*, to go no further, contain japes which must have shocked the Prioress and the Monk, if not the poor Parson. How shall we reconcile them with this Chaucer the moralist and the penitent ? Chaucer was not a hypocrite, and he was not a saint. Like many another before and after him, he believed in making the best of both worlds. Whilst he was strong and well, he reserved his religion for the confessional box and the Lady Chapel, and was content to be one of the " japeres that been the develes apes." He contrived to live at the same time a religious and a worldly life, which is no easy feat. In his old age, like Gower, he took apartments in a monastery, to devote his studies to religion and to make a good end ; and there he composed this devotional work and the retraction of his " enditings of worldly vanitees " which concludes it.

It does not strike us as a good climax to the series of tales, but no doubt to Chaucer it seemed as fit and proper as the exhortation at the end of *Troilus and Criseyde*. In a series of tales in a setting it is not the first step that requires all the art and all the judgment that the author is capable of, but the last. Boccaccio had to contend with the same difficulty, and he solved it by making his last tale that of Griselda. Chaucer might have concluded with the arrival at Canterbury, the visit of the pilgrims to the shrine, and the Life of St. Thomas à Beckett ; but instead of that he forsook verse for theology. Whatever the gain to theology, it was a sad loss to poetry ; and for most readers *The Canterbury Tales* come to an end with the tale of the Manciple. After all, without the Parson's tale, there is enough to provide the richest feast of verse-fiction in English. The Canterbury Tales are unique in their varied and sustained interest, and Chaucer's humour and good sense are a continual delight. Severally the tales are excellent, jointly they are incomparable.

VI

CHAUCER'S STYLE AND CHARACTER

§ 1

NOT only did Chaucer provide English poetry with fresh subject-matter, treated, as we have seen, with rich fancy, learned allusion, and uncommon humour; but he displayed the deftest metrical skill of any English poet before Spenser. His ability in the art of versification appears even more remarkable when we remember that, in the absence of one definite and established English poetic usage, he had to decide his own problems of diction and metre. No English dialect, before Chaucer wrote, was quite definitely the language of polite and courtly verse. Chaucer made the polite English of court, with its strong French element, so inevitable, that the other English dialects for the first time began to sound rustic and ignorant. When Chaucer began to write, the adequacy of recurring rhythm and rime was not entirely unquestioned. It was being challenged by a revival of alliterative verse in the Old English style by poets of the West of England. Chaucer's success established the two chief principles of English verse —namely, that its rhythm is determined by stress, and that its normal rhythm is rising or " iambic."

Quite reasonable would it have been for Chaucer to adopt the French tradition of syllabic scansion; but he relied on his English instinct for stress, the regularity of which he varied by slight deviations from his ideal metrical pattern. The general effect of his mode of versification is one of strength made graceful by the suppleness of free rhythmical movement. His commonest metrical variations are the insertion of additional unstressed syllables, substitution of falling rhythm for rising rhythm, variation of the position of the half-pause in the line, and use of the weak or " feminine " ending. One of these variations of rhythm now seems harsh, namely, the use of a monosyllabic first foot, as in :

Be so parfit as men finde,

or in :

In a gowne of faldyng to the knee.

But generally speaking, all Chaucer's ways of varying the rigidity of metrical pattern have endured in English poetic practice ; and, as a metrist alone, he may justly be claimed as the father of English poetry.

Chaucer's early use of the octosyllabic couplet, a metre which was common to both French and English poetry, seems to have been suggested and influenced by *Le Roman de la Rose*.   Later he adapted the French eight-line stanza to English lines of five stresses in rising rhythm.   This he used for his *A.B.C.*, *The Monk's Tale*, *The Former Age*, and for the ballade of *Fortune*, and the envoy *To Buckton*.   He also adapted a French seven-line stanza to lines of five stresses, riming ab ab, bcc, and created in English his characteristic Chaucerian stanza, sometime called " rime royal "—the metre of the *Complainte to Pity*, *Troilus and Criseyde*, *The Parlement of Fowles*, and four of his verse-tales.   Lastly he appears to have invented in English his favourite narrative verse—lines of five rising feet (" iambic pentameter ") linked by rime of the stressed syllable of the last foot and the unaccented syllable which might follow it—a metre which when written more strictly three centuries later as a series of couplets is known as the " heroic couplet."   In his complaintes and short lyrics Chaucer also produced a number of various stanzas based on arrangements of simple schemes of rime for eight, nine, or ten lines, in the manner of his French contemporaries. Chaucer's skill as a metrist prepared the way for Spenser, Shakespeare, and Milton. He developed his versification on the basis of stress with a large measure of freedom in rhythmical movement. He rang the changes upon his metrical patterns. He did not repeat them with absolute regularity, nor did he alternate his varieties. Familiar ease, not correctness, was his ideal. He found English metres halt and stiff ; he left them formal, graceful and supple. That is the inexplicable miracle of Dan Chaucer. He was not only the first, but he is one of the greatest masters of English metre and metrical arrangement.

§ 2

His lyrical poems disclose, as one might naturally anticipate, the influence of French forms. Chaucer's rondeaux and ballades were written in the style of Froissart, De Machaut, Granson, and perhaps Deschamps. The ballade and the rondeau or roundel were originally developments of dance-songs with refrains in which all the dancers joined ; but in the fourteenth century they were becoming fixed and definite poetic forms with rigid metrical patterns. The rondeau was not yet absolute in metrical structure, but commonly it was written as three short and unsymmetrical strophes linked by only two rimes. The ballade was written in three stanzas or in multiples of three ; and the fashion of adding a final strophe as an " envoi " was just beginning to be considered a grace. None of De Machaut's ballades has an envoy : many of Froissart's and Deschamps's have no envoy : none of the ballades of Charles d'Orleans and Villon is without one. The number of lines in the stanza at first varied from seven to fifteen lines of from seven to ten (eleven) syllables ; but the prevalent stanzas were those of seven lines riming ab ab, baa, and of eight lines riming ab ab, ba ba, or ab ab, bc bc ; and the ballade of three stanzas of eight lines, with an envoy became the favourite form. The rules were rigid. Not more than two, or at most three, rimes were permissible. No rime-word might be used a second time. And finally,

the scheme of rime was set by the pattern of the first
stanza, the last line of which was the refrain, and thus
became the common last line of every stanza.   Like the
Italian sonnet, the ballade elaborated and amplified one
thought or one sentiment.   And as not only the metrical
pattern of the first stanza, but the rimes also, had to be
repeated throughout, its composition demanded considerable skill, which could only be learned by practice.   In
English, such is the scarcity of riming words, it is difficult
to avoid certain inevitable and obstructive rimes ;   and
there is no small probability that sense may be sacrificed
to sound, if indeed the ballade escapes becoming an exercise
in *bouts-rimés.*

Chaucer indulged in these fixed forms of verse with
characteristic gaiety and ease.   There is a rondeau at the
end of *The Parlement of Fowles.*

> Now welcom, somer, with thy sonne softe,
> That hast this wintres weders overshake
> And driven awey the longe nightes blake ;
>
> Seynt Valentyn, that art ful high on-lofte,
> Thus singen smale foules for thy sake :
>> Now welcom, somer, with thy sonne softe,
>> That hast this wintres weders overshake.
>
> Wele have they cause for to gladen ofte,
> Sith ech of hem recovered hath his make ;
> Ful blisful mowe they singen when they wake :
>> Now welcom, somer, with thy sonne softe
>> That hast this wintres weders overshake
>> And driven awey the longe nightes blake.

It is a charming little artificial flower, which not only
indicates Chaucer's real delight in birds and springtime,
but suggests also something of the relief which the people
of the Middle Ages felt, in their cold and draughty houses,
when cold winter gave way to sunshine and warmth: The
three rondeaux of *Merciless Beauty,* two of which are
professions of courtly love and the last a jest, have also

been claimed, though without clear proof, as Chaucer's. The rime-scheme then of the type of rondeau which Chaucer wrote is abb, ab AB, abb ABB, where the capital letters denote the refrain, which is a repetition of the lines of the first strophe.

Chaucer's ballades are of three stanzas of seven or eight lines, with usually the last line of the first stanza repeated as a refrain. Sometimes, though not invariably, there is an envoy or address to the person for whom the ballade was written. Their subject-matter is courtly love—real, as in the ballade to Alceste :

> Hyde, Absalon, thy gilte tresses clere,

from the prologue to *The Legend of Good Women*,—or feigned, as in the ballade *To Rosemounde*, and in the doubtful *Against Woman Unconstant* :

> Madame, for your newe-fangelnesse,
> Many a servaunt have ye put out of grace.

Or it is an address, as in the ballade to Richard II, entitled *Lack of Steadfastness*, or in the ballade to Henry IV, entitled *The Complainte of Chaucer to his Purse*. Or it is a moral sentiment as in the ballades of *Truth* and *Gentilesse*, and in the triple ballade of *Fortune*—his three most serious poems.

The ballade *To Rosemounde* shows Chaucer mocking courtly love as he had mocked romance in *Sir Thopas*. The courtly poets of France had regarded their sovereign ladies as queens of tenderness and beauty, and had invented a semi-religious terminology with which to serve in poetry the shrine of love. They professed that their lady was incomparable and unapproachable, yet they complained of her want of pity. They offered their undying devotion and service in a language of hyperbole which was almost identical with that of Mariolatry. Chaucer accepted the tradition in his ballade to Alceste, and in *Womanly Noblesse*

("So hath my herte," etc.), if that poem be his ; but in *To Rosemounde* he transposed it from the minor key of love-longing to the major scale of the playful affection of an old man for a little girl.

The moral ballades reveal Chaucer in his reflective moods ; and they indicate that his study of Boëthius had resulted in the poet's acceptance of the philosopher's doctrines of faith, fortitude and nobility. With them, since the first four stanzas are translated from *De Consolatione Philosophiae* ii, met. 5, we may link *The Former Age*, which contrasts the honest barbarism of the golden age with the strife and baseness of Chaucer's age. It was an age of discontent and disillusion. The age of enlightenment was still to come. As yet there was no conscious goal for idealistic to struggle towards—except heaven. If they thought about progress at all, it was with regret. Chaucer's thought is that the golden age of man, the Ætas prima, lay in the dim and distant past ; and that the state of man is slowly but steadily growing worse. The only compensation was that if morals had deteriorated, the present comforts of life were better worth than the husks and uninspiring cold water of primitive simplicity. *The Former Age* is written in the eight-line stanza of Chaucer's *A.B.C.* —an early and free translation of a prayer to the Virgin-Mother which the Cistercian monk Guillaume de Guileville had inserted in his *Pèlinerage de la Vie Humaine*. De Guileville's prayer was written in twelve-line octosyllabic stanzas, each beginning with a successive letter of the alphabet. Chaucer kept the alphabetic arrangement, but simplified slightly the stanza.

The envoys to Scogan and to Buckton are playful letters in verse. The Scogan whom Chaucer addresses was evidently a courtier ; and he is supposed to have been Henry Scogan, a Norfolk squire, who acted as tutor to the four sons of Henry IV—chiefly because in his *Moral Balade* [1]

---

[1] See Skeat's *Chaucer*, Vol. VII, " Chaucerian and other pieces," No. 7, p. 237.

he calls Chaucer his " maistre " and quotes the ballade of *Gentilesse*. The *Envoy to Scogan* chides Scogan for neglecting his lady, and asks for his interest, all in a most friendly and sportive vein. Chaucer's " counceil touching mariage " was addressed probably to Robert Buckton, an esquire of Queen Anne's household, who married in the winter of 1396–7. But the identity of the recipients of these envoys matters little. It is as characteristic examples of Chaucer's wit that we read them. Both poems have some structural resemblance to ballade-form, but neither is a real ballade.

§ 3

There is nothing which captivates one and carries one away in these later minor poems of Chaucer. True they express a good deal of playful humour, and once, in *Truth*, Chaucer utters from the heart his last confession of faith ; but on the whole they are lacking in dignity and passion. The brazen trump of passion was an instrument which Chaucer never learned to sound. He could warble the flute-like melancholy of pathos, but the anguish and exultation of fierce emotion was beyond his powers. It may be that he was naturally suave and urbane ; or it may be that his years as a servant at court taught him to be politic, and habituated him to repress anger and to conceal emotion. The fact remains, Chaucer is lacking in passion.

If poetry, as has oft been stated, must be " simple, sensuous, and passionate," then Chaucer is not a poet, or at best only a poor one. But there is no convincing reason why the honourable term poetry should be restricted and confined to describe only the quickening eloquence and the fine frenzy of the poets of passion and of love. Emotion is poetry, it is true ; but so is imagination. Lyric is undoubtedly poetry, granted ; but so is fiction, so is satire, and so is fable. Simplicity, beauty and passion are not the only or the invariable marks of good poetry. There is another order of poetry, more mature than the sensuous and passionate kind, more reflective, whimsical and humorous, and at times tinged with an ironic ridicule, the product of a native geniality which has stood the shock of repeated disappointments and disillusion ; a mode of poetry which is at once polite, intellectual, and imaginative, rather than simple, sensuous, and passionate ; an order of poetry which springs not from courageous revolt against the spirit of the age, or from cowardly escape into the folly and frenzy of Bohemia, but from a wise and sad acceptance of the fact that what can't be cured, must be endured—or, teased into curing itself. This is the sort of poetry that Chaucer wrote. He is a poet of the same order as Horace, Ovid, and Phaedrus. His spirit is akin to the humour and satire of Molière, Lafontaine, and Voltaire.

He began as a writer of allegory. Then he was attracted by a new kind of romance—the epics of Boccaccio. Later still he became a writer of verse-tales ; and *The Canterbury Tales* are his masterpiece and his chief claim to original genius. In pursuing allegory, he followed in the tail of the hunt, or at least we may say that he was a hundred years behind the authors of *Le Roman de la Rose*. In following Boccaccio with *Troilus and Criseyde* and *The Knight's Tale*, he was doing with a better sense of structure little more than what the French romanciers had done two hundred years before. As far as story is concerned, it is questionable whether either Chaucer or his master surpassed Chrestien de Troyes. Yet he loved the best side of romance—its insistence on noblesse and gentilesse— but he was born too late. The best romances were written ; and already literary fashion was changing. Readers desired something more real and human, something more comic, like the merry tales of the *Decameron*. Chaucer saw the ridiculous side of romance, and mocked its prowess and its fairy brides in *Sir Thopas*. When he practised romance in *Troilus and Criseyde* and in *The Knight's Tale*, he added a humanity of pity and tenderness which trans-

GEOFFREY CHAUCER

From Hoccleve's " De Regimine Principum," MS. Harley 4866, British Museum.

figured it. His true bent he found in the tales in heroic couplets which he wrote for *The Canterbury Tales*. These later tales are excellent, not only for their story and character, but for their structure and point. They are the perfection of Chaucer's narrative art. Moreover, in the prologue and links to *The Canterbury Tales* he turned from fiction to real life, and displaced in his representation of the pilgrims his rich observation and understanding of the world around him. His observations reveal him as a humorist. Even in the grave and serious he saw the incongruities between what they were and what they ought to have been. In all, he saw oddity, or inconsistency, or self-consciousness, and poked gentle fun at it. Yet he is never indignant, never really satirical and scornful. He took the friar and the summoner, nay even the pardoner, to his heart.

He was the first English poet to prize metrical form, the first to display conscious narrative art, and the first to achieve a style. He excelled all his contemporaries, and his disciples for a century after, in the selection and narrative of a fiction, and in the phrasing and rhythm of his verse. He created the novel in England, as distinguished from the old order of romance. He introduced a new familiar style which has nothing of the romantic grimness or the florid diction of Anglo-Saxon poetry, but all the ease and grace of the French, expressed by a winsome personality that never failed to make itself felt. His style is clear and melodious. He excels in the direct simplicity of good conversation rather than in the choice of beautiful and pregnant words. In this he resembles Wordsworth, rather than Shakespeare, Milton, and Keats. But though his sentences rarely swell with the copiousness of eloquence, they are almost always melodious, and often musical. His similes are short and direct, rather than studied and pressed to a conclusion. His favourite figure is apostrophe. It is a style which is coloured by classical allusions, but he rarely allowed his learning to become ponderous. Though he frequently decorated his narratives with passages descriptive of spring and the park-like woodlands his chief interest was human nature ; and it is hard to say which is more effective, the direct characterization of the Prologue to *The Canterbury Tales* or the indirect characterization of *Troilus and Criseyde*. " In short "—as James Russell Lowell said in his essay on Chaucer, a luminous criticism that no lover of Chaucer should fail to read— " Chaucer had that fine literary sense which is as rare as genius, and, united with it, as it was in him, assures an immortality of fame. It is not merely what he has to say, but even more the agreeable way he has of saying it, that captivates our attention and gives him an assured place in literature. Above all, it is not in detached passages that his charm lies, but in the entirety of expression and the cumulative effect of many particulars working toward a common end."

His allegories are so rich in fancy and at times so gay that one can not be blamed for preferring them in certain moods to his tales. Though they were written under the influence of *Le Roman de la Rose* and the French dream-fictions, they have all the variety and grace of originals, which indeed, in invention, they truly are. No English poet ever succeeded so well in putting himself on a friendly footing with his readers. His poems and allegories have all the charm of intimate letters, an effect which is never marred by his use of rime. For so naturally does he suit the sound to the sense, that rime never becomes in the least a hindrance to his narrative. Indeed, far from encumbering him, one can truly say that it is a difficulty on which he thrives. Rime only served to increase the vivacity of his expression.

Though, as we have already said, Chaucer was lacking in passion, he was not without a characteristic vein of tenderness and pity. He was particularly susceptible to beauty in distress, as his tales of Constance and of Griselde show ; but perhaps his most sentimental poem is his Prioress's tale, which is truly excellent of its kind. But the most characteristic marks of his style are humour and good sense. " He is a perpetual fountain of good sense," said Dryden in the Preface to his *Fables*. " As he knew what to say, so he knows also when to leave off." Few English poets have been so amply endowed with the greatest blessing of the gods, a sense of humour ; and not only was he blessed with the comic spirit, but he had the good sense to direct his humour into proper channels, on the right occasion, and at the right time. His prevailing mood is genial and playful, but he could be jovial with the Host, satirical with the Friar and Pardoner, and cynical with the Merchant. It is his humour which makes the Prologue to *The Canterbury Tales* pure delight. His descriptions of the pilgrims are most convincing, and highly natural. They are not an aggregation of oddities, they are life seen from without by an impartial and whimsical commentator. The tales never reach the sublime, but equally they rarely lose sight of the ridiculous. Matthew Arnold held it to be a defect that Chaucer was lacking in depth and seriousness. If high seriousness could flourish in the Middle Ages apart from scholastic thought, there is some truth in the charge ; though it could be met with quotations from *Fortune* and *Truth*. But Chaucer was not a philosopher : like Dr. Johnson's friend he tried, but cheerfulness would keep breaking through. Even when he considers the mysteries of fate and free-will, his sense of the ridiculous often unintentionally reveals itself, and adds a spice of seasoning to dubious lucubrations.

What then, finally, is his place in the hierarchy of poets ? If he is not of the first order, what is his rank, and where shall we place him ? In eloquence and sublimity, Milton, though he lacked Chaucer's unfailing sense of humour, utterly surpassed him. Shakespeare too had more of the fire and force of passion. In delicacy of feeling and rapture, Wordsworth, though a less entertaining writer, was his superior. Keats, though often luscious in style, felt ecstasies and melancholies of which Chaucer was incapable. Chaucer is not to be compared with the Elizabethans, because he lived before the great age of English drama. He is not to be compared with the moderns, because in his age poetry included fiction; and, moreover, his was not a lyrical genius. But in two fields, narrative poetry, and the familiar style, he stands second to none. His *Troilus and Criseyde*, an inexplicable achievement of imaginative sympathy and understanding, will remain a classic as long as the world is interested in fiction. His *Canterbury Tales* ennoble him as one of the three or four great narrative poets of the world, below Homer and Dante, above Boccaccio and Ovid, and perhaps above Virgil. In an age when English poetry needed invigoration, he gave it new life and showed it fresh paths. He compelled the English that he spoke to sing, and lent it power to charm. He made poetry English. He made English poetry.

APPENDIX I

THE LANGUAGE AND METRE OF CHAUCER

I. LANGUAGE

Note.—*ĕ* denotes a final unmute *-e*. (*n*) denotes a final mute *n*.

1. SPELLING

Chaucer's language was the dialect of official London, of the clerks and sergeants of the court, in the latter part of the fourteenth century. Though it has been called a "well of English undefiled," it contained a comparatively large proportion of words borrowed from Anglo-French, and bore traces of Scandinavian influence. Its system of spelling was strongly influenced by French practice. Spelling was not approved or fixed by any authority. Every author and every scribe spelled much as he pleased, so that we must expect to find the same words spelled in different ways, e.g. *stoon*, pl. *stones, stonis*; *pit*, pl. *pyttes*, sing. *pytte*; *y-boren, y-bore, bore*; *dwellyng, dwellinge*. In the A-text of the Prologue to *The Legend of Good Women* (Globe ed.), the endings *-es, -eth, -en* regularly are spelled *-is, -ith, -in*. The vowel *i* was often written *y*, particularly when it was long in quantity; *v* was written *u*; and *u* and *n* were written alike, e.g. untrewĕ; so that a word such as armeĕ might be read either as *armée* or as *arivée*; hence *u* was written *o* before *n* and *m*, e.g. *yong, come*(*n*). Before a vowel, and at the end of a word, *u* was written as *w*, e.g. *knowe*(*n*), *cow*. The groups *ch* and *sh* were usually written *cch* and *sch*. Long consonants were written double, e.g. the *n* in *sonné* was longer than the *n* in *son*(*e*).

2. QUANTITY

It is difficult in reading Chaucer to distinguish between long and short vowels in the stressed syllables. Some vowels that are short in modern English were long in Chaucer's day, e.g. *sŏkĕ* (sick), *drŏpĕ* (drop), *deeth* (death). Length may be recognized in various ways : (1) by double vowels, e.g. *heed* (head), *loude* (loudly), *woot* (wot) ; (2) by the vowel standing before a single consonant followed by a vowel, i.e. in an " open " syllable, e.g. *ty-me, dro-pe, dame* ; (3) by a double vowel in the spelling of the modern English word, e.g. *brest, deth, frend, herte* ; and (4) by etymology, the rules being that in stressed syllables O.E. long vowels remained long unless they were shortened by a following consonant-group, e.g. O.E. *wĭs*, M.E. *wīs*, but *wĭsdom* ; O.E. *cēpan*, M.E. *keepe(n)*, but *kĕpte*, (the groups *-ld, -nd, -rd, -ng* were exceptions : before these groups short vowels became long in O.E., and long vowels remained long, e.g. *ōld, frēnd, hēng*) ; and further that in " open " syllables short *a*, *e*, and *o* became long, e.g. O.E. *măcian*, M.E. *mā-ken* ; O.E. *bĕran*, M.E. *bē-ren* ; O.E. *drŏpa*, M.E. *drō-pe*.

3. PRONUNCIATION

The exact pronunciation of Chaucer's English is now unknown, but it is believed that fourteenth-century spelling was a phonetic imitation of English sounds as heard by people who had been educated with French as their mother-tongue. Chaucer spelled his English more or less phonetically. Unfortunately Chaucer's spelling was altered slightly in the fifteenth century when most of the Chaucer manuscripts were written, partly because the sounds of the long vowels were in process of change, partly because the final *-e* had become mute, and partly because some of the manuscripts were written by provincial scribes whose native dialect differed from Chaucer's English. Hence the spelling of the manuscripts differs to a greater or lesser degree from what Chaucer originally wrote. But as most editors of Chaucer endeavour to reproduce what Chaucer must have written, rather than what the copyists wrote, we shall not be greatly in error if we observe the following rules of pronunciation.

(i) *Consonants*

Initial *k*, *g*, and *w* were pronounced, e.g. the *k* in *knowe* like the *c* in *clawe*, or the *k* in Ger. *knabe* ; similarly *gnof, write(n)*. Medial and final *-gh* was [χ], the equivalent of Scots *ch*, e.g. *bright, night, doughter, lough* (laughed). Medial and final *r* was probably trilled, e.g. *stark, licour, fether*. Medial and final *-gge* often was equivalent to modern English *-dge*, e.g. *brigge, leggen* (to lay), *logge* ; but not in *dogge, pigge*. And *g* had the sound of *j* [dʒ] in *geaunt, gentil, geste, gipser* and *gipoun.*

(ii) *Vowels*

The vowel *i* was often written *y*, and medial and final *eu, ou* were written *ew, ow*. The short vowels *a, e, i(y), o, u* were pronounced as in " pat," " pet," " pit," " pot," " put," but short *u* was written as *o* before *m* and *n* for the sake of legibility, e.g. *come*(*n*), *sonné, y-ronné*(*n*). It is necessary to remember to give each vowel its proper quality before *r, warm* [warm] not waum, *herte* [hertə] not hurt, *schirte* [ʃirtə] not shurt, *turne* [turnə] not tern.

The long vowels *a, ẹe*[ɛ], *ẹe, i(y), ọo*[ɔ], *oo, ou*(*ow*), and French *u*, correspond to long *a, ea, ee*(*ie*), *i, oa*(*o*), *oo, ou*(*ow*), and *u* respectively in modern spelling. The chief difficulty is that *ee* and *oo* represent in Chaucer's English *two* sounds, the " open " and " close " sounds of *e* and *o*, [ɛ] and [e], [ɔ] and [o] —the ancestors of the different sounds and spellings of " great " and " green," " foal " and " food." In modern English the open [ɛ̄] is usually spelled ea, and the close [ē] appears as ee or ie, and similarly the open [ɔ] appears as oa or as o in an open syllable, whereas the close [o] is spelled oo. The Chaucerian spelling *ou* represents [uu], but his *u* represented a French [y] and was probably pronounced [iū]. Otherwise the spelling of the long vowels was phonetic, as the following examples show :

ā [ā] as in " art " : *name, maken, maad, place, estat, chasten.*
ē [ɛ̄] as in " airt " : *breeth, deel, deth, greet, bere*(*n*), *pees, sesoun.*
ē [ē] as in " ate " : *seed, swete, bileve, frend, feeld, pece, peple.*
ī, ȳ [i] as in " eat " : *wyf, nine, child, hye, stryf, vice.*
ō [ɔ̄] as in " ought " : *stoon, cloth, hope, y-bore*(*n*), *rose, suppose.*
ō [ō] as in " oat " : *good, foot, do, to, fool, prove.*
ou [ū] as in " hoot " : *mouth, hous, doute, flour, mount, conclusioun.*
ū [iū] as in " hue " : *due, use, fortune, vertu, mesure.*

The diphthongs offer a greater difficulty, but we can adhere to our phonetic system and pronounce as follows :

ai [ai] as in " hie " : *day, fayn, gay, delay, bataile.*
ei [ai] as in " hie " : *wey, reyn, veyne, streit.*
au [āu] as in " how " : *drawe*(*n*), *saugh, cause, sauf, chaunce, graunt.*
eu [iū] as in " hew " : *fewe, schewe*(*n*), *blew, trewe, rewme.*
ou [ōu] not quite the same as in " haw " : *doughter, owen, nought, soul, knowe*(*n*), *growe*(*n*).
oi [oi] as in " hoy " : *joy, point, destroye, oistre.*

(iii) *A few Peculiarities remain to be Noted*

O.E. *y* became M.E. *i* in the North and East Midlands, *e* in Kent, and *u* in Wessex and the West Midlands ; but these developments were not entirely local. In words containing O.E. *y* Chaucer's dialect should have *i*, but Kentish *e* and Southern *u* also occur, e.g. *liste* (it pleased) appears also as *leste* and *luste* ; similarly *myrie, merie, murie* ; *stinte*(*n*) and *stente*(*n*) ; *shirte, sherte* ; *shette* (shut) ; *berie* (bury).

O.E. *e*, O.Fr. *e*, before -*ng*, -*nk*, was in Chaucer's time in process of becoming *i* as in " think," " ink." Hence Chaucer has sometimes *i* and sometimes *e*, e.g. *thinke*(*n*), *wing*, but *streng* (string), *senge* (singe), *wenged* (winged).

O.E. *a* in some districts became *o* before nasal consonants, and everywhere in Midland and Southern before -*ng* ; cf. Eng. " long," " strong," with Scots " lang," " strang." In Chaucer's dialect *o* occurs instead of *a* before -*nd*, e.g. *hond, lond, strond* ; and in *lomb*.

O.E. *e*, O.Fr. *e*, before *r* followed by a consonant, (which in modern English are often pronounced [ā]), still remained in Chaucer's dialect. Hence spellings such as *sterre, herte, yerd, ferthing, erthe, werk, swerd, clerk, persoun* (parson), *vertu*, etc.

In words of three written syllables, medial *e* is silent, reducing the word to two spoken syllables, e.g. *ev*(*e*)*ry, everè, evenè, havenès, soverain, colerik, remenaunt, lovedè.*

(iv) *Vowels in Final Syllables*

Final -*e* was becoming mute in Chaucer's English, and had probably already disappeared in words of two syllables after

a short root-vowel, e.g. *y-cŏm(e)*, *wrĭt(e)* (p.p.), and in the
auxiliary verbs *hadd(e)*, *wer(e)*, *shold(e)*, and *wold(e)*. It was
pronounced in words of two syllables as a rule after a long root
vowel, e.g. *smālė foweles*, the *yongė sonnė*, *tỹmė*, *mākė*, *drinkė*
(inf.) ; but was often omitted in the dative sing. of nouns.
In any case, except at the cæsura and at the end of a line,
final *-e* was elided before a word beginning with a vowel
or *h*, e.g. :

> *Wel coud(e) he sitt(e) on hors, and fairė rydė*
> *He coudė songės mak(e) and wel endytė.*

Final syllables may be pronounced as follows :

Final *-e* [ə] as in " fathe(r) " : *swetė, gracė, knowė, seyė, keptė.*
Final *-ye* [iə] : *malady-ė, compaigny-ė, vileyny-ė.*
Final *-es, -eth,* and *-ed* we probably pronounced [iz], [-iθ],
and [-id].
Final *-ioun* [-iūn] : *na-ci-oun, condi-ci-oun, reli-gi-oun.*
Final *-ial* [-ial] : *spe-ci-al, cor-di-al.*
Final *-ee* [e] from French *é* occurred in a stressed syllable,
and was therefore not elided, e.g. *degree, citee, countree.*

4. ACCIDENCE

The following are the chief peculiarities of Chaucer's forms :

(i) *Nouns.*

	Sing.	Plur.
N.A.	stoon	stones
G.	stones	stones
D.	stonė	stones

Some nouns, however, ended normally in *-ė* in the nom.
sing., e.g. *endė, metė, dorė, spechė.* The genitive sing. ending is
omitted in some nouns (chiefly feminine) which take no
possessive inflexion, e.g. *his lady grace, at chirchė dore, his
doughter name.*

A few nouns form their plurals in *-en, -n* : *eyen, shoon,
brethren, doughtren, sistren, children, toon* (toes), *keen* or *kỹn*
(cows).

A few nouns are unchanged in the N.A. plural, e.g. *hors,
yeer, vers, cas.*

(ii) *Adjectives.*

When an adjective was used attributively, a distinction was made, chiefly in the singular of monosyllables, between the adjective used in an indefinite or general sense and the adjective defined and limited by a demonstrative or a possessive pronoun. The latter, called the " weak " form, was inflected with *-ė*, e.g. *an old book, som old book,* but *the oldė book, his oldė book.* The definite or " weak " form of the adjective is also used before personal names, and in the vocative, e.g. *goodė God, fairė Venus, oldė dotard, levė brother.*

Adjectives were also inflected by the addition of *-ė* for the plural, e.g. *a smal fowel,* but *smalė foweles* ; *an òld book,* but *oldė bokes.*

So that there are in Chaucer's English two forms of the adjective, as follows :

	Indefinite.	Definite.
Sing. N.A.	*an old book*	*this oldė book*
Plur. N.A.	*oldė bokes*	*thise oldė bokes*

Some adjectives, however, ended normally in *-ė* in the nom. sing., e.g. *swetė, trewė, newė, richė, ablė, straungė* ; hence *a trewė man,· a newė· book.* The weak and plural form of *high* is *hyė.*

Adjectives of two or more syllables, and adjectives used predicatively, are usually uninflected. French adjectives occasionally follow their noun, and may form their plurals in *-es,* e.g. *a knight auntrous, places delitables, romances that been royales.*

An old genitive plural in *-er* survives in *aller, alder* (of all), e.g. *oure aller cok, alderbest.*

The comparative form is ordinarily inflected with *-er,* and the superlative with the ending *-este,* e.g. *old, elder, eldeste* ; *leef, lever, leveste* ; *high, hyer, hyeste.* Final consonants were often doubled, e.g. *greet, grĕtter, grĕtteste,* and when this happened, long root-vowels were shortened.

Irregular are : *ferre* (further), *derre* (dearer), *nerre* (nearer), *lenger* and *strenger.*

(iii) *Pronouns.*

Personal : The stressed form of *I,* namely, *ich,* sometimes occurs. *Thou* is sometimes attached to the verb in

the interrogative, e.g. *wiltow*? *schaltow*? *crydestow*?
The third person differs from modern English :

Singular.

	Masc.	Fem.	Neut.
N.	*he*	*she*	*it, hit*
G.	*his*, pl. *hise*	*hir(e)*	*his*
A.D.	*him*	*hir(e), her(e)*	*it, hit*

Plural.

Masc., Fem., Neut.

N.	*they*
G.	*hir(e), her(e)*
A.D.	*hem*

Hir (her) can only be distinguished by the context from *hire*, or *here* (their).

The dative personal pronouns are used with impersonal verbs, e.g. *me mette* (I dreamed), *him liste* (he liked).

Demonstrative : *the* ; *th' ilke* (the same) ; *this*, pl. *thise* ; *that*, pl. *tho* ; *this ilke* (this same) ; *swich* (such), pl. *swiche*.

Relative : Usually *that*, (*that* . . . *he* = who ; *that* . . . *his* = whose ; *that* . . . *him* = whom) ; *which, which that, the which* (*that*). *That* is used redundantly after adverbial conjunctions, e.g. *if* (*that*), *though* (*that*), *whan* (*that*). Similarly *as* is redundant after relative adverbs, e.g. *ther* (*as*), *wher* (*as*) ; and before imperatives, e.g. *as lat* (let), *as lene* (lend).

Interrogative : *who, whos* (the relative is *which*, e.g. *licour Of which virtu*), *whom* ; *which* (what kind ?), pl. *whiche* ; *what* (why).

Indefinite : *som*, pl. *some* ; *man, men* (one), e.g. *men seith, if men smoot it* ; *who so* (if anyone) ; *he, she* (one), e.g. *if he gaf* (if one gave), *as she that* (as one who).

(iv) *Verbs.*

1. Weak verbs form their past tense by adding *-ed, -ede,* or *-dė* (*-tė*), and their past participle by adding *-ed, -d*(*-t*) to the root, e.g. *love*(*n*), *lovede, loved* ; *seye*(*n*), *seide, seyd.*

Present Tense.		Past Tense.	
Sing.	Plur.	Sing.	Plur.
(1) *makė*	*makė(n)*	*madė*	*maden*
(2) *makest*	*makė(n)*	*madest*	*maden*
(3) *maketh*	*makė(n)*	*madė(maked)*	*maden (makeden)*

Subjunctive Present : sing. *makė*, pl. *make(n)*.
Imperative Present : sing. *makė*, pl. *maketh*.
Infinitive : *makė(n)*.
Pres. Participle : *making(e)*, *makyng(e)*.
Past Participle : *y-maked*, *maad*.
Verbal Noun : *making*.

2. Strong verbs form their past tenses and their past participles by gradation of vowels, e.g. *bere(n)*, *bar*, *bere(n)*, *y-bore(n)* ; *smyte(n)*, *smoot*, *smite(n)*, *smiten*, etc.

Present Tense.		Past Tense.	
Sing.	Plur.	Sing.	Plur.
(1) *spekė*	*spekė(n)*	*spak*	*speken*
(2) *spekest*	*spekė(n)*	*spak(e)*	*speken*
(3) *speketh*	*spekė(n)*	*spak*	*speken*

Subjunctive Present : sing. *spekė*, pl. *speke(n)*.
Imperative Present : sing. *spek*, pl. *speketh*.
Infinitive : *spekė(n)*.
Pres. Participle : *speking(e)*, *spekyng(e)*.
Past Participle : *y-spoken*, *spokė(n)*.
Verbal Noun : *speking*.

In the 3rd sing. present, the ending *-th* may contract with a preceding dental consonant to *-t*, e.g. *bit, rit, sit, chĕst*, for *biddeth, rideth, sitteth, cheseth*.

The past participle often retains the old prefix *y-*, e.g. *y-bore(n)*, *y-come(n)*, *y-cleped*, *y-kept*.

The past tenses of strong verbs often differ from the corresponding modern English forms : Chaucer has *saugh, seigh, sigh, sye* (saw) ; *bad, bede* (bade) ; *sat, sete* (sat) ; *cam, come* (came) ; *bigan, bigonne* (began) ; *drank, dronke* (drank) ; *song* (sang) ; *smoot, smite* (smote) ; *chees* (chose) ; *lees* (lost) ; *wex* (waxed) ; *wesh* (washed) ; *lough* (laughed) ; *slough* (slew) ; *fel, fil* (fell) ; *heng* (hung) ; *sleep, slepte* (slept).

The gerundial infinitive, which denotes purpose, is preceded by *for to*, e.g. *for to delen with . . . swich poraille*.

The root-vowel is shortened in the past tenses of many of the weak verbs, owing to the doubling of the consonant, e.g. *fedĕ, fĕdde* ; *ledĕ, lădde* ; *metĕ, mĕtte* ; *havĕ, hădde* ; *slepĕ, slĕpte*. In others it differs in the past tense, e.g. *recchĕ, raughte* ; *seche, soughte*.

(v) *Adverbs.*

Many have the same form as the weak adjective, e.g. *depĕ* (deeply), *hyĕ* (highly), *loudĕ* ; or have an unmutated vowel, e.g. *swetĕ* (adj.), *swotĕ*, or *sootĕ* (adv.).

Some are formed by the addition of *-ly* to the adjective, e.g. *swetely, trewely, shortly, gladly.*

As (considering, concerning) is used before prepositions, e.g. *as by his facultee, as of so litel space,* almost without meaning.

II. METRE

1. FINAL -ĕ

In Chaucer's English, final *-e* was not always mute, as in modern English, but was frequently pronounced. Usually the rhythm of the verse will indicate the places where it must be pronounced. It can only occur in an unstressed syllable. Final *-e* in Chaucerian spelling is of two origins : (1) it represents an earlier final syllable or inflexion (O.E. *-a, -e, -u, -an, -um, -en,* O.Fr. *-e*) ; or (2) it was a scribal device to indicate a preceding long vowel, as in N. *stone* for *stoon,* N. *mede* for *meed* ; and hence was inserted in pronominal monosyllables where it was never pronounced, as in *youre, thise, some, hise* ; *here, there* ; and sometimes indeed simply capriciously, as in *pytte* (pit), *Aprille.* For this reason some knowledge of English etymology is an advantage to the reader ; for, whereas inflexional *-ĕ* was pronounced [ə] (except where it was elided before a word beginning with a vowel or *h*), scribal *-e* did not represent a real syllable, and should not be pronounced.

Inflexional *-ĕ* may be distinguished grammatically. It is :

(1) The normal N. sing. ending of certain nouns and adjectives, e.g. *son(ĕ), timĕ, chirchĕ, damĕ, servicĕ* ; *grenĕ, trewĕ, gravĕ* ; and A.G.D. ending of others, e.g. *spechĕ, sorwĕ, dedĕ.*

(2) In monosyllabic adjectives the plural ending, e.g. *oldĕ*

bokes, fernė halwes ; and also the singular ending after *the, that, this, his, her*, etc., e.g. *the yongė sonnė, his halfė cours, this ilkė knyght* ; and before personal names, e.g. *fairė Venus*.

(3) An ending of adverbs : *fairė, smertė.*

(4) The ending of many forms of the verb :

Infinitive : *rydė, wrytė, seyė, tellė.*

Present tense, 1st sing. : *I rydė, wrytė, seyė, tellė.*

Present tense, plur. : *we rydė, wrytė, seggė, tellė.*

Wk. past tense, 1st, 3rd, sing. and pl. : *seyd(ė), toldė, hadd(ė), keptė.*

St. past tense, plural : *we ridė, writė, spekė, comė, foundė.*

St. past participle : *y-rid(ė), writ(ė), spokė, comė, foundė.*

But it was usually mute after a short root-vowel, e.g. *stir(e), com(e), son(e)* (son), *bol(e)* (bull) ; and in the 2nd sing. past indic. of st. verbs e.g. *thou spăke, băre*, etc.

2. Stress

The correct reading of Chaucer's verse depends largely on the recognition and observance of the natural stress of words. The stressed syllables may usually be recognized by the rhythm of the verse, about which we shall speak later ; and to a lesser degree by the modern accentuation which is often, though in the case of French words frequently not, the same.

In unprefixed words of English origin, the stress falls on the root-syllable, e.g. *timė, fáder, slépen, goóth, frายneth*, etc.

In words compounded with a prefix, the stress varies. In verbs, the stress falls on the root-syllable, e.g. *a-rýsen, bigínnen, for-géten, fore-seén, under-táken, out-táken, ykórven, ybóren*. In nouns and adjectives, the stress falls on the prefix, e.g. *án-swere, fóre-heed, oút-ridere, óver-este, wán-town, úndergrowe* ; except in the case of those formed with the prefixes *a-, bi-, for-, mis-, un-*, and *y-*, which have the stress on the root-syllable, e.g. *a-boód, bi-hálf, for-gétful, for-gífnesse, misháp, un-coúth, y-wýmpled*.

In words to which a suffix is added, the stress falls on the root-syllable, e.g. *freéndshipe, wísdom, stóny, bóldely, múchel, lóvyere* ; except that present participles and verbal nouns *may* take a full metrical stress on the suffix, e.g. *wépinge* or *wep-ínge*, and similarly *reken-íng, cloóth-mak-íng*, etc., etc.

Semi-compound words composed of epithet + noun had level stress on both roots, e.g. *a stoón wáll*, not *a stoón wall* ; but where the two words were so closely united that the composition was felt to be complete, stronger stress fell on the first component, e.g. *plówman, gárleek, yéldehalle, fýr-reed* ; except that if the second component was a word of two syllables following a monosyllable, the metrical stress could fall on the root-syllable of the second component, e.g. *quik-sílver, grehoúndes.*

French words usually have French accentuation on the last syllable, or on the last but one if *-é* follows, e.g. *cás, grácé, vertú, corágé, licoúr, armeé, accórdé, devýsé, enquéré, recéyvé.* But dissyllabic nouns may take English stress on the first syllable, if the metre requires it : *pitée* or *píte, manére* or *máner.* Polysyllabic nouns, besides having stress on the last syllable, throw the accent back two syllables, e.g. *émperoúr, mélodýé, ímpossíble, imáginácioún, sóvereýniteé.* Present participles in *-aunt* usually retain the stress on the syllable which is accented in the present stem of the verb, *accórde, accórdaunt* ; *súffre, súffraunt* ; but the corresponding nouns take the stress on the penultimate syllable : *áccordaúnce, suffraúnce, chévissaúnce, óbservaúnce, rémembraúnce,* etc.

3. METRE

Chaucer's commonest metres are :

(1) The Octosyllabic couplet, as in *The Book of the Duchess,* and *The Hous of Fame.*
(2) The 7-line (decasyllabic) stanza, riming ababbcc, as in *Troilus and Criseyde, The Clerk's Tale,* etc., etc.
(3) The 8-line (decasyllabic) stanza, riming ababbcbc, as in *Chaucer's A.B.C., The Monk's Tale,* etc.
(4) The Decasyllabic couplet, as in *The Legend of Good Women, The Knight's Tale,* etc., etc.

Besides these, Chaucer wrote other decasyllabic stanzas— of six lines in the Envoy to *The Clerk's Tale,* of nine lines in *The Complainte of Mars,* and in *The Complainte of Anelida. The Complainte to his Lady* contains a section in *terza rima,* and the latter half of this poem is in stanzas of ten lines. Chaucer's ballades are written both in the seven-line stanza and in the more common ballade stanza of eight lines ; some have no envoy.   There is a roundel at the end of *The Parlement of Fowles* ; and *Merciless Beauty* consists of three of these formal little lyrics.   Chaucer's tale of *Sir Thopas* is written in the *rime couée* of the romancers—with variations in the shape of short tails.

4. RHYTHM

Chaucer's rhythm depends on the alternation of unstressed and stressed syllables, and upon the half-way pause in the line.

(i) *Octosyllabic couplet* : The normal line has four rising or "iambic" feet :

> Upón my bédde I sát upríght.

But the normal line is varied both by the addition of an unstressed syllable at the end (the so-called "feminine" ending) :

> So whán I saẃ I míght not slépė,

and by the suppression of the first unstressed syllable :

> " Sír," quod Í, " this gáme is doón."

There is usually a natural half pause (*cæsura*) in the line, but its position is varied constantly, e.g. :

After the 2nd syllable : Allás ! ‖ and Í wol télle thee whý.
    ,,   3rd   ,,   : The béstė ‖ thát might bérė lýf.
    ,,   4th   ,,   : What aýleth hím ‖ to sítten hére ?
    ,,   5th   ,,   : That né(v)er was foúndė ‖ ás it télles.
    ,,   6th   ,,   : Therwíth Fortúnė seýde ‖ " Check hére ! "

An extra syllable may sometimes be inserted before the pause, e.g. :

> But fórth they rómed ‖ right wónder fáste.

And inversion of the position of the unstressed and stressed syllables of the first foot is sometimes found :

$$— \cdot \cdot — \cdot — \cdot —$$

How that I líve, for daý ne níghte.

(ii) *Decasyllabic couplet* : the normal line has five rising or " iambic " feet :

$$\cdot — \cdot — \cdot — \cdot — \cdot —$$

A Kníght ther wás, and thát a wórthy mán.

The normal line is varied by the addition of an unstressed syllable at the end (the " feminine " ending) :

$$\cdot — \cdot — \cdot — \cdot — \cdot — \cdot$$

Wel coúde he sítte on hórs, and faíre rýdè ;

also, more rarely, by the suppression of the first unstressed syllable :

$$— \cdot — \cdot — \cdot — \cdot —$$

Év(e)rich fór the wísdom thát he cán ;

or, more rarely still, by both combined :

$$— \cdot — \cdot — \cdot — \cdot$$

Whán that Áprill wíth his shoúres soótè.

There is a natural half-pause (*cæsura*) in the line. These pauses are sometimes marked by the punctuation of modern editions ; but, whether indicated or not, they are there, and they are as essential to the rhythm as the recurring stresses. The half-pause is found often after the fourth or the fifth syllable, but its position is varied constantly—a grace which gives Chaucer's verse remarkable ease and fluidity. Examples are :

After the 2nd syllable : At níght ‖ were cóme intó that hóstelrýè.
    ,,   3rd   ,,   : At métè ‖ wél ytaúght was shé withálle.
    ,,   4th   ,,   : A mánly mán ‖ to beén an ábbot áble.
    ,,   5th   ,,   : When Zéphirús eek ‖ wíth his swétè breéth.
    ,,   6th   ,,   : With hím ther wás his sóne ‖ a yóng Squiér.

After the 7th syllable : Syngínge he wás or floýtinge ‖ ál the day.

„ 8th „ : That Í was óf hir félaw(e)shípe ‖ anoón.

An extra syllable may sometimes be inserted before the pause (the so-called " weak " or " feminine " *cæsura*) ; and before the pause there is naturally no elision of -*é* before a vowel or *h*, e.g. :

Hir nósė trétys ‖ hir eýen gréye as glás.

But sórė weép she ‖ if oón of hém were deéd.

Inversion of the position of the unstressed and stressed syllables of the first foot is sometimes found, e.g. :

$$— \cdot \cdot — \ \| \ \cdot — \cdot — \cdot —$$

Únder his bélt ‖ he bár ful thríftilý :

Caúght in a tráppė ‖ if ít were deéd or bléddė ;

and more rarely in other feet in the line :

Troúthe and honoúr, ‖ frédom and cúrteisýė.

Lastly, it will be noticed that the couplet is rarely a complete sentence or phrase. The sense flows on from line to line, so that until the period finally is reached (which always comes at the end of a line) each line forms a part of a longer iambic sentence, which is united with others to form a verse-paragraph.

(iii) *The 7-line stanza* : The seven decasyllabic lines have the same rhythms as the lines of the decasyllabic couplet (q.v.). The lines of the stanza rime with each other according to the following pattern : ababbcc. Each stanza is complete in itself (with rare exceptions) ; and each stanza has a half-pause (*volta*) corresponding to the half-pause in the line.

We may describe Chaucer's versification as follows :

(1) The Chaucerian stanza is normally, but not invariably, terminated by a full pause after the seventh line.

(2) The Chaucerian stanza ordinarily has a half-pause or *volta*, determinable not by punctuation, but by the sense. This half-pause is followed by an amplification, a re-statement, or by the consequences of, or a contrast to the preceding lines ;

and is recognizable by the fact that it is a break in the unity of the stanza, if not a break in narrative.

(3) There is no fixed place for this half-pause. Chaucer observed it wherever it best suited his purpose ; but it will be found in about 90 per cent of his stanzas. Usually it occurs at the end of a line. More rarely it is found in the middle of a line. The varied position of this half-pause indicates that the stanzas were not written to be sung.

(4) The commonest type of stanza is that based on what must have been the original type, described by Ten Brink as two *pedes* (ab, ab), and a *cauda* (bcc), that is, a musical phrase repeated twice and ending in a half cadence, followed by an answering phrase of unequal length leading to a full cadence, as in Luther's hymn *Nun freut euch* (1529), commonly sung in England to the hymn " Great God, what do I see and hear ? " This type of stanza consists of a quatrain followed by a tercet. I call it the 4 : 3 type, and about 40 per cent of Chaucer's stanzas are of this type.

The second stanza of *The Clerk's Tale* will illustrate it :

> A markis whylom lord was of that londe,
> As were his worthy eldres him bifore ;
> And obeisant and redy to his honde
> Were alle his liges, bothe lasse and more. ||
> Thus in delyt he liveth, and hath don yore,
> Biloved and drad, thurgh favour of fortune,
> Bothe of his lordes and of his commune.

(5) Other common types are, secondly, a tercet (aba) followed by a quatrain of two couplets (bb cc). I call this the 3 : 4 type. We might exemplify from the first stanza of *The Parlement of Fowles* :

> The lyf so short, the craft so long to lerne,
> Th' assay so hard, so sharp the conquering,
> The dredful joye, that alwey slit so yerne, ||
> All this mene I by love, that my feling
> Astonyeth with his wonderful worching
> So sore ywis, that when I on him thinke,
> Nat wot I wel wher that I wake or winke.

About 20 per cent of Chaucer's stanzas are of this type ; but the proportion rises in his later work to about 30 per cent of the stanzas in a given poem. Thirdly, there is another common type—a quintet (ababb) followed by a couplet (cc). I call this the 5 : 2 type. As an example I take the first stanza of *The Prioress's Tale* :

> Ther was in Asie, in a greet citee,
> Amonges Cristen folk, a Jewerye,
> Sustened by a lord of that contree
> For foule usure and lucre of vilanye,
> Hateful to Crist and to his companye ; ||
> And thurgh the strete men mighte ryde or wende,
> For it was free, and open at either ende.

Slightly less than 20 per cent of Chaucer's stanzas are of this type, and the percentage in each poem differs considerably.

(6) Irregular types are, fourthly, a couplet (ab) followed by a quintet (abbcc). This type, which I call the 2 : 5 type, is naturally ungraceful, and therefore rare. Here is an example from *The Prioress's Tale* :

> I seye that in a wardrobe they him threwe
> Where-as these Jewes purgen hir entraille. ||
> O cursed folk of Herodes al newe,
> What may your yvel entente yow availle ?
> Mordre wol out, certein, it wol nat faille,
> And namely ther th' onour of God shal sprede,
> The blood out cryeth on your cursed dede.

Fifthly, the stanza with an interlinear half-pause. There is of course no fixed place for the pause. This example is from *The Man of Law's Tale* :

> In sterres, many a winter ther-biforn,
> Was writen the deeth of Ector, Achilles,
> Of Pompey, Julius, er they were born ;
> The stryf of Thebes ; and of Ercules,
> Of Sampson, Turnus, and of Socrates
> The deeth ; || but mennes wittes been so dulle,
> That no wight can wel rede it atte fulle.

This type is also rare, for the half-pause usually occurs at the end of a line. Sixthly, the stanza with no half-pause.

This type is very rare. The example is taken from *Troilus and Criseyde*, I, 10:

> Now fil it so, that in the toun ther was
> Dwellinge a lord of greet auctoritee,
> A greet devyn, that cleped was Calkas,
> That in science so expert was, that he
> Knew wel that Troye sholde destroyed be,
> By answere of his god, that highte thus,
> Daun Phebus or Apollo Delphicus.

There are also a few anomalous stanzas, such as 1 : 6, 6 : 1, and stanzas with two well-defined pauses.

To summarize these observations, the seven-line stanza was usually written by Chaucer with one half-pause or *volta*. Consequently, there are many structural types. The chief types are the 4 : 3 (abab, bcc), the 3 : 4 (aba, bbcc), the 5 : 2 (ababb, cc). Rare and irregular types are the 2 : 5 (ab, abbcc), the stanza with an interlinear *volta*, the stanza with no *volta*, the stanza with two well-defined pauses and possibly rarer anomalous stanzas.

(iv) The eight-line stanza will similarly be found to have a *volta*, which often, but by no means regularly, comes after the end of the fourth line.

APPENDIX II

A SHORT LIST OF CHAUCER MANUSCRIPTS

BRITISH MUSEUM.

Additional 5140 - C. Tales.

,, 10340 - Boece, *Truth.

,, 16165 - Boece, Anelida, Ballades of Complaint and of a Reeve, Proverbs: (by Shirley).

,, 22139 - Truth, Gentilesse, Lack of Steadfastness, Purse.

,, 23002 - Astrolabe.

,, 25718 - C. Tales.

,, 28617 - Legend of G. Women.

,, 34360 - C. to his Lady, *Womanly Noblesse.

,, 35286 (Ashburnham 125) C. Tales.·

Cotton, Cleopatra D 7 Truth, Gentilesse, Lack of Steadfastness, Against Women Inconstant.

Egerton 2726 - C. Tales.

,, 2863 - - C. Tales.

,, 2864 - - C. Tales.

Harley 78 - - C. to Pity, to his Lady.

,, 1239 - - Troilus.

,, 1758 - - C. Tales.

,, 2251 - - Fortune, Purse.

,, *2280 - - Troilus.

,, 2392 - - Troilus.

,, 3758 - - Against Women Inconstant.

,, 3943 - - Troilus.

,, 4912 - - Troilus.

,, 7333 - - C. Tales, Anelida, P. of Fowles, C. of Mars, Truth, Gentilesse, Lack of Steadfastness, Purse: (after Shirley)

,, *7334 - - C. Tales.

,, 7335 - - C. Tales.

Harley 7578 -	- C. to Pity, A.B.C., Ballades of a Reeve, Gentilesse, Lack of Steadfastness, Against Women Inconstant, Purse.
Lansdowne 699	- Fortune, Truth.
,, *851	- C. Tales.
Royal 17 D XV	- C. Tales.
,, 18 C II -	- C. Tales.
Sloane 291 -	- Astrolabe.
,, 1685 -	- C. Tales.
,, 1686 -	- C. Tales.

BODLEIAN LIBRARY, OXFORD

Ashmole 59 -	- C. of Venus, Fortune, Gentilesse : (by Shirley).
*Bodley 638 -	- C. to Pity, A.B.C., Duchess, Anelida, H. of Fame, P. of Fowles, Legend of G. Women, Fortune.
Digby 72 -	- Astrolabe.
,, 181 -	- Troilus, Anelida, P. of Fowles.
*Fairfax 16 -	- C. to Pity, A.B.C., Duchess, Anelida, H. of Fame, P. of Fowles, Legend of G. Women, C. of Mars, Venus, Fortune, Truth, Lack of Steadfastness, Against Women Inconstant. To Scogan, *Buckton, Purse, Proverbs.
Laud 416 -	- P. of Fowles.
,, 470 -	- A.B.C.
,, 600 -	- C. Tales.
,, 739 -	- C. Tales.
Arch. Selden B 14 -	C. Tales.
,, B 24 -	Troilus, P. of Fowles, Legend of G. Women, C. of Mars, Venus, Truth.
,, supra 56	Troilus.
*Tanner 346 -	- C. to Pity, Duchess, Anelida, P. of Fowles, Legend of G. Women, C. of Mars, Venus.
Rawlinson, Poet. 163 -	Troilus, *To Rosemounde.
,, 165 -	Troilus.

CORPUS CHRISTI COLLEGE, OXFORD

*MS. 198   -   -   C. Tales.

ST. JOHN'S COLLEGE, OXFORD

MS. lvii -   -   -   P. of Fowles.

CAMBRIDGE UNIVERSITY LIBRARY

*Dd 4 24 -   -   -   C. Tales.
Dd 3 53 -   -   -   Astrolabe.
Dd 12 51 -   -   -   Astrolabe.
Ff 1 6   -   -   -   C. to Pity, P. of Fowles, Venus,
                                 Purse.
Ff 5 30 -   -   -   A.B.C., Anelida.
*Gg 4 27 -   -   -   A.B.C., Troilus, P. of Fowles,
                                 *Legend of Good Women (A),
                                 C. Tales, Truth, To Scogan.
Hh 4 12 -   -   -   P. of Fowles, Former Age.
*Ii 1 38   -   -   -   Boece.
Ii 3 21   -   -   -   Boece, Former Age, Fortune.
Ii 3 26   -   -   -   C. Tales.
Mm 2 5   -   -   -   C. Tales.

CORPUS CHRISTI COLLEGE, CAMBRIDGE

MS. 61   -   -   -   Troilus.

ST. JOHN'S COLLEGE, CAMBRIDGE

MS. G 21   -   -   A.B.C.
  ,, *LI -   -   -   Troilus.

MAGDALEN COLLEGE, CAMBRIDGE

*Pepys 2006   -   -   A.B.C., Anelida, H. of Fame, P. of
                                 Fowles, Legend of G. Women,
                                 C. of Mars, Venus, Fortune,
                                 *Merciless Beauty, To Scogan,
                                 Purse.

TRINITY COLLEGE, CAMBRIDGE

R 3 3   -   -   -   C. Tales.
R 3 15   -   -   -   C. Tales.

R 3 19   -   -   - C. to Pity, P. of Fowles, Legend of G. Women.

*R 3 20   -   -   - Anelida, P. of Fowles, C. of Mars, Venus, *To Adam, Fortune, Truth, Gentilesse, Lack of Steadfastness : (by Shirley).

R 15 18 -   -   - Astrolabe.

GLASGOW UNIVERSITY LIBRARY

Bannatyne 1568   - Lack of Steadfastness.
Hunter Q 2 25   - A.B.C.
,,   U 1 1 -   - C. Tales.
,,   V 3 7 -   - *Romaunt of the Rose.

PRIVATE LIBRARIES

*Campsall -   -   - Troilus.
*Ellesmere -   -   - C. Tales, (Truth).
*Hengwrt 154 (Peniarth) C. Tales.
,,   393   ,,   Boece.
Longleat 258   -   - C. to Pity, Anelida, P. of Fowles, C. of Mars.
*Petworth   -   - C. Tales.
Phillipps 8252 (Cheltenham)   Troilus.
Phillipps 9053   ,,   C. to his Lady.
Sion College L 40 2a/3   A.B.C.

APPENDIX III

BIBLIOGRAPHY

I. TEXTUAL

I

(A complete list of the publications of the Chaucer Society is issued
by the Oxford University Press.)

CHAUCER SOCIETY : The Six-Text Edition of *The Canterbury
Tales*, from MSS. Ellesmere, Hengwrt, Cambridge
Gg 4 27, Corpus, Petworth, and Lansdowne 851.
1868–84.

   Edition of MS. Harley 7334. 1885.

   Edition of MS. Cambridge Dd 4 24. 1901–2.

   The Parallel-Text Edition of *Troilus and Criseyde*, from
MSS. Campsall, Harley 2280, and Cambridge Gg 4 27.
1881–2.

   The Parallel-Text Edition of Chaucer's Minor Poems.
1871–86.

The Ellesmere Chaucer in facsimile. Manchester Univ. Press.
1911.

Francis Thynne's *Chaucer* (1532) in facsimile. Oxford Univ.
Press. 1905.

II

TYRWHITT, T. : The Canterbury Tales. Oxford. 1775–8.

WRIGHT, T. : The Canterbury Tales. Percy Society. 1847.

SKEAT, W. W. : The Complete Works of Geoffrey Chaucer.
Oxford. 1894.

   Supplement to the Works of Geoffrey Chaucer. Oxford.
1897.

   The Works of Chaucer (Oxford Poets). 1895.

POLLARD, A. W., and others : The Works of Chaucer (Globe
Edition). 1898.

III

FURNIVALL, F. J. : A Temporary Preface to the Six-Text
Edition, Chaucer Society. 1868.

KOCH, J. : A Detailed Comparison of the eight MSS. of *The Canterbury Tales*. Heidelberg. 1913.
Textkritische Bemerkungen zu Chaucer's *Canterbury Tales*, in *Englische Studien*, xlvii, p. 338. 1914.
POLLARD, A. W., and others : Introduction to the " Globe " Chaucer. Macmillan. 1898.
SKEAT, W. W. : Introductions (*passim*) to The Complete Works of Chaucer. Oxford. 1894.

II. GRAMMATICAL

EMERSON, O. F. : Introduction to *A Middle English Reader*. Macmillan. 1905, 1915.
POLLARD, A. W. : " Chaucer's Language " in *Chaucer, The Prologue*, p. 1. Macmillan. 1903.
SISAM, K. : Appendix to *Fourteenth Century Verse and Prose*, Oxford. 1921.
SKEAT, W. W. : Introduction and Glossary, being Skeat's *Chaucer*, Vol. vi. Oxford. 1894.
SWEET, H. : Second Middle English Primer. Oxford. 1905.
TEN BRINK, B. : The Language and Metre of Chaucer (trans. Miss M. Bentinck Smith). Macmillan. 1901.
WRIGHT, J. : An Elementary Middle English Grammar. Oxford Univ. Press. 1923.

III. CRITICAL

I

BRUSENDORFF, A. : The Chaucer Tradition. Oxford Univ. Press. 1925.
FANSLER, A. : Chaucer and the Roman de la Rose. New York (Columbia Univ. Press). 1914.
FURNIVALL, F. J., and CLOUSTON, W. A. : Originals and Analogues of the Canterbury Tales. Chaucer Society. 1888.
HAMMOND, Miss E. P. : Chaucer, a Bibliographical Manual. New York. 1908.
HINCKLEY, H. B. : Notes on Chaucer. Northampton, U.S.A. 1907.

KER, W. P.: English Literature, Medieval. Williams and
   Norgate. 1912.
KOCH, J.: Der gegenwärtige Stand der Chaucerforschung, in
   Anglia, xlix, p. 193. 1925.
ROSSETTI, W.: Chaucer's Troilus and Criseyde compared with
   Boccaccio's Filostrato. Chaucer Society. 1883.
SPURGEON, Miss C. F. E.: Five Hundred Years of Chaucer
   Criticism and Allusion. Cambridge Univ. Press. 1925.
TEN BRINK, B.: Chaucer. Münster (Russell). 1870.
TYRWHITT, T.: Preface to The Canterbury Tales. Oxford.
   1775.
WRIGHT, T.: Preface to The Canterbury Tales. Percy
   Society. 1847.
YOUNG, K.: The Origin and Development of the story of
   Troilus and Criseyde. Chaucer Society. 1904.

II

ARNOLD, Matthew: The Study of Poetry, in *Essays in
   Criticism* (Second Series) (1888).
BLAKE, William: Descriptive Catalogue, in the " Oxford "
   Blake, p. 432 (1809).
DRYDEN, John: Preface to the Fables, in the " Globe "
   Dryden, p. 493 (1699).
HAZLITT, William: On Chaucer and Spenser, in *Lectures on
   the English Poets* (1818).
HUNT, Leigh: " Chaucer," in *Essays*, Ed. A. Symons, 1887.
LOWELL, James Russell: Chaucer, in *My Study Windows*
   (1871).

IV. BIOGRAPHICAL

JUSSERAND, J. J.: A Literary History of the English People,
   vol. i. Unwin. 1894.
KIRK, R. E. G., and others: Life Records of Chaucer. Chaucer
   Society. 1900.
KITTREDGE, G. L.: Chaucer and his Poetry. Cambridge,
   U.S.A. 1915.
LEGOUIS, E.: Geoffrey Chaucer (" Écrivains Étrangers ").
   Paris (Blond). 1910.
LOUNSBURY, T. R.: Studies in Chaucer. New York (Harpers).
   1892.

NICOLAS, Sir H. : Life of Chaucer in " Aldine " Chaucer, vol. i. Bell. 1866.

POLLARD, A. W. : Chaucer. Macmillan. 1893.

TEN BRINK, B. : English Literature, vol. ii. (trans. W. C. Robinson). Bell. 1893.

WELLS, J. E. : A Manual of the Writings in Middle English. Yale Univ. Press. 1916, 1920.

V. HISTORICAL

ABRAM, A. : English Life and Manners in the Later Middle Ages. Routledge. 1913.

BESANT, W. : Sir Richard Whittington. Chatto and Windus. 1894.

COULTON, G. G. : Chaucer and his England. Methuen. 1908. Social Life in England. Cambridge Univ. Press. 1919.

JUSSERAND, J. J. : English Wayfaring Life in the Middle Ages. Unwin. 1888.

LEACH, A. F. : The Schools of Medieval England. Methuen. 1915.

POWER, Miss Eileen : Medieval People. Methuen. 1924.

QUILLER-COUCH, Sir A. T. : The Age of Chaucer. Dent. 1926.

SMITH, S. Armitage : John of Gaunt. Constable. 1904.

TAYLOR, H. O. : The Mediaeval Mind. Macmillan. 1911.

TREVELYAN, G. M. : England in the Age of Wycliffe. Longmans. 1899, 1909.

UNWIN, G. : Finance and Trade under Edward III. Manchester Univ. Press. 1918.

INDEX

ERRATA

Page 26, line 11 ; *for* ‘ *complainte* ’ *read Complainte.*

Page 32, line 21 ; *for* ‘ £20 ’ *read* 20 marks.

Page 36, line 18 ; *for* ‘ plent ’ *read* blent.

Page 62, line 31 ; *for* ‘ aвd ’ *read* and.

Page 98, line 14 ; *for* ‘ Thesus ’ *read* Theseus.

Page 142, line 37 ; *for* ‘ he ’ *read* the.